FANTASTIC FOUR

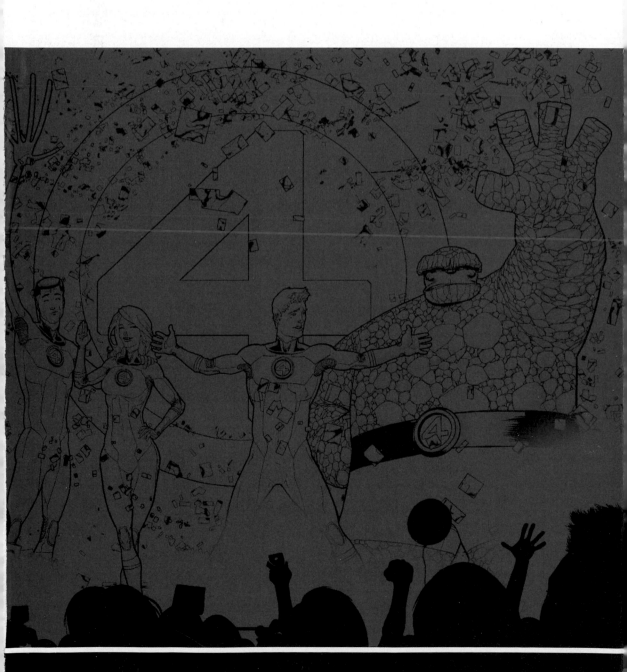

COLLECTION EDITOR: **JENNIFER GRÜNWALD**
ASSISTANT EDITOR: **CAITLIN O'CONNELL**
ASSOCIATE MANAGING EDITOR: **KATERI WOODY**
EDITOR, SPECIAL PROJECTS: **MARK D. BEAZLEY**
VP PRODUCTION & SPECIAL PROJECTS: **JEFF YOUNGQUIST**
BOOK DESIGN: **JEFF POWELL**

SVP PRINT, SALES & MARKETING: **DAVID GABRIEL**
DIRECTOR, LICENSED PUBLISHING: **SVEN LARSEN**
EDITOR IN CHIEF: **C.B. CEBULSKI**
CHIEF CREATIVE OFFICER: **JOE QUESADA**
PRESIDENT: **DAN BUCKLEY**
EXECUTIVE PRODUCER: **ALAN FINE**

FANTASTIC FOUR: FANTASTIC ORIGINS. Contains material originally published in magazine form as FANTASTIC FOUR: SEASON ONE and FANTASTIC FOUR #570. First printing 2019. ISBN 978-0-7851-5642-0. Published by MARVEL WORLDWIDE, INC., a subsidiary of MARVEL ENTERTAINMENT, LLC. OFFICE OF PUBLICATION: 135 West 50th Street, New York, NY 10020. **Printed in Canada.** DAN BUCKLEY, President, Marvel Entertainment; JOHN NEE, Publisher; JOE QUESADA, Chief Creative Officer; TOM BREVOORT, SVP of Publishing; DAVID BOGART, Associate Publisher & SVP of Talent Affairs; DAVID GABRIEL, SVP of Sales & Marketing, Publishing; JEFF YOUNGQUIST, VP of Production & Special Projects; DAN CARR, Executive Director of Publishing Technology; ALEX MORALES, Director of Publishing Operations; DAN EDINGTON, Managing Editor; SUSAN CRESPI, Production Manager; STAN LEE, Chairman Emeritus. For information regarding advertising in Marvel Comics or on Marvel.com, please contact Vit DeBellis, Custom Solutions & Integrated Advertising Manager, at vdebellis@marvel.com. For Marvel subscription inquiries, please call 888-511-5480. **Manufactured between 6/7/2019 and 7/9/2019 by SOLISCO PRINTERS, SCOTT, QC, CANADA.**

10 9 8 7 6 5 4 3 2 1

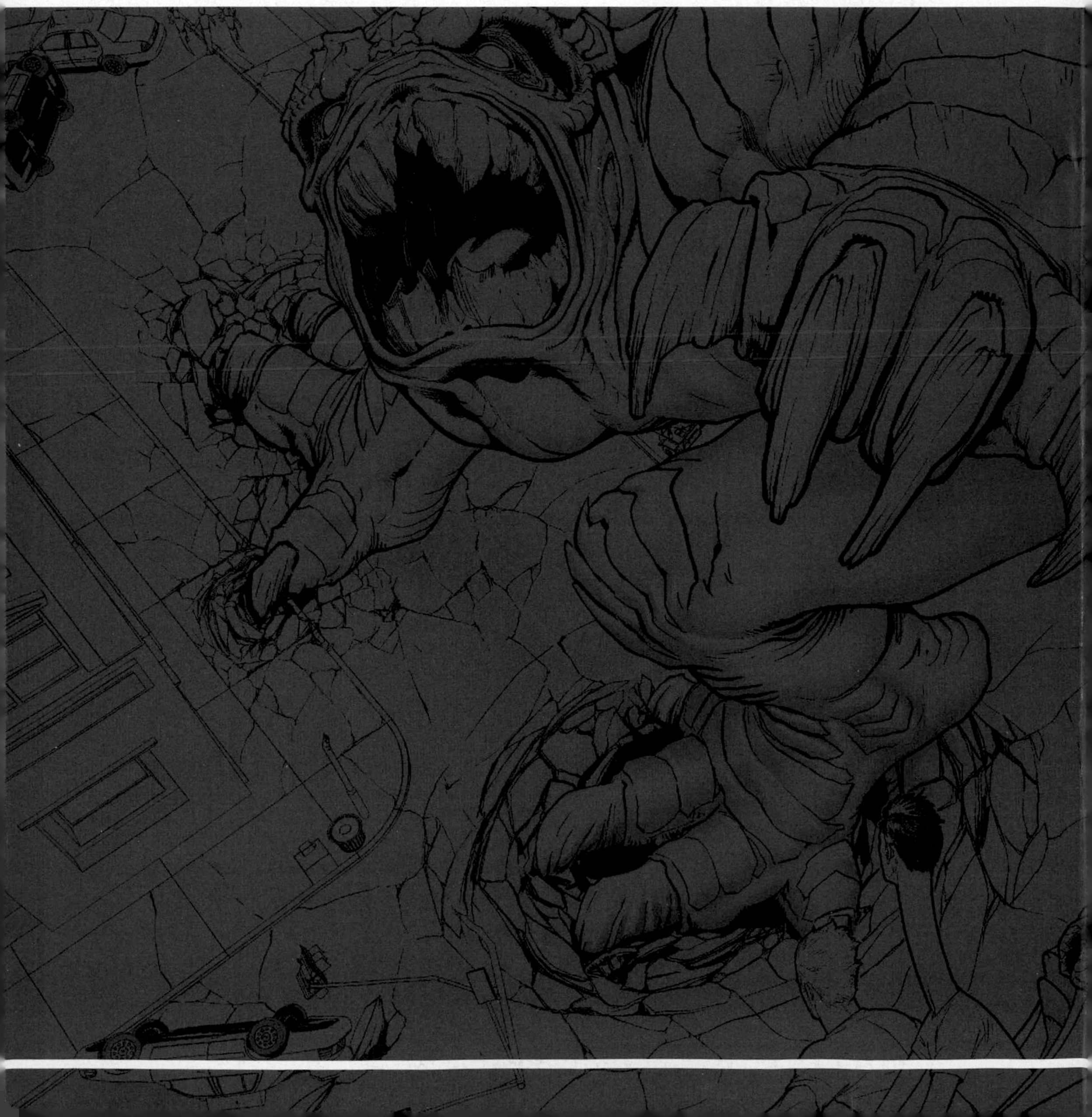

FANTASTIC FOUR

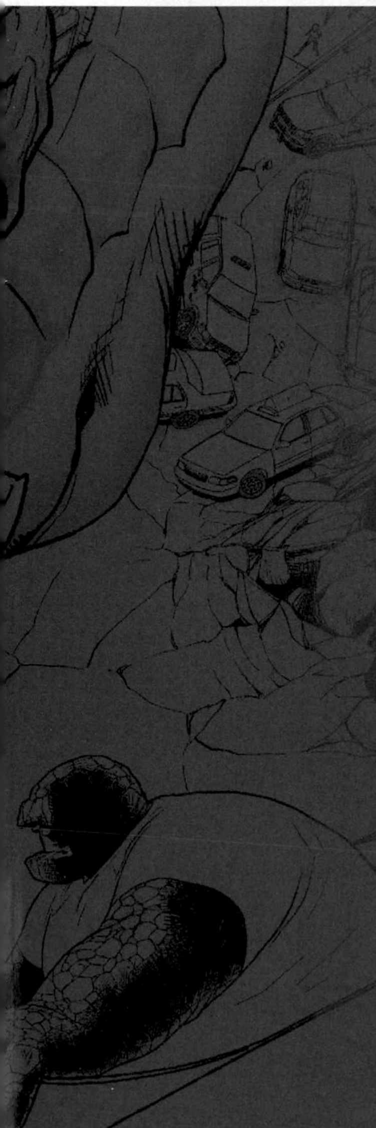

WRITER
ROBERTO AGUIRRE-SACASA
ARTIST
DAVID MARQUEZ
COLOR ARTIST
GURU-eFX
LETTERER
VC'S CLAYTON COWLES
COVER ARTIST
JULIAN TOTINO TEDESCO

ASSISTANT EDITOR
JOHN DENNING
EDITOR
LAUREN SANKOVITCH
EXECUTIVE EDITOR
TOM BREVOORT

FANTASTIC FOUR CREATED BY STAN LEE & JACK KIRBY

FANTASTIC ORIGINS

SUSAN STORM — HEART

JOHNNY STORM — BODY

DR. REED RICHARDS — MIND

BEN GRIMM — SOUL

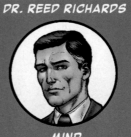

HERE THEY COME...

SOON, THEY WILL BE...

THE FANTASTIC FOUR

BUT NOT YET.

RIGHT NOW, IT'S:

Teatime at the Four Seasons.

OH, CLAUDETTE, THAT'S *BRILLIANT*--

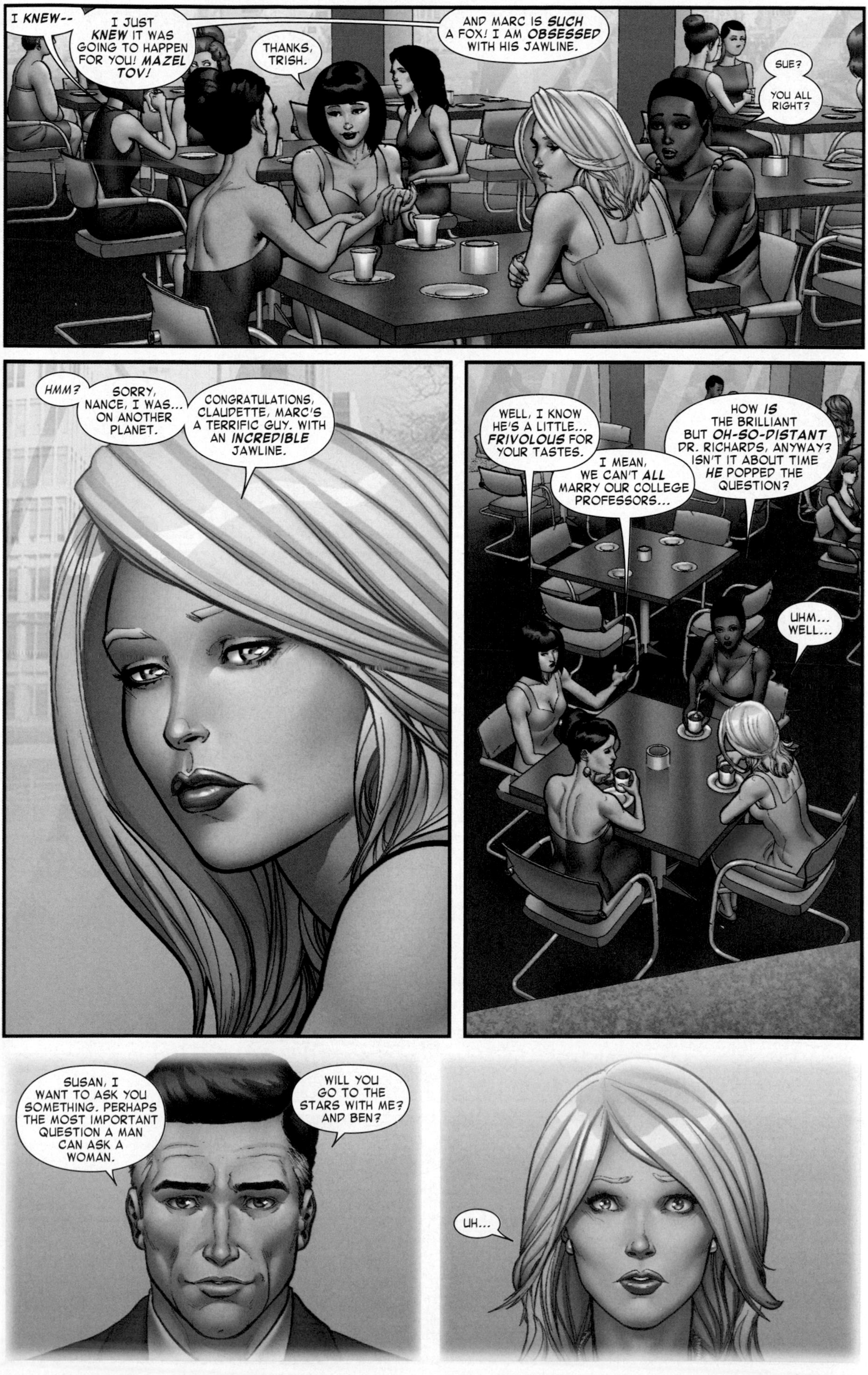
I KNEW--
I JUST KNEW IT WAS GOING TO HAPPEN FOR YOU! MAZEL TOV!
THANKS, TRISH.
AND MARC IS SUCH A FOX! I AM OBSESSED WITH HIS JAWLINE.
SUE?
YOU ALL RIGHT?
HMM?
SORRY, NANCE, I WAS... ON ANOTHER PLANET.
CONGRATULATIONS, CLAUDETTE, MARC'S A TERRIFIC GUY. WITH AN INCREDIBLE JAWLINE.
WELL, I KNOW HE'S A LITTLE... FRIVOLOUS FOR YOUR TASTES.
I MEAN, WE CAN'T ALL MARRY OUR COLLEGE PROFESSORS...
HOW IS THE BRILLIANT BUT OH-SO-DISTANT DR. RICHARDS, ANYWAY? ISN'T IT ABOUT TIME HE POPPED THE QUESTION?
UHM... WELL...
SUSAN, I WANT TO ASK YOU SOMETHING. PERHAPS THE MOST IMPORTANT QUESTION A MAN CAN ASK A WOMAN.
WILL YOU GO TO THE STARS WITH ME? AND BEN?
UH...

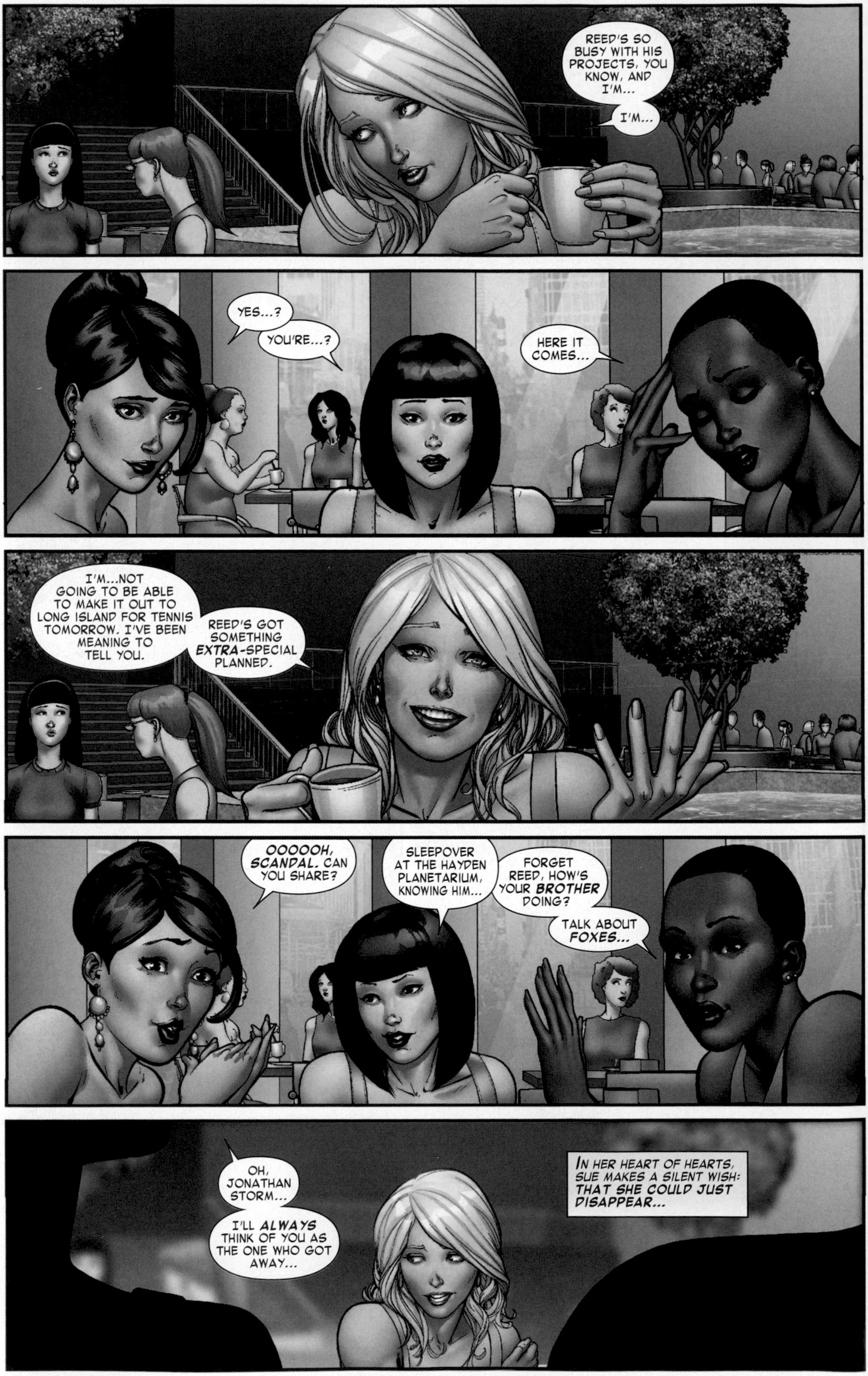
REED'S SO BUSY WITH HIS PROJECTS, YOU KNOW, AND I'M...
I'M...
YES...?
YOU'RE...?
HERE IT COMES...
I'M...NOT GOING TO BE ABLE TO MAKE IT OUT TO LONG ISLAND FOR TENNIS TOMORROW. I'VE BEEN MEANING TO TELL YOU.
REED'S GOT SOMETHING EXTRA-SPECIAL PLANNED.
OOOOOH, SCANDAL. CAN YOU SHARE?
SLEEPOVER AT THE HAYDEN PLANETARIUM, KNOWING HIM...
FORGET REED, HOW'S YOUR BROTHER DOING?
TALK ABOUT FOXES...
OH, JONATHAN STORM...
I'LL ALWAYS THINK OF YOU AS THE ONE WHO GOT AWAY...
IN HER HEART OF HEARTS, SUE MAKES A SILENT WISH: THAT SHE COULD JUST DISAPPEAR...

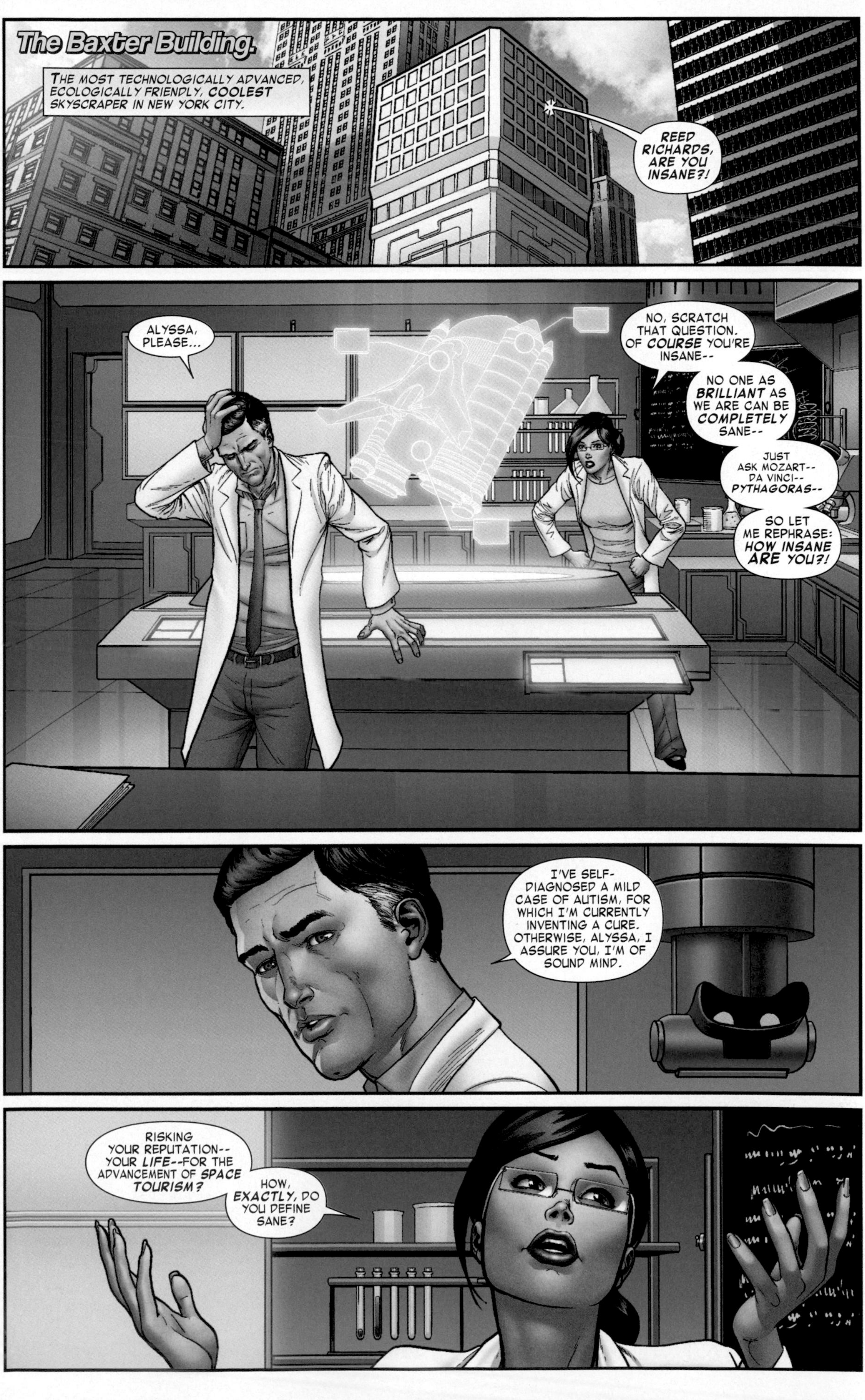
The Baxter Building.
THE MOST TECHNOLOGICALLY ADVANCED, ECOLOGICALLY FRIENDLY, COOLEST SKYSCRAPER IN NEW YORK CITY.
REED RICHARDS, ARE YOU INSANE?!
ALYSSA, PLEASE...
NO, SCRATCH THAT QUESTION. OF COURSE YOU'RE INSANE--
NO ONE AS BRILLIANT AS WE ARE CAN BE COMPLETELY SANE--
JUST ASK MOZART-- DA VINCI-- PYTHAGORAS--
SO LET ME REPHRASE: HOW INSANE ARE YOU?!
I'VE SELF-DIAGNOSED A MILD CASE OF AUTISM, FOR WHICH I'M CURRENTLY INVENTING A CURE. OTHERWISE, ALYSSA, I ASSURE YOU, I'M OF SOUND MIND.
RISKING YOUR REPUTATION-- YOUR LIFE--FOR THE ADVANCEMENT OF SPACE TOURISM?
HOW, EXACTLY, DO YOU DEFINE SANE?

OBVIOUSLY, SPACE TOURISM IS NOT THE GOAL. THE GOAL IS... EVERYTHING ELSE I'M DOING HERE.

SPACE TOURISM IS A *BUSINESS* VENTURE. TO SUBSIDIZE THE REST OF MY WORK.

OUR WORK, REED--MY GOD, YOU'RE INSANE *AND* HUBRISTIC.

IF YOU NEED MONEY, INVENT AN ANTI-AGING SKIN CREAM-- *LITERALLY.*

WHAT ABOUT THE RISKS?

STATISTICALLY, LESS THAN DRIVING A CAR.

ESPECIALLY ON THE VAN WYCK.

JOKE ALL YOU WANT, BUT I'M TRACKING COSMIC STORMS FOR THE NEXT THREE TO EIGHT REVOLUTIONS.

WHY TOMORROW? WHY NOT WAIT?

REED RICHARDS DOESN'T SAY WHAT HE'S THINKING, WHICH IS: BECAUSE I WANT TO BE FIRST.

SO, INSTEAD, HE SAYS NOTHING.

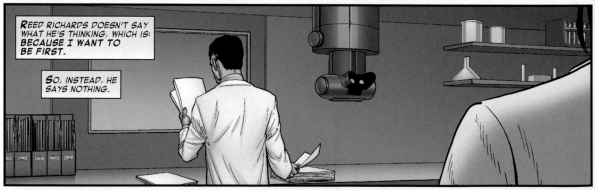

YOU'RE GOING TO BE VILIFIED, YOU KNOW. IF NOT ARRESTED.

YOU DON'T HAVE PERMITS, YOU DON'T HAVE PERMISSION, YOU DON'T HAVE *CLEARANCE*--

WHO'S EVEN *FLYING* WITH YOU?

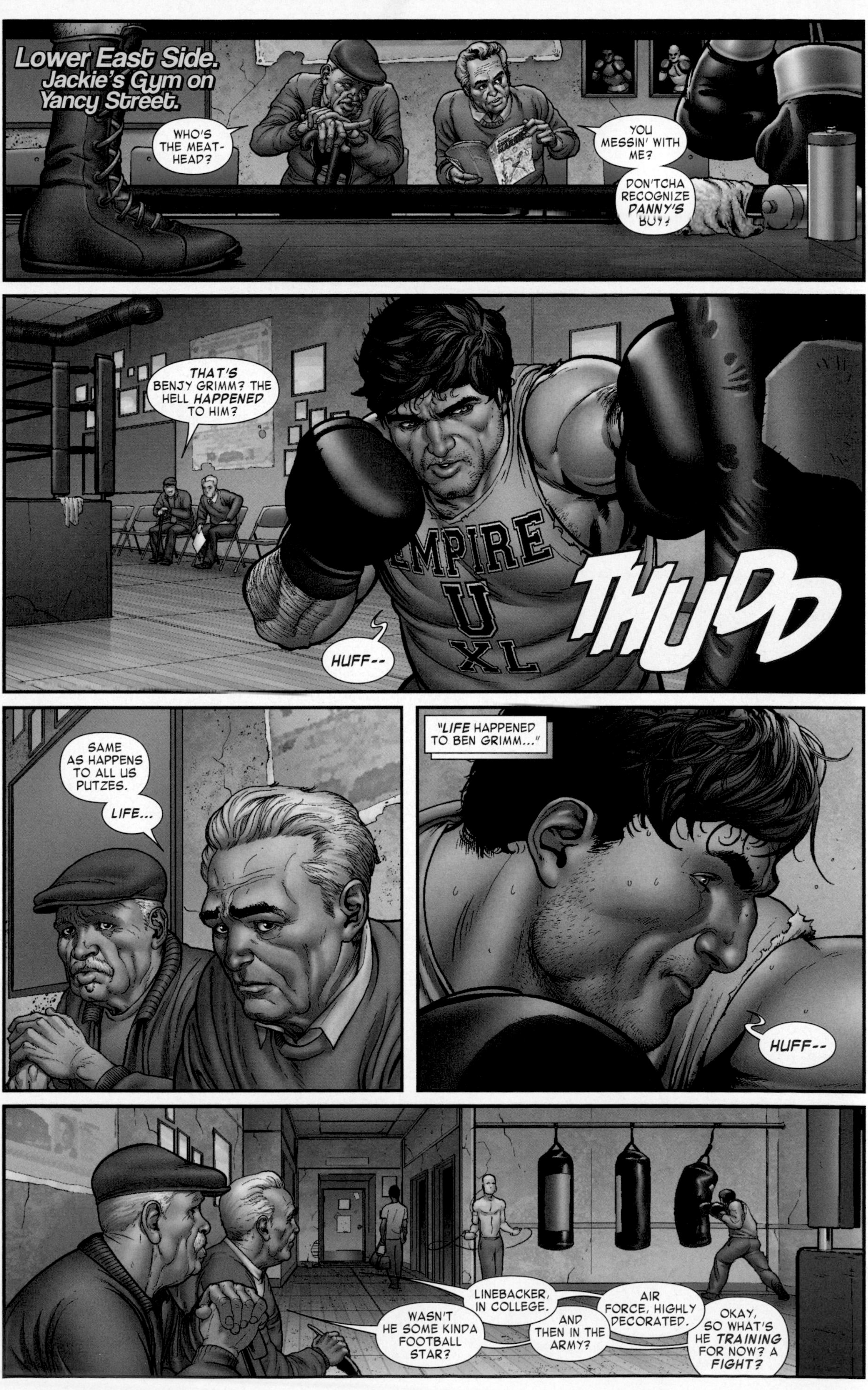
Lower East Side. Jackie's Gym on Yancy Street.
WHO'S THE MEAT-HEAD?
YOU MESSIN' WITH ME?
DON'TCHA RECOGNIZE DANNY'S BOY?
THAT'S BENJY GRIMM? THE HELL HAPPENED TO HIM?
EMPIRE U XL
THUDD
HUFF--
SAME AS HAPPENS TO ALL US PUTZES.
LIFE...
"LIFE HAPPENED TO BEN GRIMM..."
HUFF--
WASN'T HE SOME KINDA FOOTBALL STAR?
LINEBACKER, IN COLLEGE.
AND THEN IN THE ARMY?
AIR FORCE, HIGHLY DECORATED.
OKAY, SO WHAT'S HE TRAINING FOR NOW? A FIGHT?

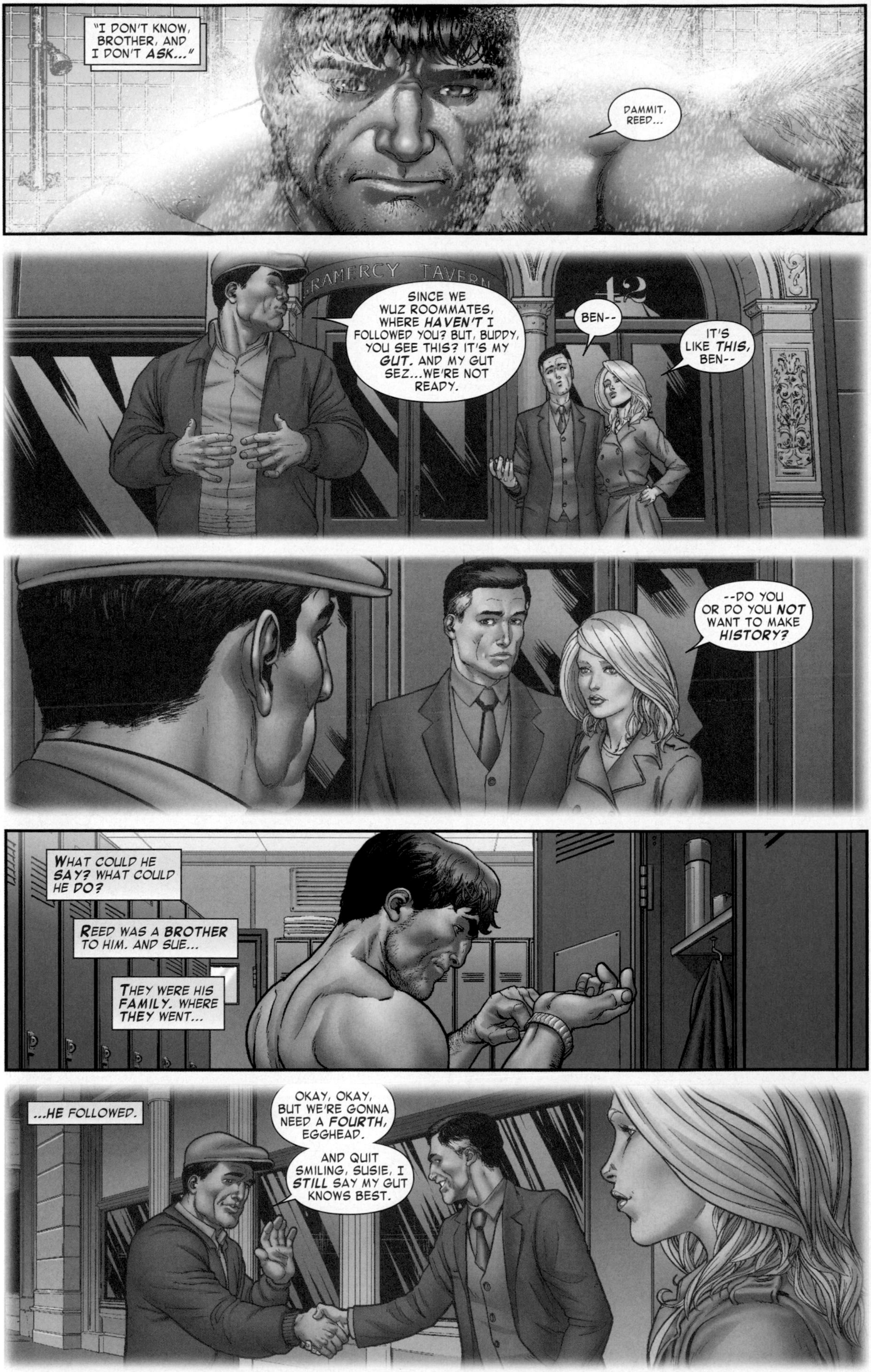
"I DON'T KNOW, BROTHER, AND I DON'T ASK..."
DAMMIT, REED...
SINCE WE WUZ ROOMMATES, WHERE HAVEN'T I FOLLOWED YOU? BUT, BUDDY, YOU SEE THIS? IT'S MY GUT. AND MY GUT SEZ...WE'RE NOT READY.
GRAMERCY TAVERN
42
BEN--
IT'S LIKE THIS, BEN--
--DO YOU OR DO YOU NOT WANT TO MAKE HISTORY?
WHAT COULD HE SAY? WHAT COULD HE DO?
REED WAS A BROTHER TO HIM. AND SUE...
THEY WERE HIS FAMILY. WHERE THEY WENT...
...HE FOLLOWED.
OKAY, OKAY, BUT WE'RE GONNA NEED A FOURTH, EGGHEAD.
AND QUIT SMILING, SUSIE, I STILL SAY MY GUT KNOWS BEST.

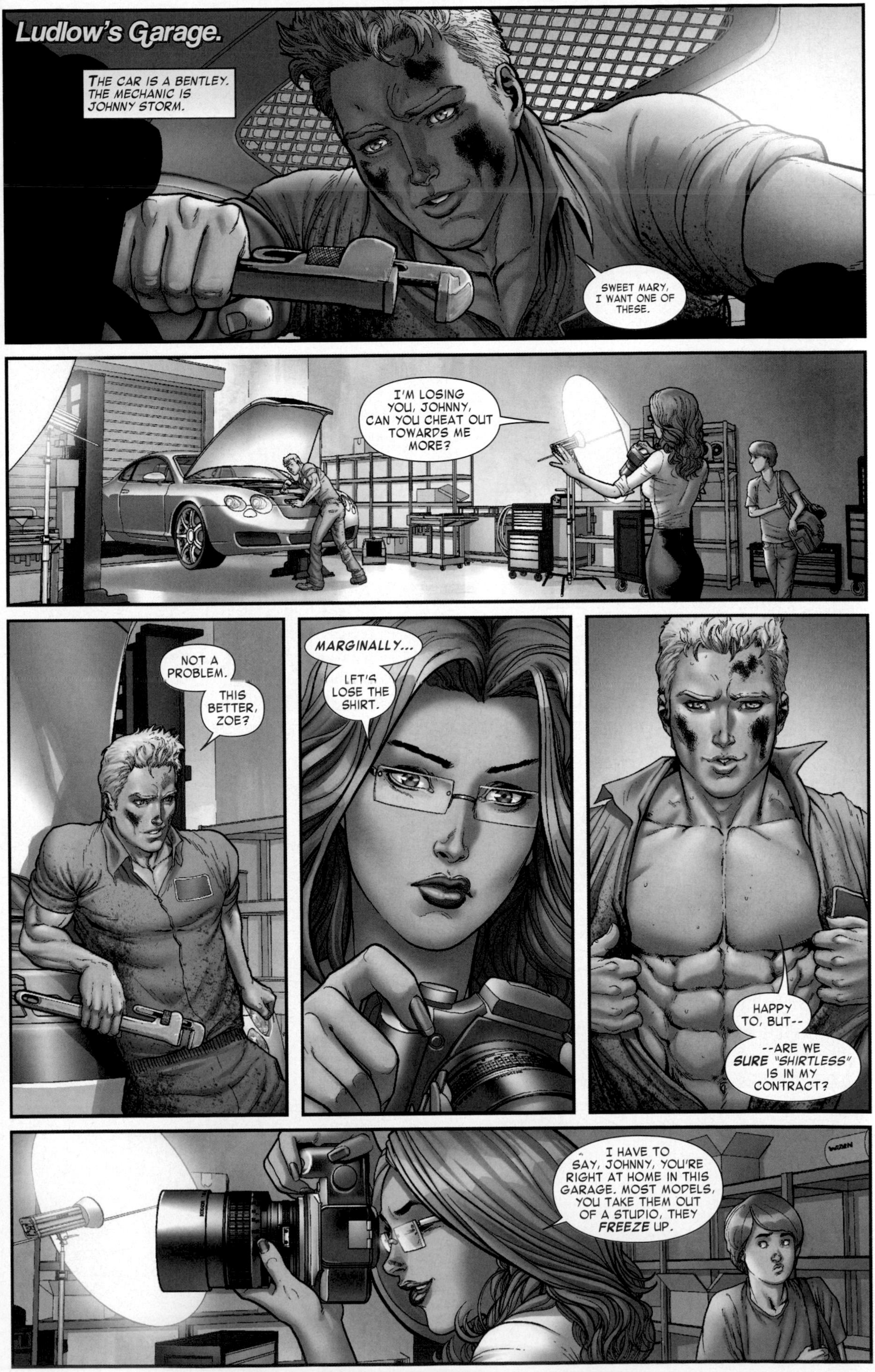
Ludlow's Garage.
THE CAR IS A BENTLEY. THE MECHANIC IS JOHNNY STORM.
SWEET MARY, I WANT ONE OF THESE.
I'M LOSING YOU, JOHNNY, CAN YOU CHEAT OUT TOWARDS ME MORE?
NOT A PROBLEM.
THIS BETTER, ZOE?
MARGINALLY...
LET'S LOSE THE SHIRT.
HAPPY TO, BUT--
--ARE WE SURE "SHIRTLESS" IS IN MY CONTRACT?
I HAVE TO SAY, JOHNNY, YOU'RE RIGHT AT HOME IN THIS GARAGE. MOST MODELS, YOU TAKE THEM OUT OF A STUDIO, THEY FREEZE UP.

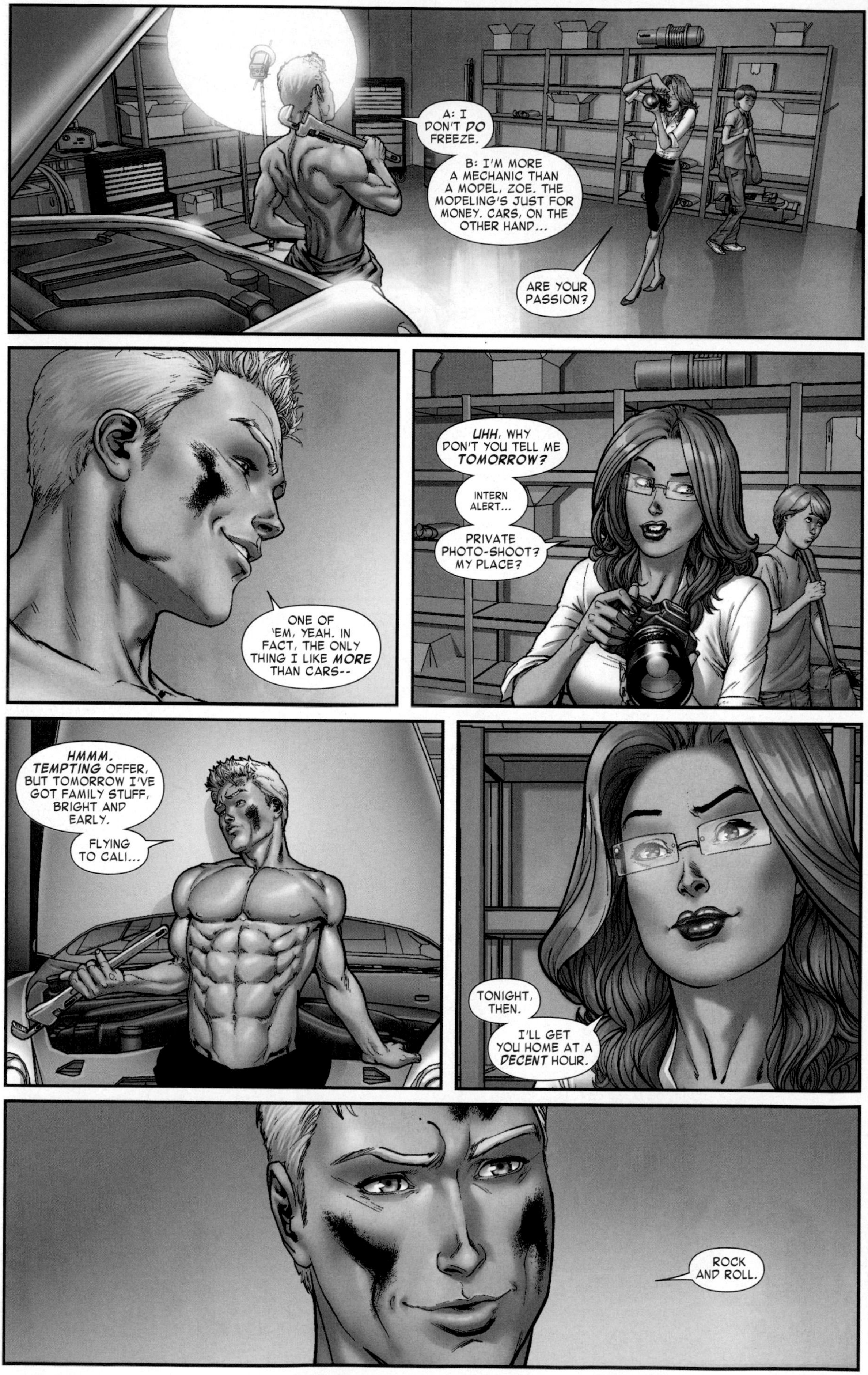
A: I DON'T DO FREEZE.
B: I'M MORE A MECHANIC THAN A MODEL, ZOE. THE MODELING'S JUST FOR MONEY. CARS, ON THE OTHER HAND...
ARE YOUR PASSION?
ONE OF 'EM, YEAH. IN FACT, THE ONLY THING I LIKE MORE THAN CARS--
UHH, WHY DON'T YOU TELL ME TOMORROW?
INTERN ALERT...
PRIVATE PHOTO-SHOOT? MY PLACE?
HMMM. TEMPTING OFFER, BUT TOMORROW I'VE GOT FAMILY STUFF, BRIGHT AND EARLY.
FLYING TO CALI...
TONIGHT, THEN.
I'LL GET YOU HOME AT A DECENT HOUR.
ROCK AND ROLL.

THE LAST FEW MONTHS, THE FARMERS OF STOCKTON, CALIFORNIA, HAVE WONDERED ABOUT THE MYSTERIOUS SILO BUILT ON A NONDESCRIPT PARCEL OF LAND, JUST BARELY VISIBLE FROM THE 5.

...FOUR...THREE...TWO...ONE...

NUESCH ORCHARDS

ON THIS BRIGHT, CLEAR, JUNE DAY...

...THEY'RE STILL WONDERING.

"UHHGH, I THINK I'M GONNA BE SICK..."

GIVE ME A BREAK, JOHNNY. THIS TAKEOFF'S FAR SMOOTHER THAN ANY OF OUR RIDES IN THE SIMULATOR.

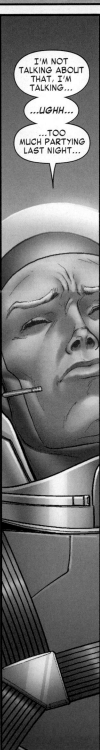

I'M NOT TALKING ABOUT THAT, I'M TALKING...

...UGHH...

...TOO MUCH PARTYING LAST NIGHT...

I WASN'T GOING TO COMMENT, BUT NOW THAT YOU MENTION IT, I DON'T REMEMBER HEARING YOU COME IN...

IN CASE ANYONE'S WONDERIN', WE'RE EGGZACTLY FIFTEEN SECONDS BEHIND THE SPACE SHUTTLE...

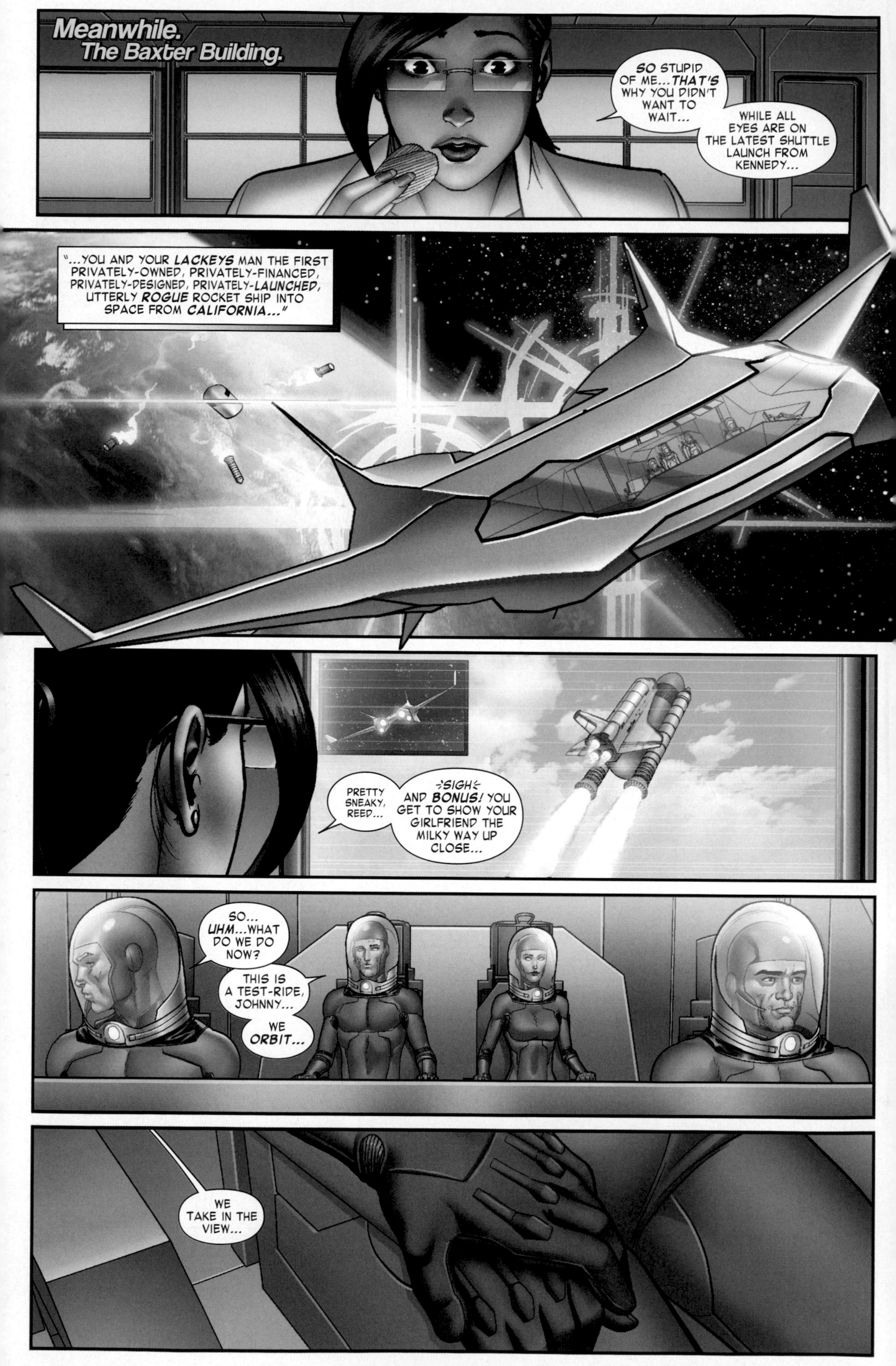
Meanwhile. The Baxter Building.
SO STUPID OF ME...THAT'S WHY YOU DIDN'T WANT TO WAIT...
WHILE ALL EYES ARE ON THE LATEST SHUTTLE LAUNCH FROM KENNEDY...
"...YOU AND YOUR LACKEYS MAN THE FIRST PRIVATELY-OWNED, PRIVATELY-FINANCED, PRIVATELY-DESIGNED, PRIVATELY-LAUNCHED, UTTERLY ROGUE ROCKET SHIP INTO SPACE FROM CALIFORNIA..."
PRETTY SNEAKY, REED...
SIGH AND BONUS! YOU GET TO SHOW YOUR GIRLFRIEND THE MILKY WAY UP CLOSE...
SO... UHM...WHAT DO WE DO NOW?
THIS IS A TEST-RIDE, JOHNNY...
WE ORBIT...
WE TAKE IN THE VIEW...

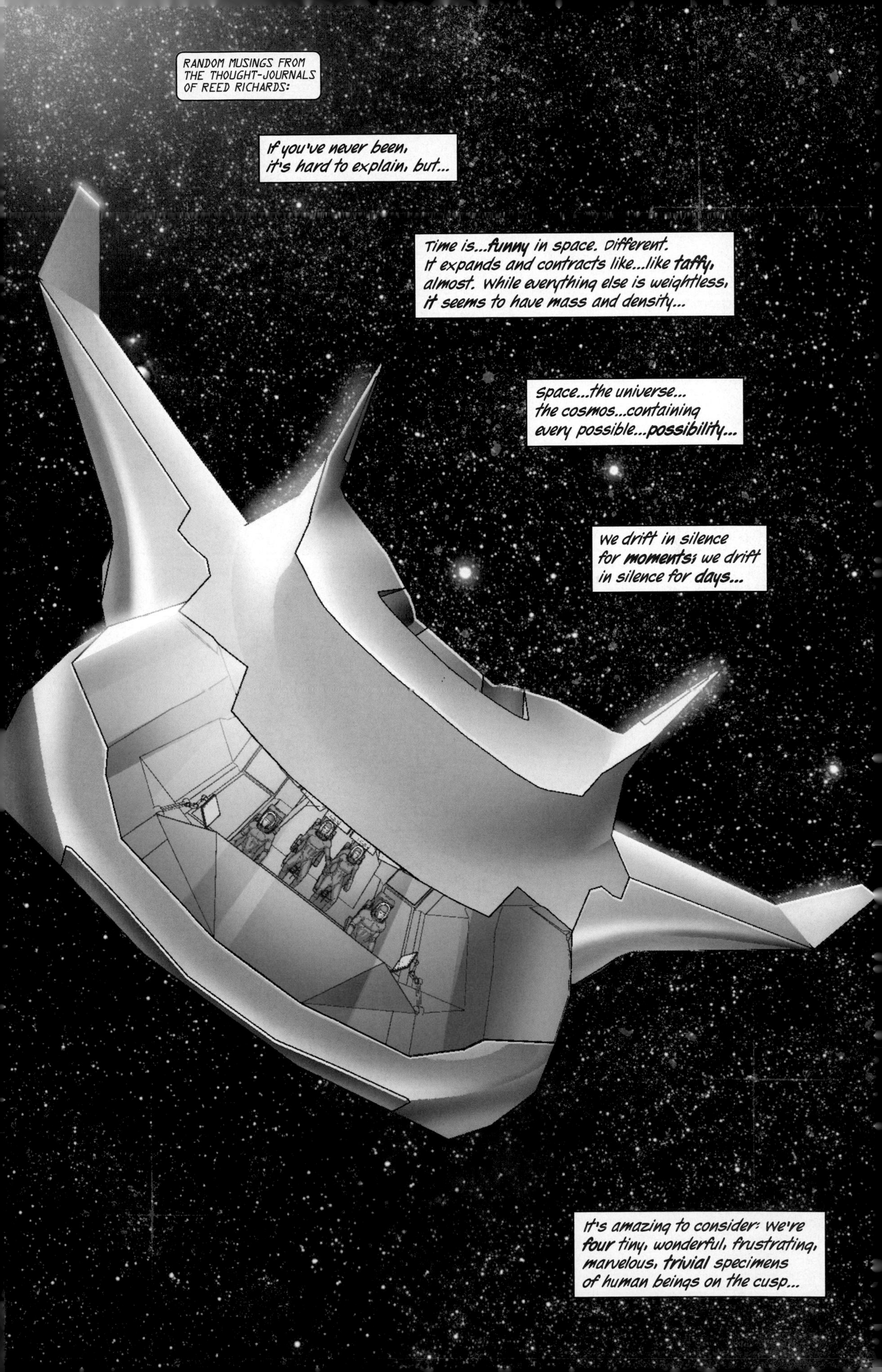
RANDOM MUSINGS FROM THE THOUGHT-JOURNALS OF REED RICHARDS:
If you've never been, it's hard to explain, but...
Time is...funny in space. Different. It expands and contracts like...like taffy, almost. While everything else is weightless, it seems to have mass and density...
Space...the universe... the cosmos...containing every possible...possibility...
We drift in silence for moments; we drift in silence for days...
It's amazing to consider: We're four tiny, wonderful, frustrating, marvelous, trivial specimens of human beings on the cusp...

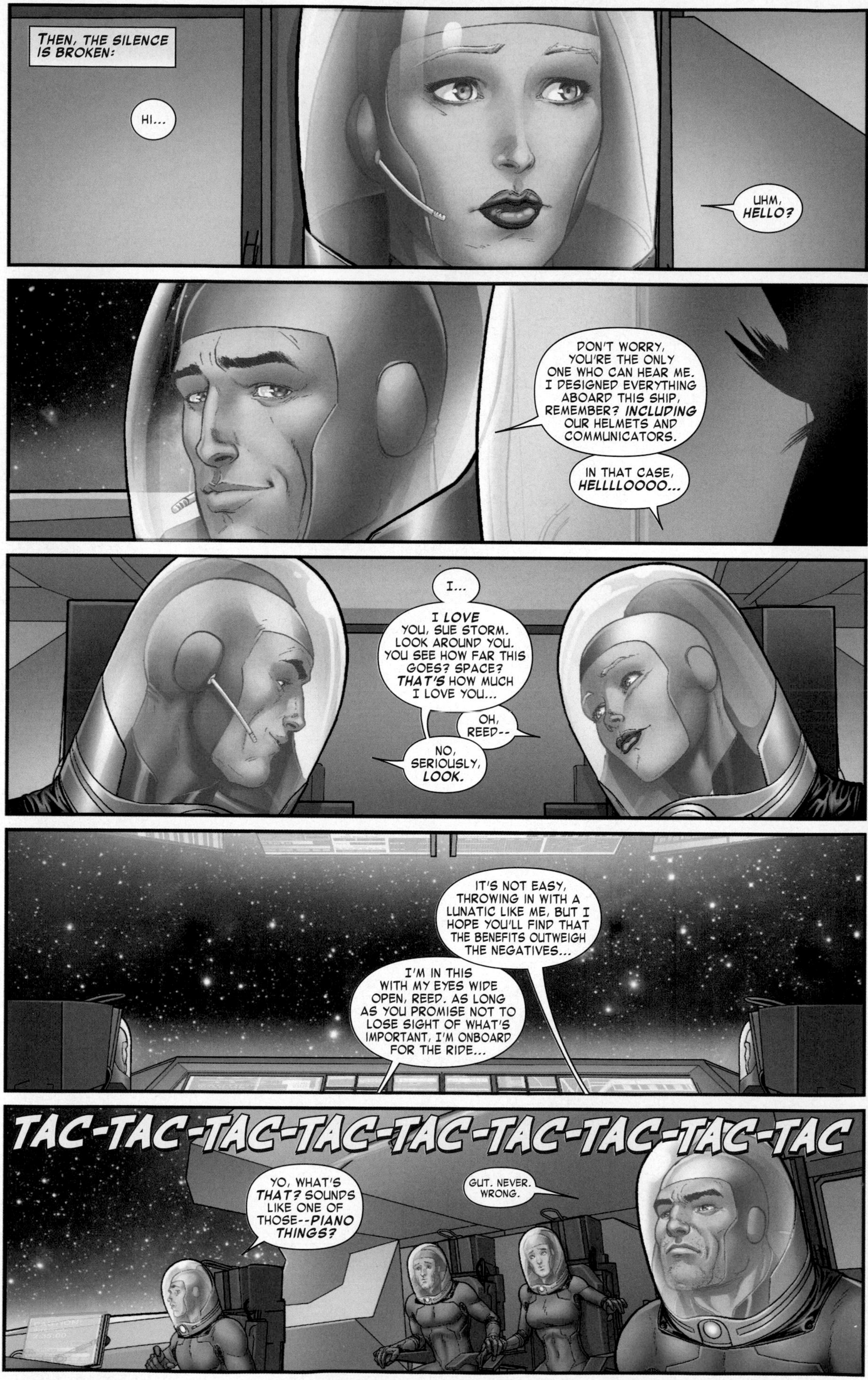
THEN, THE SILENCE IS BROKEN:
HI...
UHM, HELLO?
DON'T WORRY, YOU'RE THE ONLY ONE WHO CAN HEAR ME. I DESIGNED EVERYTHING ABOARD THIS SHIP, REMEMBER? INCLUDING OUR HELMETS AND COMMUNICATORS.
IN THAT CASE, HELLLLOOOO...
I...
I LOVE YOU, SUE STORM. LOOK AROUND YOU. YOU SEE HOW FAR THIS GOES? SPACE? THAT'S HOW MUCH I LOVE YOU...
OH, REED--
NO, SERIOUSLY, LOOK.
IT'S NOT EASY, THROWING IN WITH A LUNATIC LIKE ME, BUT I HOPE YOU'LL FIND THAT THE BENEFITS OUTWEIGH THE NEGATIVES...
I'M IN THIS WITH MY EYES WIDE OPEN, REED. AS LONG AS YOU PROMISE NOT TO LOSE SIGHT OF WHAT'S IMPORTANT, I'M ONBOARD FOR THE RIDE...
TAC-TAC-TAC-TAC-TAC-TAC-TAC-TAC-TAC
YO, WHAT'S THAT? SOUNDS LIKE ONE OF THOSE--PIANO THINGS?
GUT. NEVER. WRONG.

HE MEANS A METRONOME, REED THINKS--

--JUST AS THE *FOUR* FLY INTO ONE OF THE COSMIC STORMS ALYSSA MOY HAD PREDICTED...

We're being *bombarded* by cosmic rays--

BEN, CAN YOU AVERT?

WHAT DO YOU THINK I'M *TRYIN'* TA DO? SUZIE, HANG ON--

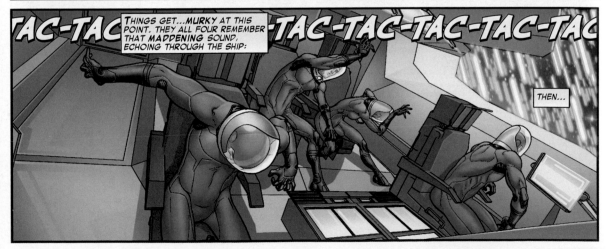

TAC-TAC-TAC-TAC-TAC-TAC-TAC-TAC

THINGS GET...MURKY AT THIS POINT. THEY ALL FOUR REMEMBER THAT *MADDENING* SOUND, ECHOING THROUGH THE SHIP:

THEN...

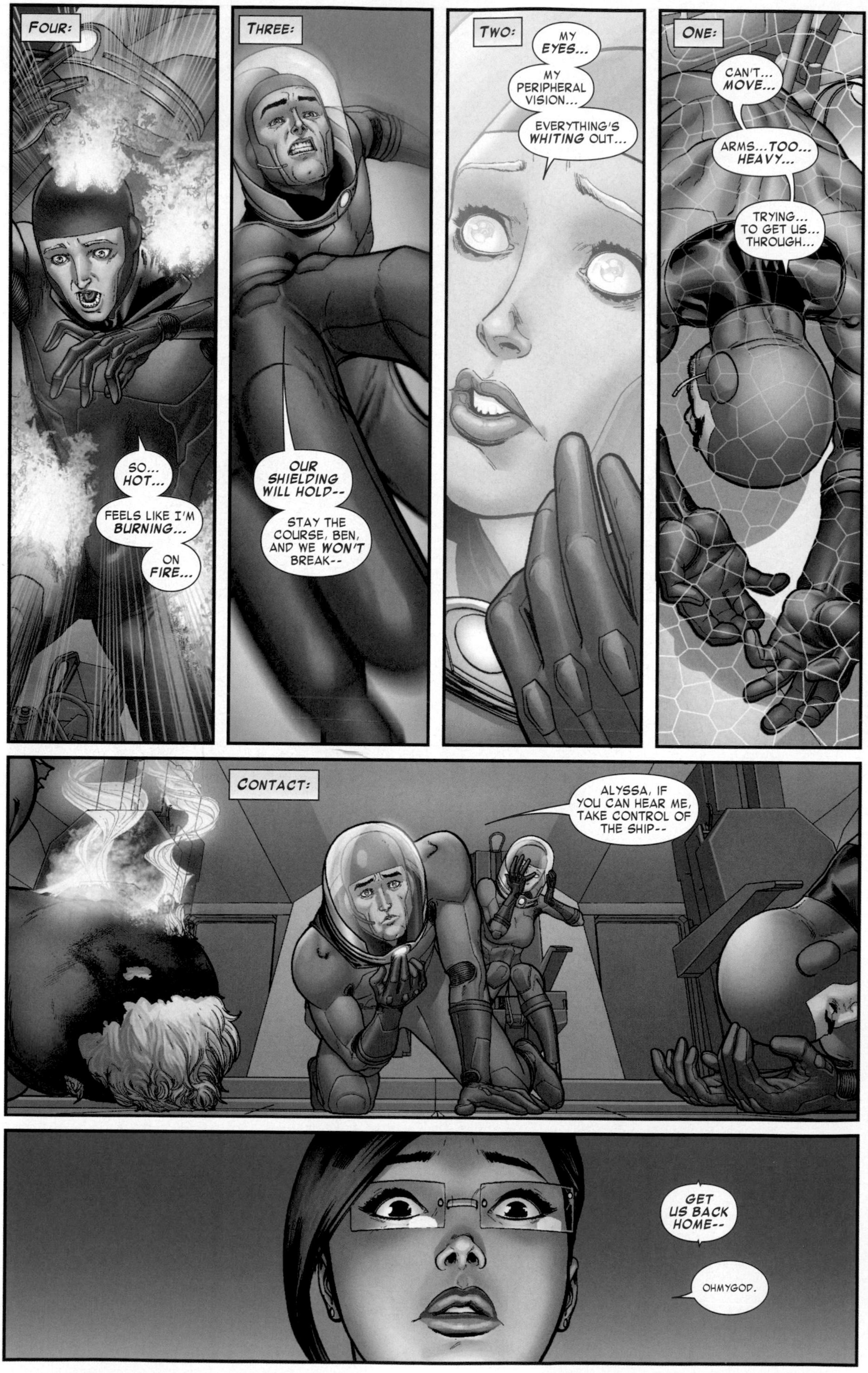
FOUR:
SO... HOT...
FEELS LIKE I'M BURNING...
ON FIRE...
THREE:
OUR SHIELDING WILL HOLD--
STAY THE COURSE, BEN, AND WE WON'T BREAK--
TWO:
MY EYES...
MY PERIPHERAL VISION...
EVERYTHING'S WHITING OUT...
ONE:
CAN'T... MOVE...
ARMS... TOO... HEAVY...
TRYING... TO GET US... THROUGH...
CONTACT:
ALYSSA, IF YOU CAN HEAR ME, TAKE CONTROL OF THE SHIP--
GET US BACK HOME--
OHMYGOD.

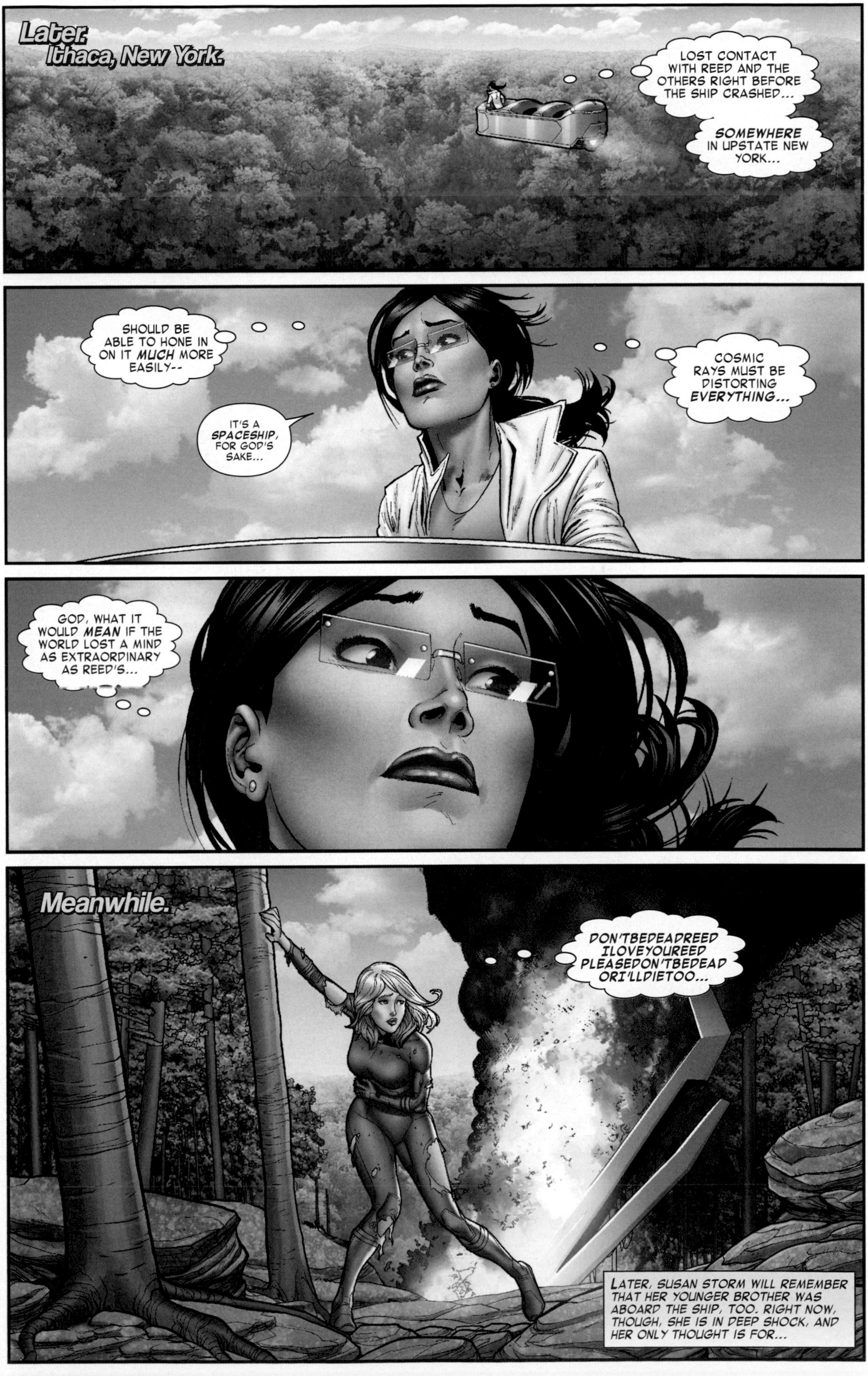

Later.
Ithaca, New York.
LOST CONTACT WITH REED AND THE OTHERS RIGHT BEFORE THE SHIP CRASHED...
SOMEWHERE IN UPSTATE NEW YORK...
SHOULD BE ABLE TO HONE IN ON IT MUCH MORE EASILY--
IT'S A SPACESHIP, FOR GOD'S SAKE...
COSMIC RAYS MUST BE DISTORTING EVERYTHING...
GOD, WHAT IT WOULD MEAN IF THE WORLD LOST A MIND AS EXTRAORDINARY AS REED'S...
Meanwhile.
DON'TBEDEADREED ILOVEYOUREED PLEASEDON'TBEDEAD ORI'LLDIETOO...
LATER, SUSAN STORM WILL REMEMBER THAT HER YOUNGER BROTHER WAS ABOARD THE SHIP, TOO. RIGHT NOW, THOUGH, SHE IS IN DEEP SHOCK, AND HER ONLY THOUGHT IS FOR...

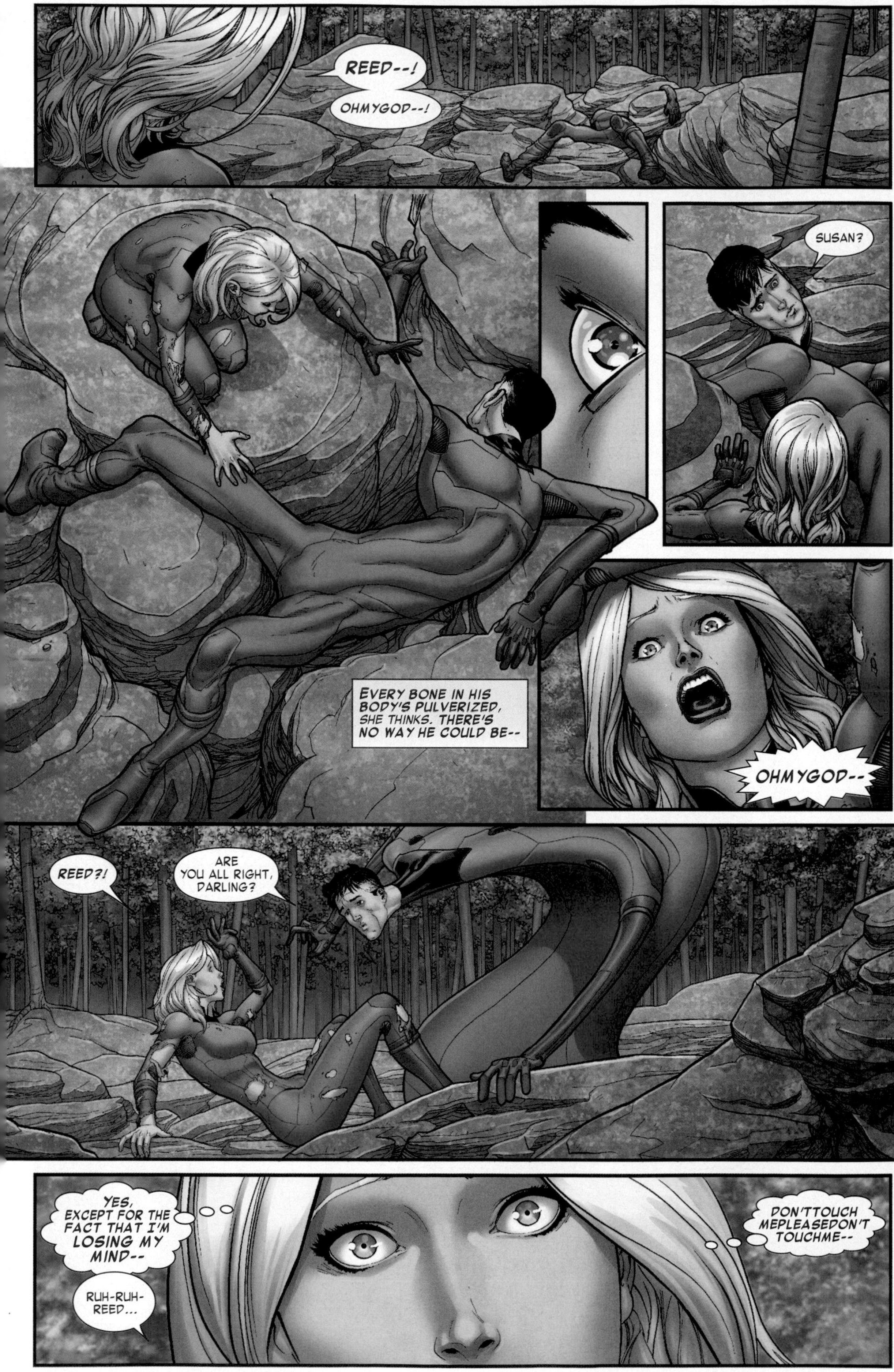
REED--!
OHMYGOD--!
SUSAN?
EVERY BONE IN HIS BODY'S PULVERIZED, SHE THINKS. THERE'S NO WAY HE COULD BE--
OHMYGOD--
REED?!
ARE YOU ALL RIGHT, DARLING?
YES, EXCEPT FOR THE FACT THAT I'M LOSING MY MIND--
RUH-RUH-REED...
DON'TTOUCH MEPLEASEDON'T TOUCHME--

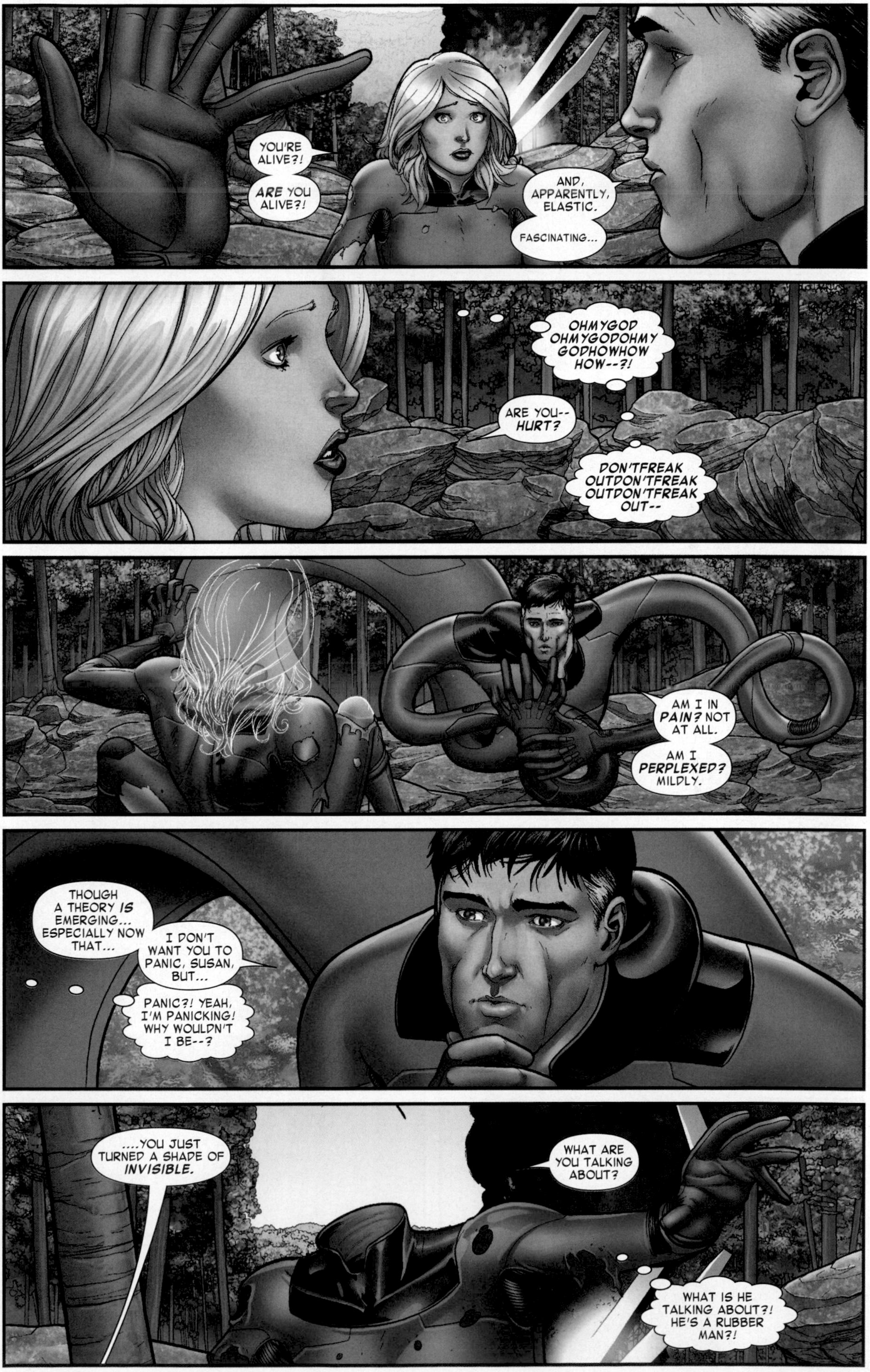

YOU'RE ALIVE?!
ARE YOU ALIVE?!
AND, APPARENTLY, ELASTIC.
FASCINATING...
OHMYGOD OHMYGODOHMY GODHOWHOW HOW--?!
ARE YOU-- HURT?
DON'TFREAK OUTDON'TFREAK OUTDON'TFREAK OUT--
AM I IN PAIN? NOT AT ALL.
AM I PERPLEXED? MILDLY.
THOUGH A THEORY IS EMERGING... ESPECIALLY NOW THAT...
I DON'T WANT YOU TO PANIC, SUSAN, BUT...
PANIC?! YEAH, I'M PANICKING! WHY WOULDN'T I BE--?
....YOU JUST TURNED A SHADE OF INVISIBLE.
WHAT ARE YOU TALKING ABOUT?
WHAT IS HE TALKING ABOUT?! HE'S A RUBBER MAN?!

OH. OH, DEAR...

OH, REED...

REEEEEEEEEEED...

THE COSMIC RAYS...

ALYSSA WAS RIGHT...

ALYSSA WAS RIGHT ABOUT WHAT?

HM? SORRY, IT'S A BIT DISCONCERTING--

I READ H.G. WELLS'S *"THE INVISIBLE MAN"* WHEN I WAS THREE AND NOW I'M *LIVING* IT...

REED! WHAT WAS ALYSSA RIGHT ABOUT?

ALYSSA WAS CONCERNED WE MIGHT COME INTO CONTACT WITH COSMIC ENERGY...SHE WARNED AGAINST OUR FLIGHT...

OBVIOUSLY THE COSMIC RAYS HAVE ALTERED US IN DIFFERENT, *RADICAL* WAYS...

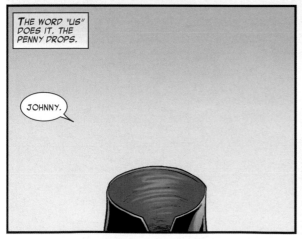

THE WORD "US" DOES IT. THE PENNY DROPS.

JOHNNY.

BEN.

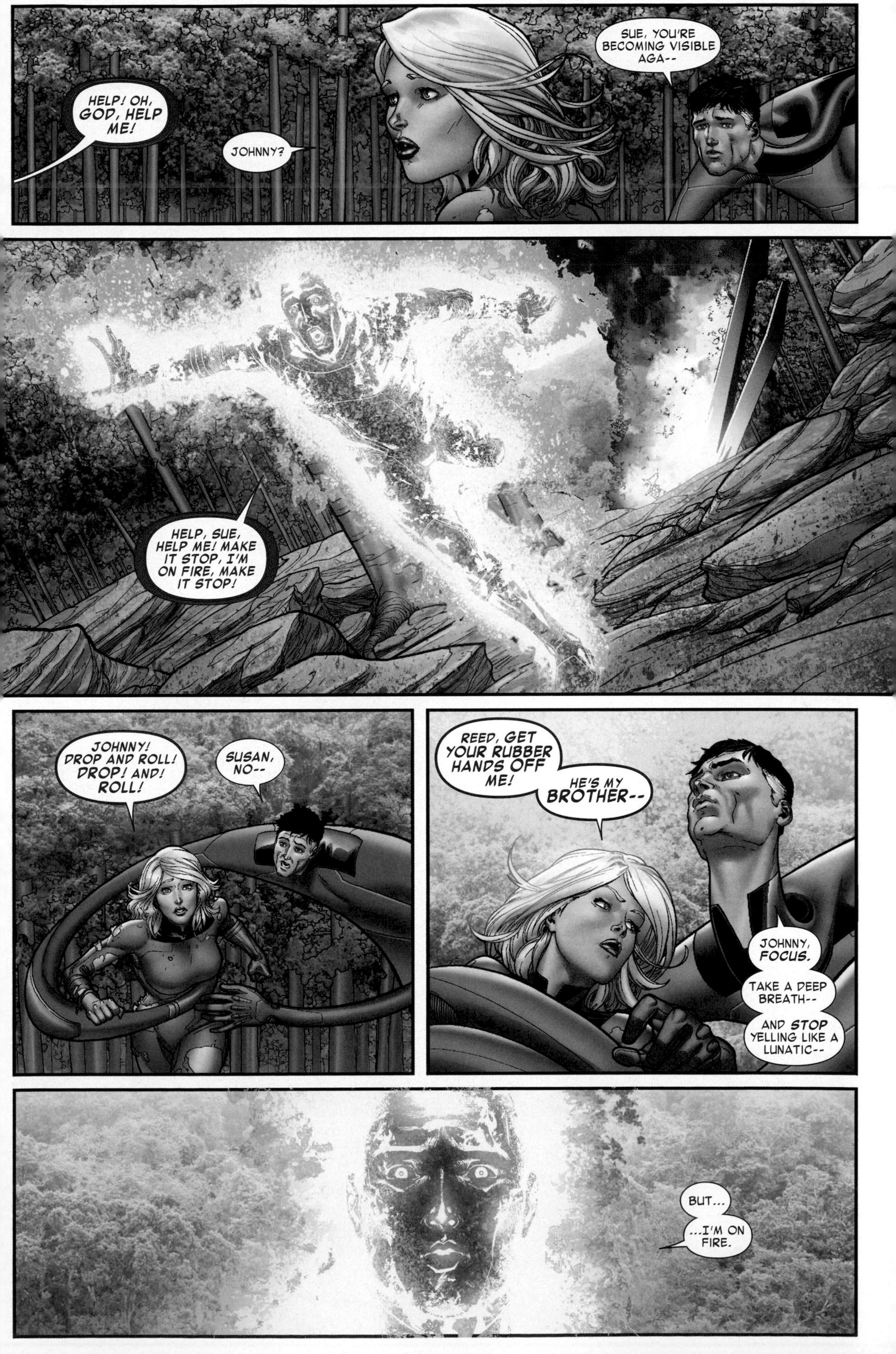
HELP! OH, GOD, HELP ME!
JOHNNY?
SUE, YOU'RE BECOMING VISIBLE AGA--
HELP, SUE, HELP ME! MAKE IT STOP, I'M ON FIRE, MAKE IT STOP!
JOHNNY! DROP AND ROLL! DROP! AND! ROLL!
SUSAN, NO--
REED, GET YOUR RUBBER HANDS OFF ME!
HE'S MY BROTHER--
JOHNNY, FOCUS.
TAKE A DEEP BREATH--
AND STOP YELLING LIKE A LUNATIC--
BUT...
...I'M ON FIRE.

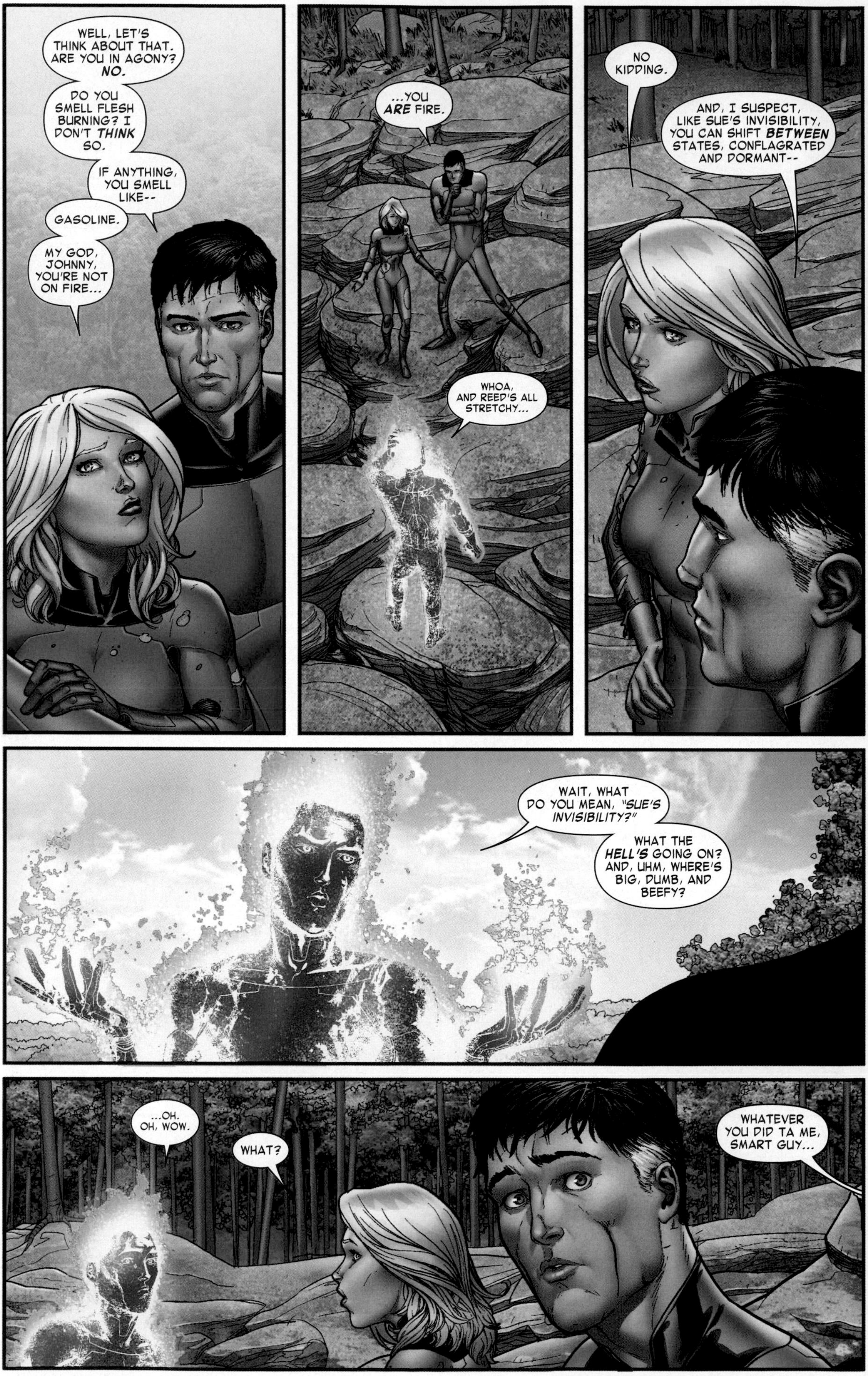
WELL, LET'S THINK ABOUT THAT. ARE YOU IN AGONY? NO.
DO YOU SMELL FLESH BURNING? I DON'T THINK SO.
IF ANYTHING, YOU SMELL LIKE--
GASOLINE.
MY GOD, JOHNNY, YOU'RE NOT ON FIRE...
...YOU ARE FIRE.
WHOA, AND REED'S ALL STRETCHY...
NO KIDDING.
AND, I SUSPECT, LIKE SUE'S INVISIBILITY, YOU CAN SHIFT BETWEEN STATES, CONFLAGRATED AND DORMANT--
WAIT, WHAT DO YOU MEAN, "SUE'S INVISIBILITY?"
WHAT THE HELL'S GOING ON? AND, UHM, WHERE'S BIG, DUMB, AND BEEFY?
...OH. OH, WOW.
WHAT?
WHATEVER YOU DID TA ME, SMART GUY...

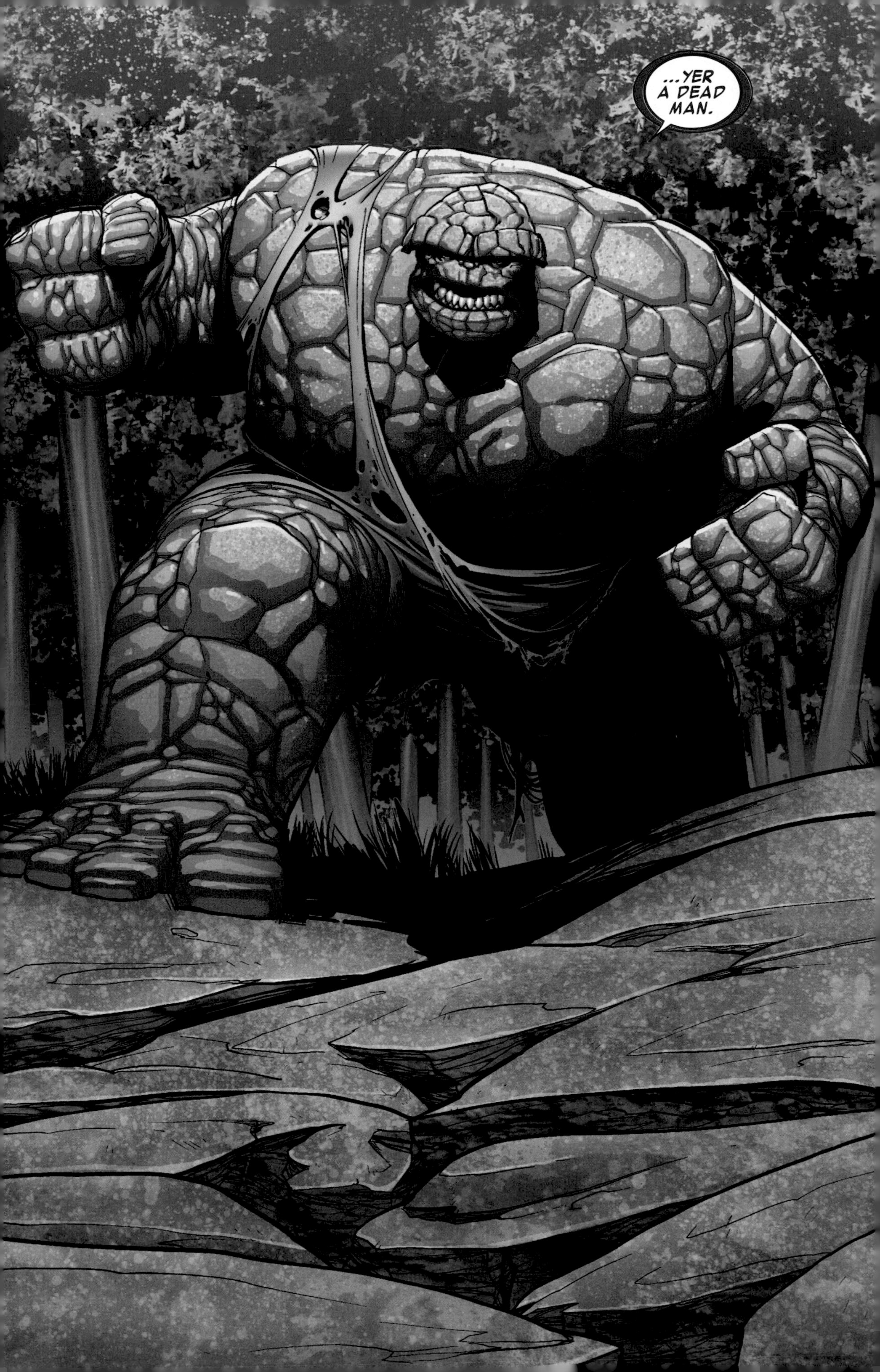
...YER A DEAD MAN.

BEN--

BEN, *CONTROL YOURSELF*--

WILL DO--

AS SOON AS YER A *PUDDLE*--

IS THAT *REALLY* BEN?

...

WHAT THE HECK DID HE *BECOME,* SUE?

I DON'T KNOW, BUT IT'S *NOT GOOD,* AND HE *BLAMES* REED--

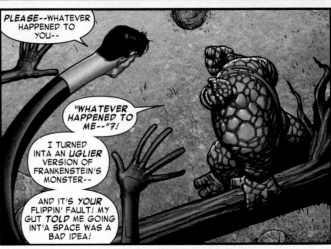

PLEASE--WHATEVER HAPPENED TO YOU--

"WHATEVER HAPPENED TO ME--"?!

I TURNED INTA AN *UGLIER* VERSION OF FRANKENSTEIN'S MONSTER--

AND IT'S *YOUR* FLIPPIN' FAULT! MY GUT *TOLD* ME GOING INT'A SPACE WAS A *BAD* IDEA!

A SECOND'S HESITATION, THEN:

WE WERE *ALL* CHANGED, BEN--YOU, ME, JOHNNY, SUE--

BUT SUE CAN PHASE BETWEEN VISIBILITY AND INVISIBILITY--AND JOHNNY CAN CONTROL HIS *FLAME* (AT LEAST I *THINK* HE CAN)--

HAVE YOU TRIED *WILLING* YOURSELF BACK TO--TO--?

LOOKING NORMAL? YEAH, I *TRIED*--

GUESS WHAT, *GENIUS? DIDN'T WORK*--

WELL THEN, *TRY HARDER*--

I WILL-- LIKE I SAID, *AFTER* I KILL YOU FOR BEING SUCH A--

THAT'S ENOUGH!

BOTH OF YOU, *STOP!*

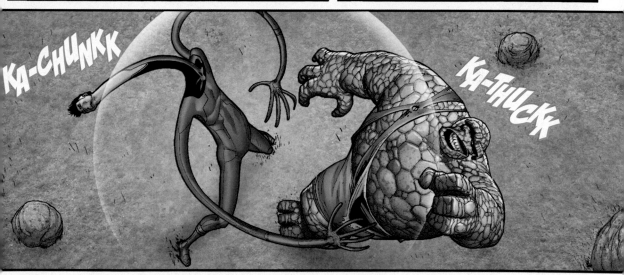

KA-CHUNKK

KA-THUCKK

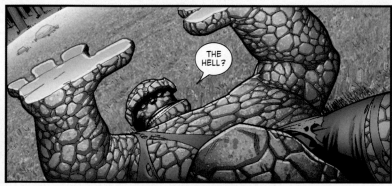

THE HELL?

I... I'M...NOT SURE. M-MAYBE?

INVISIBLE FORCE-FIELD.

SUSAN... IS THIS YOU?

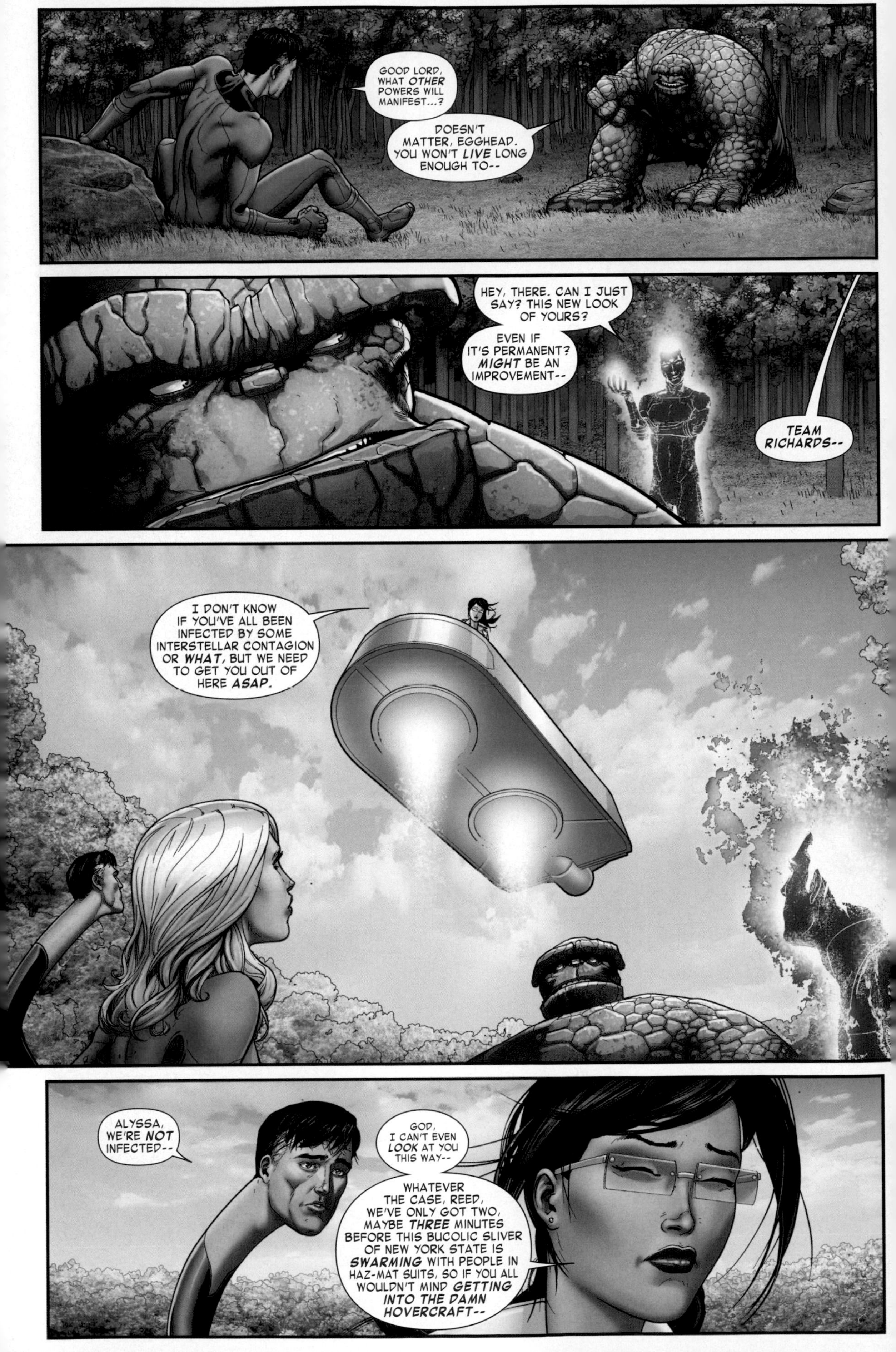
GOOD LORD, WHAT *OTHER* POWERS WILL MANIFEST...?
DOESN'T MATTER, EGGHEAD. YOU WON'T *LIVE* LONG ENOUGH TO--
HEY, THERE. CAN I JUST SAY? THIS NEW LOOK OF YOURS?
EVEN IF IT'S PERMANENT? *MIGHT* BE AN IMPROVEMENT--
TEAM RICHARDS--
I DON'T KNOW IF YOU'VE ALL BEEN INFECTED BY SOME INTERSTELLAR CONTAGION OR *WHAT*, BUT WE NEED TO GET YOU OUT OF HERE *ASAP*.
ALYSSA, WE'RE *NOT* INFECTED--
GOD, I CAN'T EVEN *LOOK* AT YOU THIS WAY--
WHATEVER THE CASE, REED, WE'VE ONLY GOT TWO, MAYBE *THREE* MINUTES BEFORE THIS BUCOLIC SLIVER OF NEW YORK STATE IS *SWARMING* WITH PEOPLE IN HAZ-MAT SUITS, SO IF YOU ALL WOULDN'T MIND *GETTING INTO THE DAMN HOVERCRAFT--*

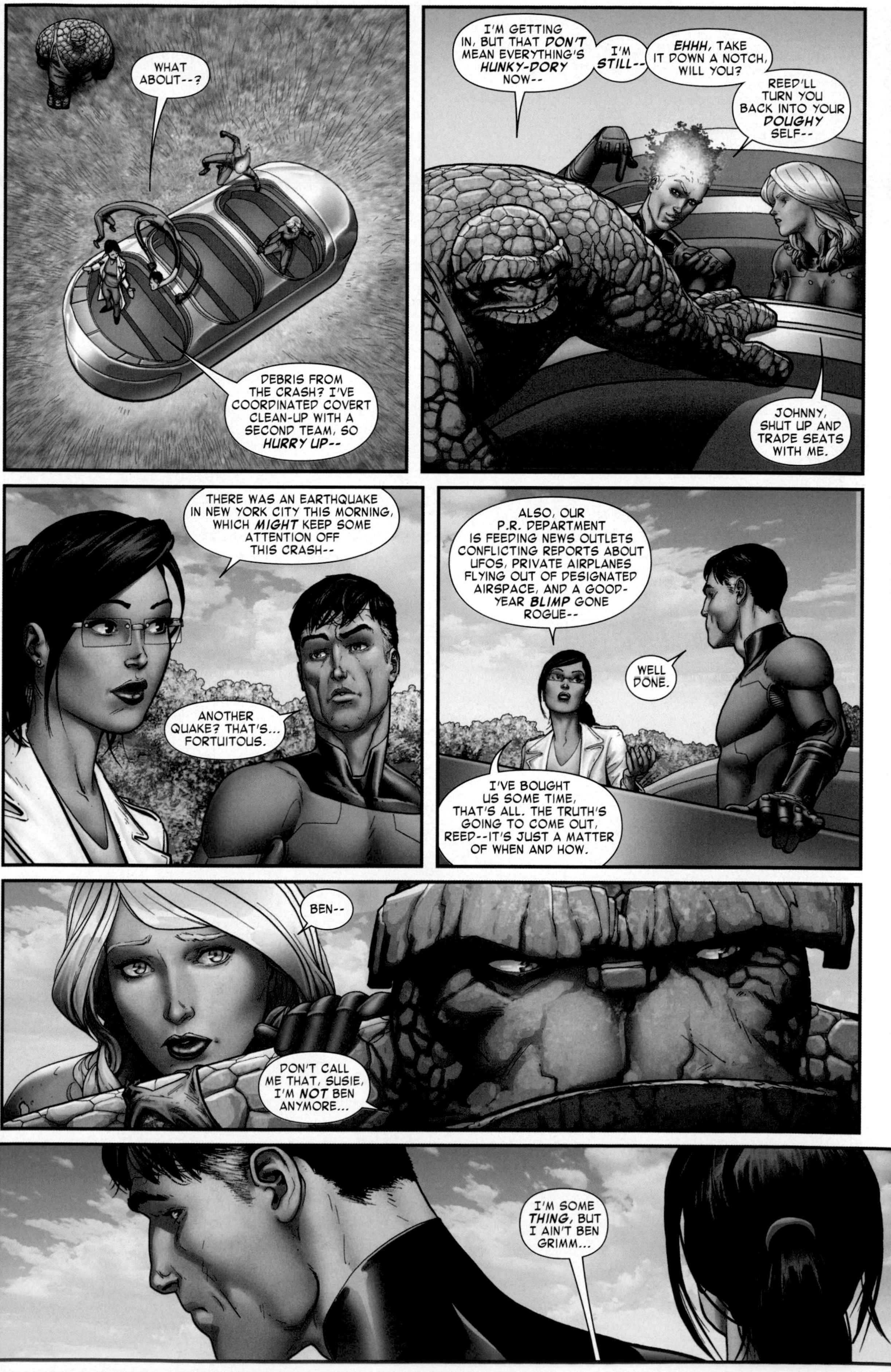
WHAT ABOUT--?
DEBRIS FROM THE CRASH? I'VE COORDINATED COVERT CLEAN-UP WITH A SECOND TEAM, SO HURRY UP--
I'M GETTING IN, BUT THAT DON'T MEAN EVERYTHING'S HUNKY-DORY NOW--
I'M STILL--
EHHH, TAKE IT DOWN A NOTCH, WILL YOU?
REED'LL TURN YOU BACK INTO YOUR DOUGHY SELF--
JOHNNY, SHUT UP AND TRADE SEATS WITH ME.
THERE WAS AN EARTHQUAKE IN NEW YORK CITY THIS MORNING, WHICH MIGHT KEEP SOME ATTENTION OFF THIS CRASH--
ANOTHER QUAKE? THAT'S... FORTUITOUS.
ALSO, OUR P.R. DEPARTMENT IS FEEDING NEWS OUTLETS CONFLICTING REPORTS ABOUT UFOS, PRIVATE AIRPLANES FLYING OUT OF DESIGNATED AIRSPACE, AND A GOOD-YEAR BLIMP GONE ROGUE--
WELL DONE.
I'VE BOUGHT US SOME TIME, THAT'S ALL. THE TRUTH'S GOING TO COME OUT, REED--IT'S JUST A MATTER OF WHEN AND HOW.
BEN--
DON'T CALL ME THAT, SUSIE, I'M NOT BEN ANYMORE...
I'M SOME THING, BUT I AIN'T BEN GRIMM...

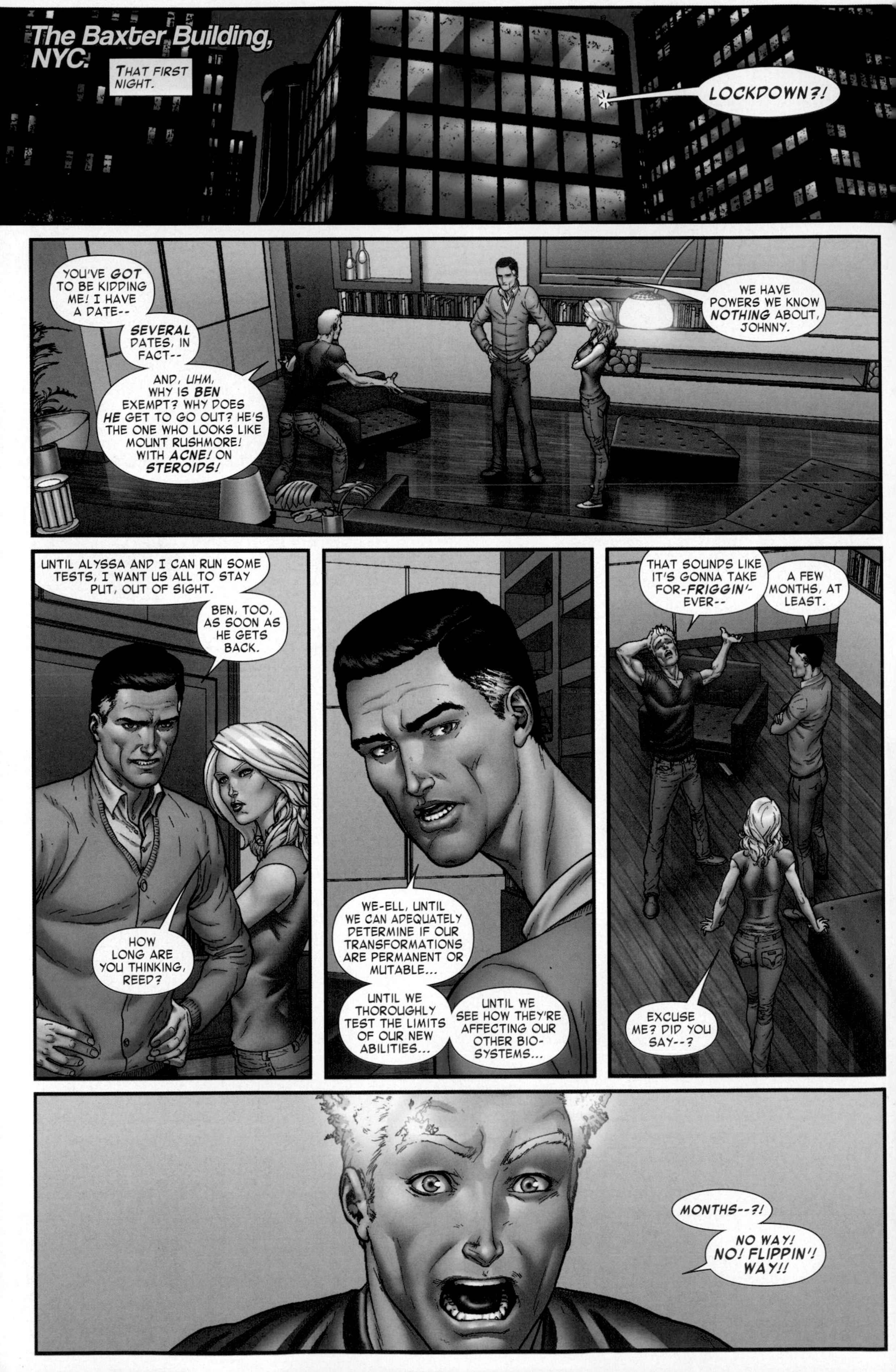

The Baxter Building, NYC.
THAT FIRST NIGHT.
LOCKDOWN?!
YOU'VE GOT TO BE KIDDING ME! I HAVE A DATE--
SEVERAL DATES, IN FACT--
AND, UHM, WHY IS BEN EXEMPT? WHY DOES HE GET TO GO OUT? HE'S THE ONE WHO LOOKS LIKE MOUNT RUSHMORE! WITH ACNE! ON STEROIDS!
WE HAVE POWERS WE KNOW NOTHING ABOUT, JOHNNY.
UNTIL ALYSSA AND I CAN RUN SOME TESTS, I WANT US ALL TO STAY PUT, OUT OF SIGHT.
BEN, TOO, AS SOON AS HE GETS BACK.
HOW LONG ARE YOU THINKING, REED?
WE-ELL, UNTIL WE CAN ADEQUATELY DETERMINE IF OUR TRANSFORMATIONS ARE PERMANENT OR MUTABLE...
UNTIL WE THOROUGHLY TEST THE LIMITS OF OUR NEW ABILITIES...
UNTIL WE SEE HOW THEY'RE AFFECTING OUR OTHER BIO-SYSTEMS...
THAT SOUNDS LIKE IT'S GONNA TAKE FOR-FRIGGIN'-EVER--
A FEW MONTHS, AT LEAST.
EXCUSE ME? DID YOU SAY--?
MONTHS--?!
NO WAY! NO! FLIPPIN'! WAY!!

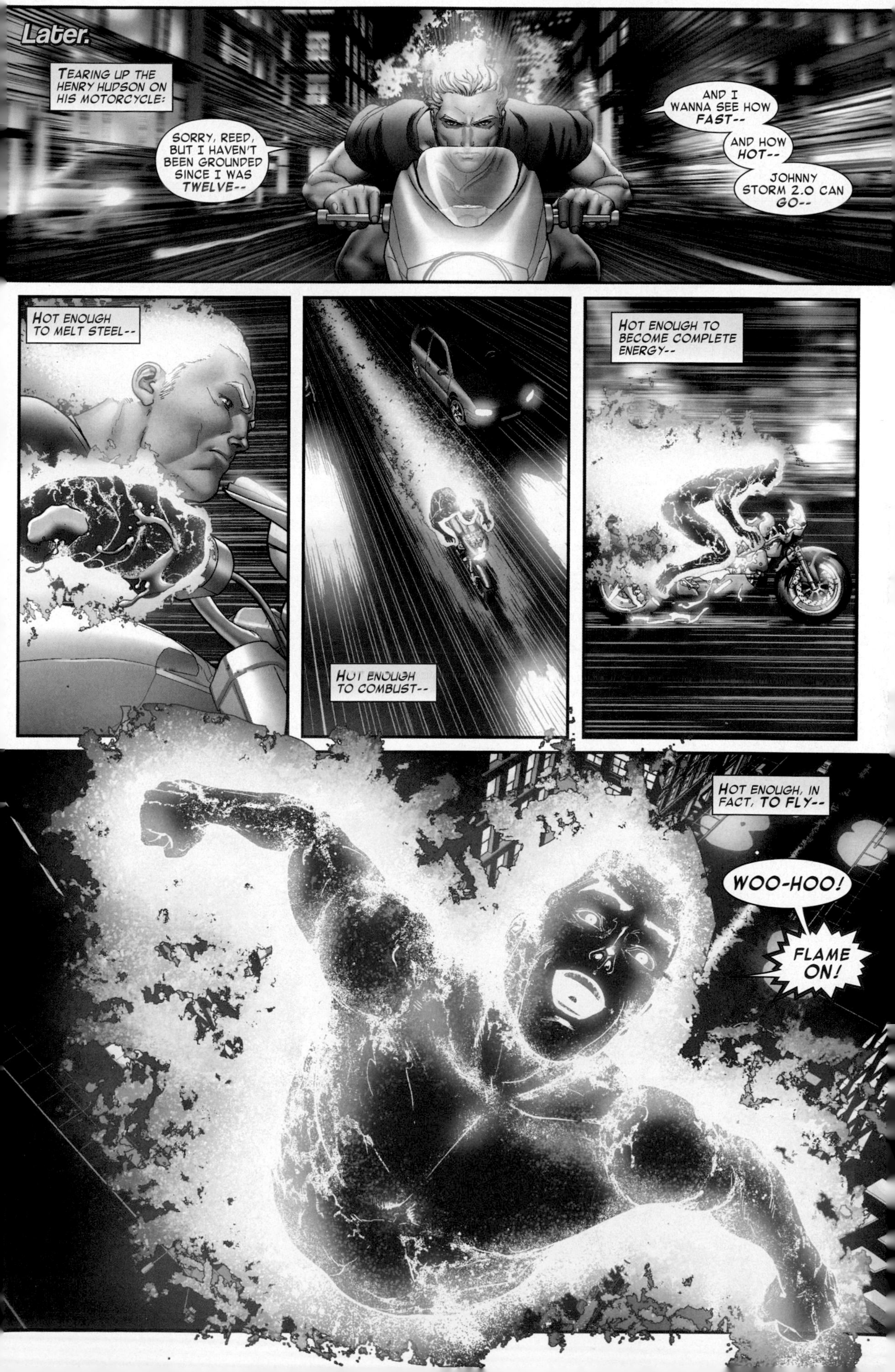
Later.
Tearing up the Henry Hudson on his motorcycle:
SORRY, REED, BUT I HAVEN'T BEEN GROUNDED SINCE I WAS TWELVE--
AND I WANNA SEE HOW FAST--
AND HOW HOT--
JOHNNY STORM 2.0 CAN GO--
Hot enough to melt steel--
Hot enough to combust--
Hot enough to become complete energy--
Hot enough, in fact, to fly--
WOO-HOO!
FLAME ON!

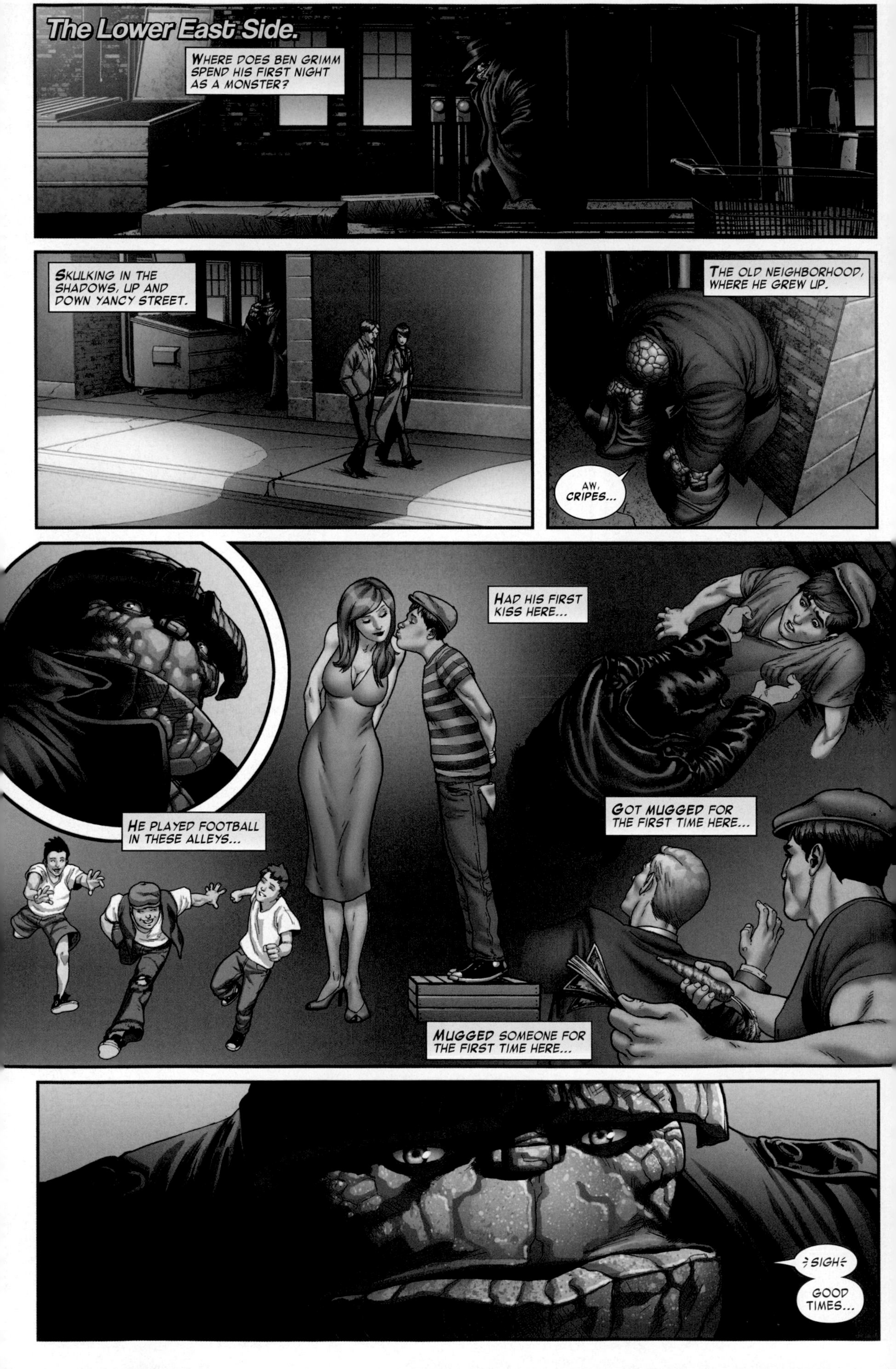
The Lower East Side.
WHERE DOES BEN GRIMM SPEND HIS FIRST NIGHT AS A MONSTER?
SKULKING IN THE SHADOWS, UP AND DOWN YANCY STREET.
THE OLD NEIGHBORHOOD, WHERE HE GREW UP.
AW, CRIPES...
HE PLAYED FOOTBALL IN THESE ALLEYS...
HAD HIS FIRST KISS HERE...
GOT MUGGED FOR THE FIRST TIME HERE...
MUGGED SOMEONE FOR THE FIRST TIME HERE...
SIGH
GOOD TIMES...

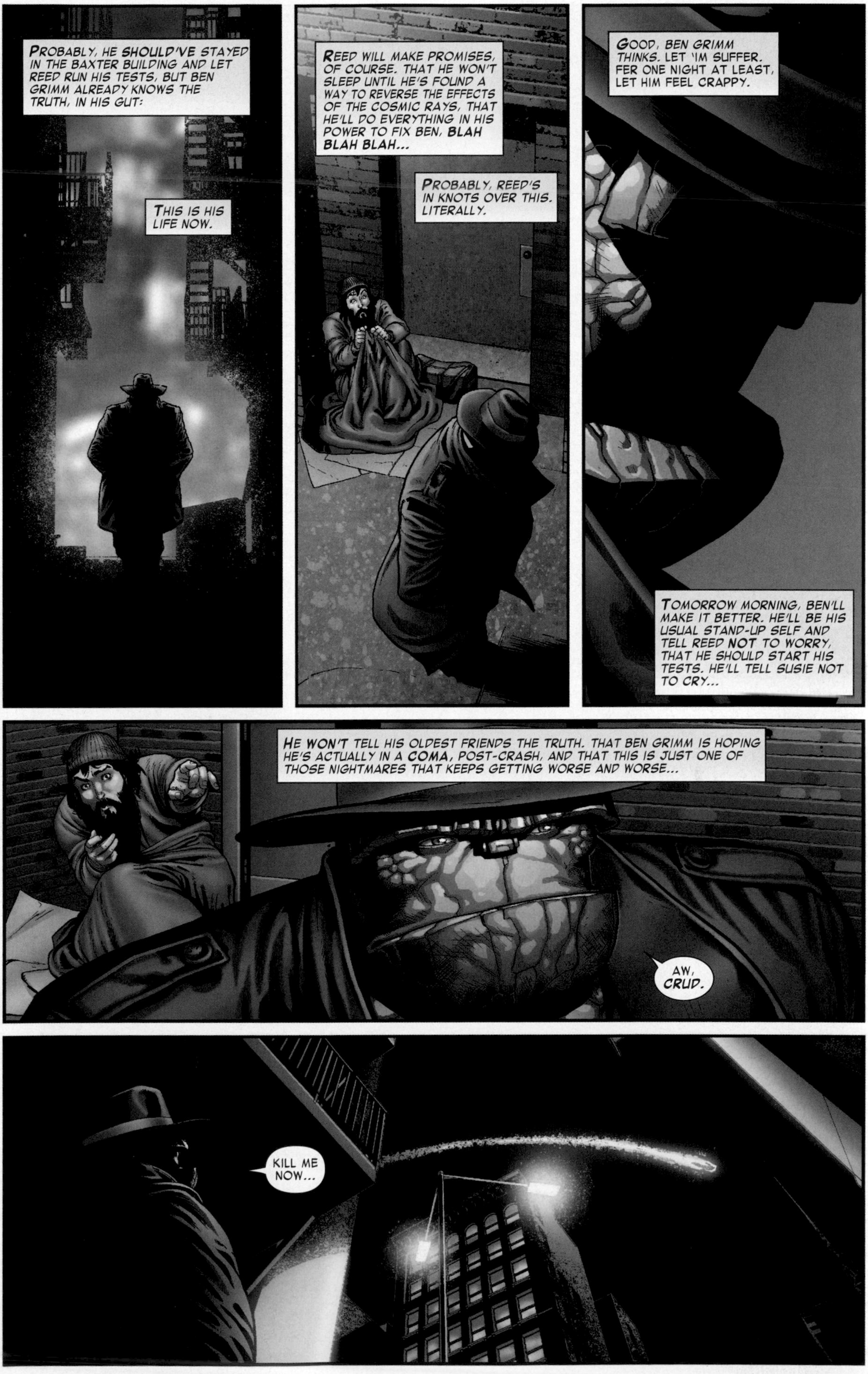
PROBABLY, HE SHOULD'VE STAYED IN THE BAXTER BUILDING AND LET REED RUN HIS TESTS, BUT BEN GRIMM ALREADY KNOWS THE TRUTH, IN HIS GUT:
THIS IS HIS LIFE NOW.
REED WILL MAKE PROMISES, OF COURSE. THAT HE WON'T SLEEP UNTIL HE'S FOUND A WAY TO REVERSE THE EFFECTS OF THE COSMIC RAYS, THAT HE'LL DO EVERYTHING IN HIS POWER TO FIX BEN, BLAH BLAH BLAH...
PROBABLY, REED'S IN KNOTS OVER THIS. LITERALLY.
GOOD, BEN GRIMM THINKS. LET 'IM SUFFER. FER ONE NIGHT AT LEAST, LET HIM FEEL CRAPPY.
TOMORROW MORNING, BEN'LL MAKE IT BETTER. HE'LL BE HIS USUAL STAND-UP SELF AND TELL REED NOT TO WORRY, THAT HE SHOULD START HIS TESTS. HE'LL TELL SUSIE NOT TO CRY...
HE WON'T TELL HIS OLDEST FRIENDS THE TRUTH. THAT BEN GRIMM IS HOPING HE'S ACTUALLY IN A COMA, POST-CRASH, AND THAT THIS IS JUST ONE OF THOSE NIGHTMARES THAT KEEPS GETTING WORSE AND WORSE...
AW, CRUD.
KILL ME NOW...

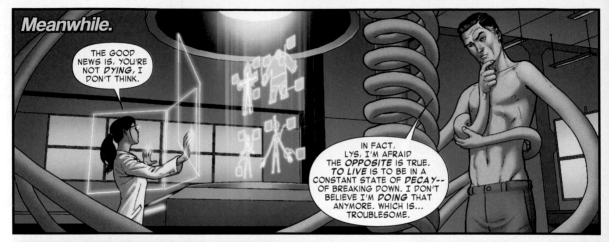

Meanwhile.

THE GOOD NEWS IS, YOU'RE NOT *DYING*, I DON'T THINK.

IN FACT, LYS, I'M AFRAID THE *OPPOSITE* IS TRUE. *TO LIVE* IS TO BE IN A CONSTANT STATE OF *DECAY*-- OF BREAKING DOWN. I DON'T BELIEVE I'M *DOING* THAT ANYMORE. WHICH IS... TROUBLESOME.

AGREED.

ON THE OTHER HAND, JOHNNY *MIGHT* BE HYPER-METABOLIZING HIMSELF TOWARDS AN EARLY GRAVE... *OR NOT.*

AND BEN *MIGHT* CONTINUE CALCIFYING INTO A MOTIONLESS, LIFELESS STATUE...*OR NOT.* WHO KNOWS? THEY LEFT BEFORE--

THEY'RE BLOWING OFF STEAM, BUT-- THEY'LL BE BACK.

AS FOR SUSAN...SHE *RESPECTFULLY* DECLINED MY OFFER TO GIVE HER A PHYSICAL.

CAN YOU BLAME HER?

IF YOU'RE IMPLYING SUE'S BEEN *THREATENED* BY ME, OR *JEALOUS* OF ME, SHE *NEEDN'T* BE ANYMORE. YOU'RE BOUND FOR LIFE NOW, THE TWO OF YOU-- THE *FOUR* OF YOU, REALLY.

YOU SURVIVED... I'M NOT EVEN SURE *WHAT*, YET, BUT SOMETHING EXTRAORDINARY.

ME, I'M LIKE THE *FIFTH* BEATLE WHO DIDN'T GET FAMOUS.

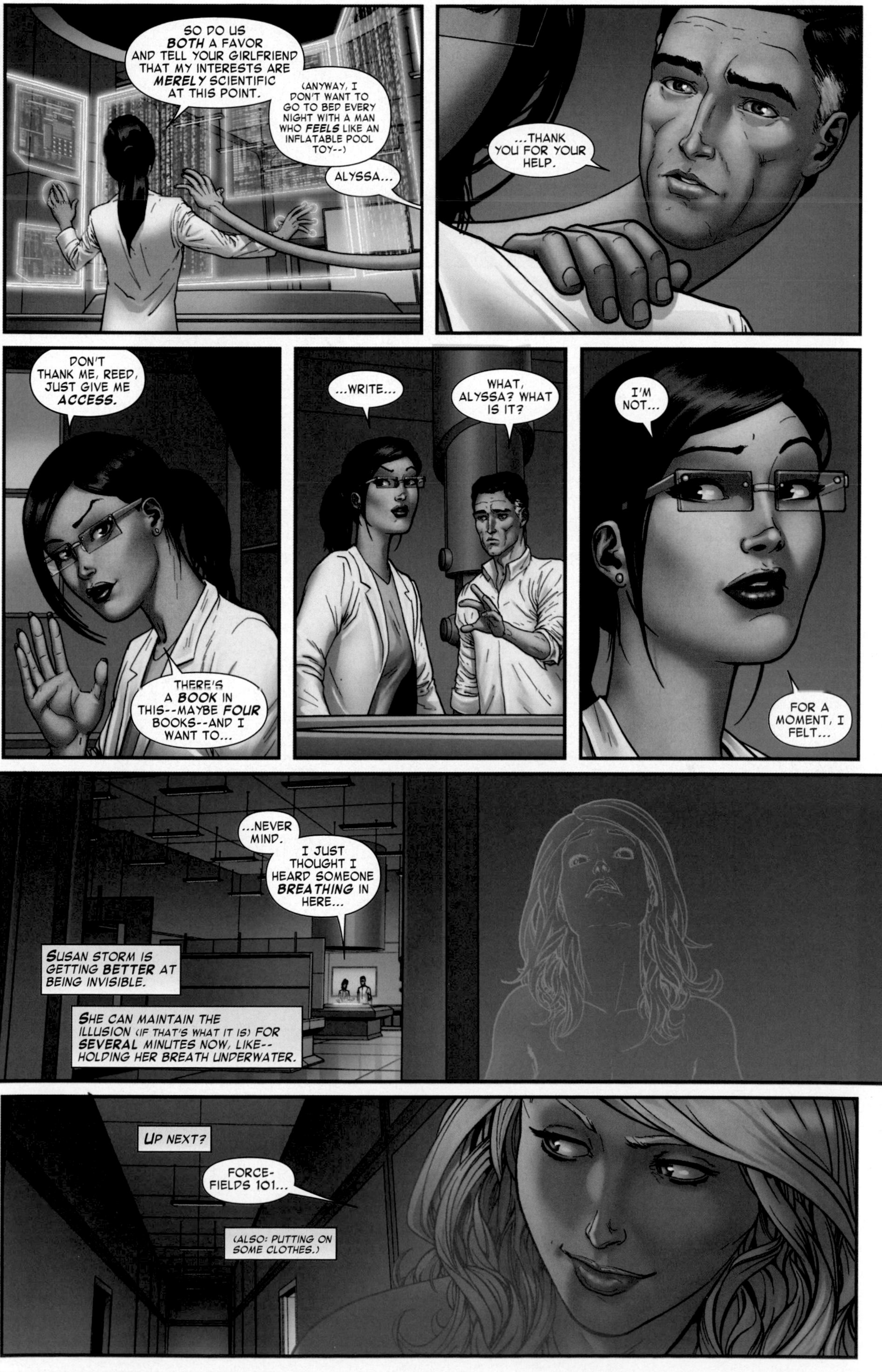
SO DO US BOTH A FAVOR AND TELL YOUR GIRLFRIEND THAT MY INTERESTS ARE MERELY SCIENTIFIC AT THIS POINT.
(ANYWAY, I DON'T WANT TO GO TO BED EVERY NIGHT WITH A MAN WHO FEELS LIKE AN INFLATABLE POOL TOY--)
ALYSSA...
...THANK YOU FOR YOUR HELP.
DON'T THANK ME, REED, JUST GIVE ME ACCESS.
THERE'S A BOOK IN THIS--MAYBE FOUR BOOKS--AND I WANT TO...
...WRITE...
WHAT, ALYSSA? WHAT IS IT?
I'M NOT...
FOR A MOMENT, I FELT...
...NEVER MIND.
I JUST THOUGHT I HEARD SOMEONE BREATHING IN HERE...
SUSAN STORM IS GETTING BETTER AT BEING INVISIBLE.
SHE CAN MAINTAIN THE ILLUSION (IF THAT'S WHAT IT IS) FOR SEVERAL MINUTES NOW, LIKE--HOLDING HER BREATH UNDERWATER.
UP NEXT?
FORCE-FIELDS 101...
(ALSO: PUTTING ON SOME CLOTHES.)

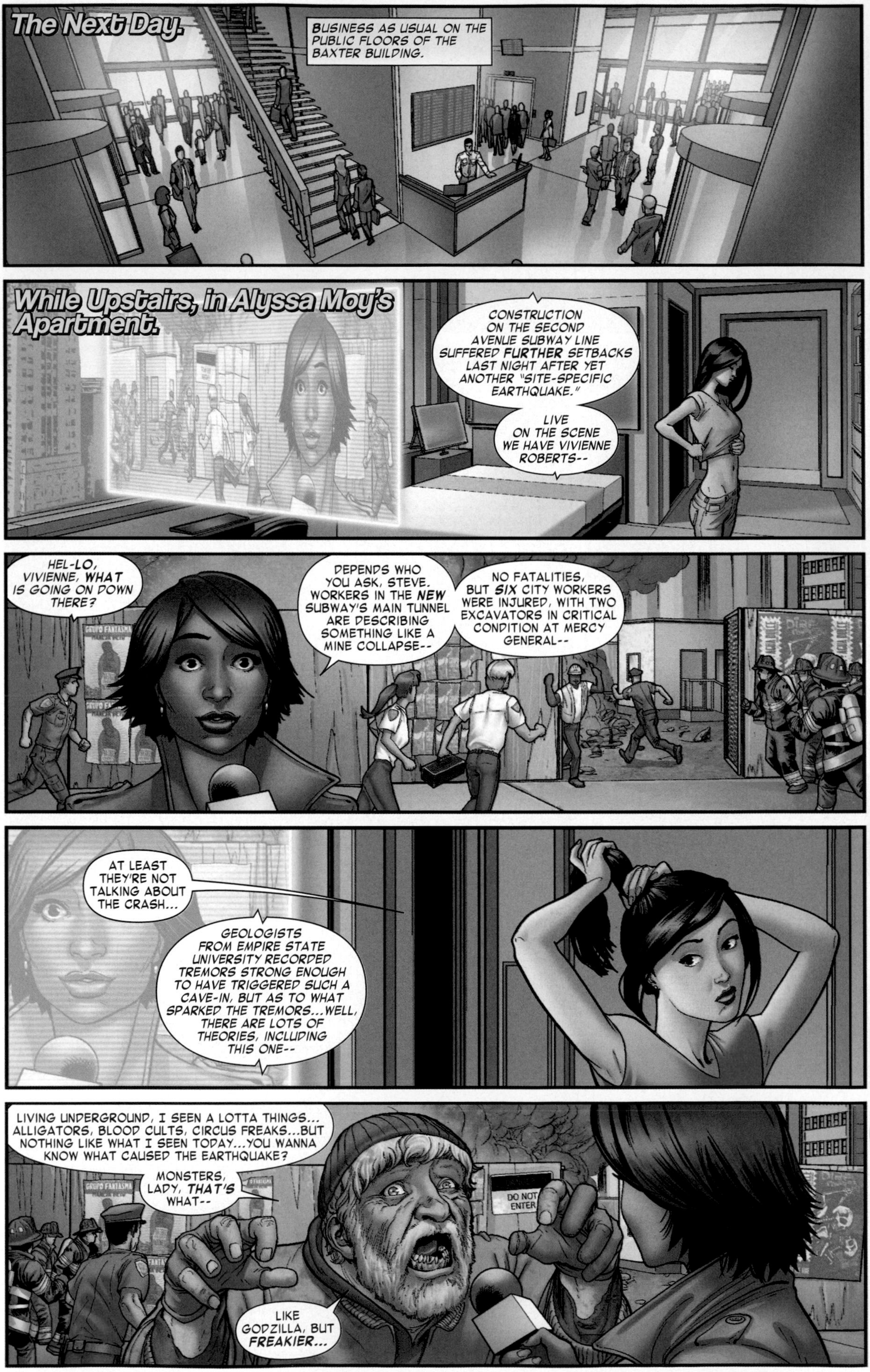
The Next Day.
BUSINESS AS USUAL ON THE PUBLIC FLOORS OF THE BAXTER BUILDING.
While Upstairs, in Alyssa Moy's Apartment.
CONSTRUCTION ON THE SECOND AVENUE SUBWAY LINE SUFFERED FURTHER SETBACKS LAST NIGHT AFTER YET ANOTHER "SITE-SPECIFIC EARTHQUAKE."
LIVE ON THE SCENE WE HAVE VIVIENNE ROBERTS--
HEL-LO, VIVIENNE, WHAT IS GOING ON DOWN THERE?
DEPENDS WHO YOU ASK, STEVE. WORKERS IN THE NEW SUBWAY'S MAIN TUNNEL ARE DESCRIBING SOMETHING LIKE A MINE COLLAPSE--
NO FATALITIES, BUT SIX CITY WORKERS WERE INJURED, WITH TWO EXCAVATORS IN CRITICAL CONDITION AT MERCY GENERAL--
GRUPO FANTASMA
AT LEAST THEY'RE NOT TALKING ABOUT THE CRASH...
GEOLOGISTS FROM EMPIRE STATE UNIVERSITY RECORDED TREMORS STRONG ENOUGH TO HAVE TRIGGERED SUCH A CAVE-IN, BUT AS TO WHAT SPARKED THE TREMORS...WELL, THERE ARE LOTS OF THEORIES, INCLUDING THIS ONE--
LIVING UNDERGROUND, I SEEN A LOTTA THINGS... ALLIGATORS, BLOOD CULTS, CIRCUS FREAKS...BUT NOTHING LIKE WHAT I SEEN TODAY...YOU WANNA KNOW WHAT CAUSED THE EARTHQUAKE?
MONSTERS, LADY, THAT'S WHAT--
DO NOT ENTER
LIKE GODZILLA, BUT FREAKIER...

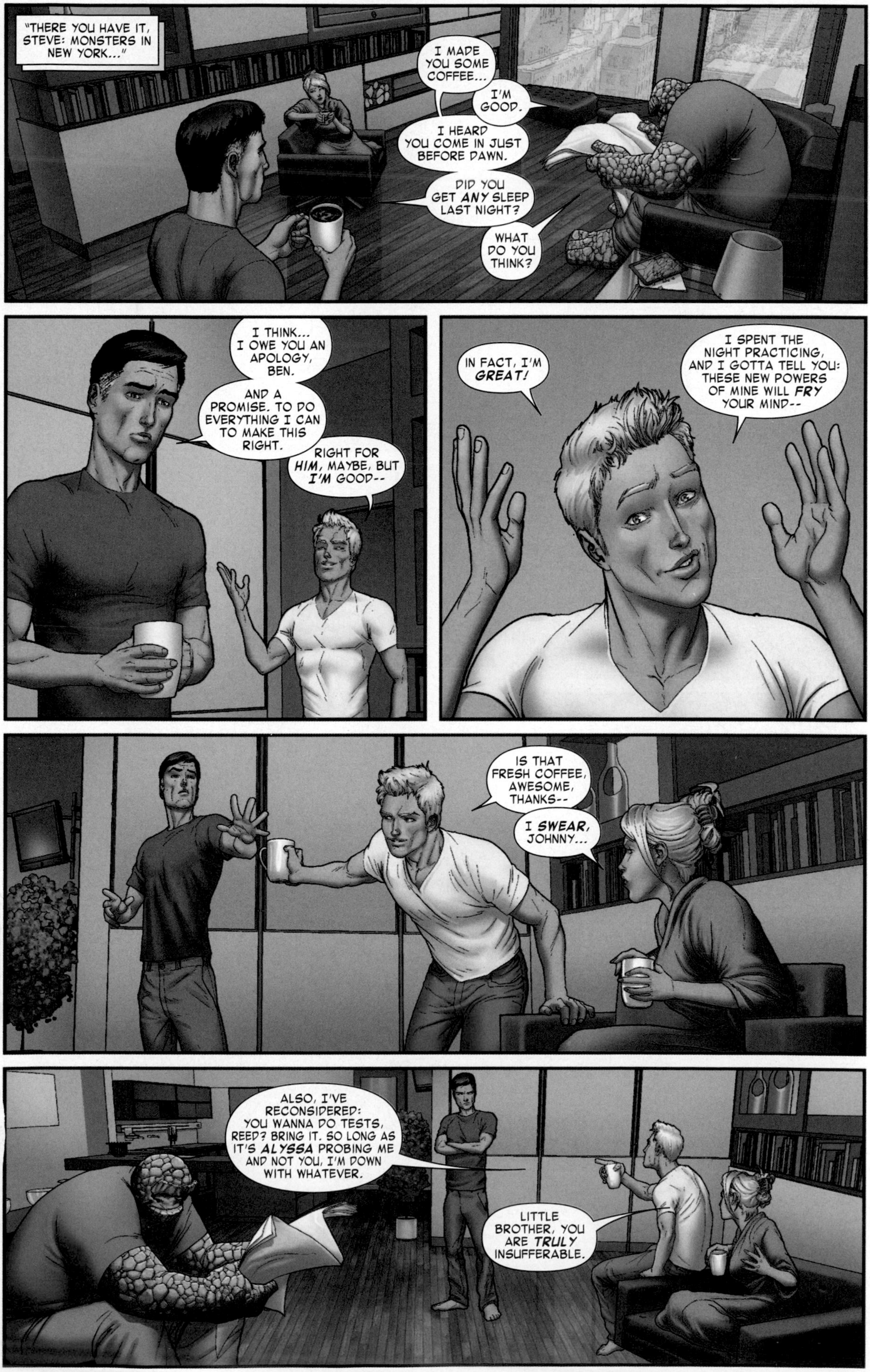
"THERE YOU HAVE IT, STEVE: MONSTERS IN NEW YORK..."
I MADE YOU SOME COFFEE...
I'M GOOD.
I HEARD YOU COME IN JUST BEFORE DAWN.
DID YOU GET *ANY* SLEEP LAST NIGHT?
WHAT DO YOU THINK?
I THINK... I OWE YOU AN APOLOGY, BEN.
AND A PROMISE. TO DO EVERYTHING I CAN TO MAKE THIS RIGHT.
RIGHT FOR *HIM*, MAYBE, BUT *I'M* GOOD--
IN FACT, I'M *GREAT!*
I SPENT THE NIGHT PRACTICING, AND I GOTTA TELL YOU: THESE NEW POWERS OF MINE WILL *FRY* YOUR MIND--
IS THAT FRESH COFFEE, AWESOME, THANKS--
I *SWEAR*, JOHNNY...
ALSO, I'VE RECONSIDERED: YOU WANNA DO TESTS, REED? BRING IT. SO LONG AS IT'S *ALYSSA* PROBING ME AND NOT YOU, I'M DOWN WITH WHATEVER.
LITTLE BROTHER, YOU ARE *TRULY* INSUFFERABLE.

MOY HERE, HOLO-CONFERENCING. WE HAVE A GOOD NEWS/ BAD NEWS/GOOD NEWS SITUATION, PEOPLE, SO... PAY ATTENTION.

THE *GOOD* NEWS IS, NO ONE'S TALKING ABOUT YOU FOUR OR THE CRASH--

THE *BAD* NEWS IS, THERE'S A MONSTER RAMPAGING IN MIDTOWN--

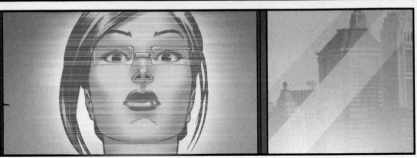

HOW'S THAT?

DETAILS ARE SKETCHY, BUT APPARENTLY CONSTRUCTION ON THE SECOND AVENUE SUBWAY HAS AWOKEN SOME KIND OF PREHISTORIC MONSTER--

(SOME POOR NEWSCASTER WOMAN WAS JUST EATEN...)

BY ODD COINCIDENCE, IT'S HEADED RIGHT FOR THE BAXTER BUILDING--

THE LAST FEW WEEKS, I *HAVE* BEEN CHARTING STRANGE SEISMIC ACTIVITY THROUGHOUT THE ISLAND...

AND THIS IS HAPPENING RIGHT NOW?

AS WE STAND HERE WASTING TIME. NEEDLESS TO SAY, THIS PRESENTS A UNIQUE OPPORTUNITY TO GET AHEAD OF THE STORY.

AS WELL AS SAVE LIVES--

HOVERCAR'S FUELED AND IDLING, REED.

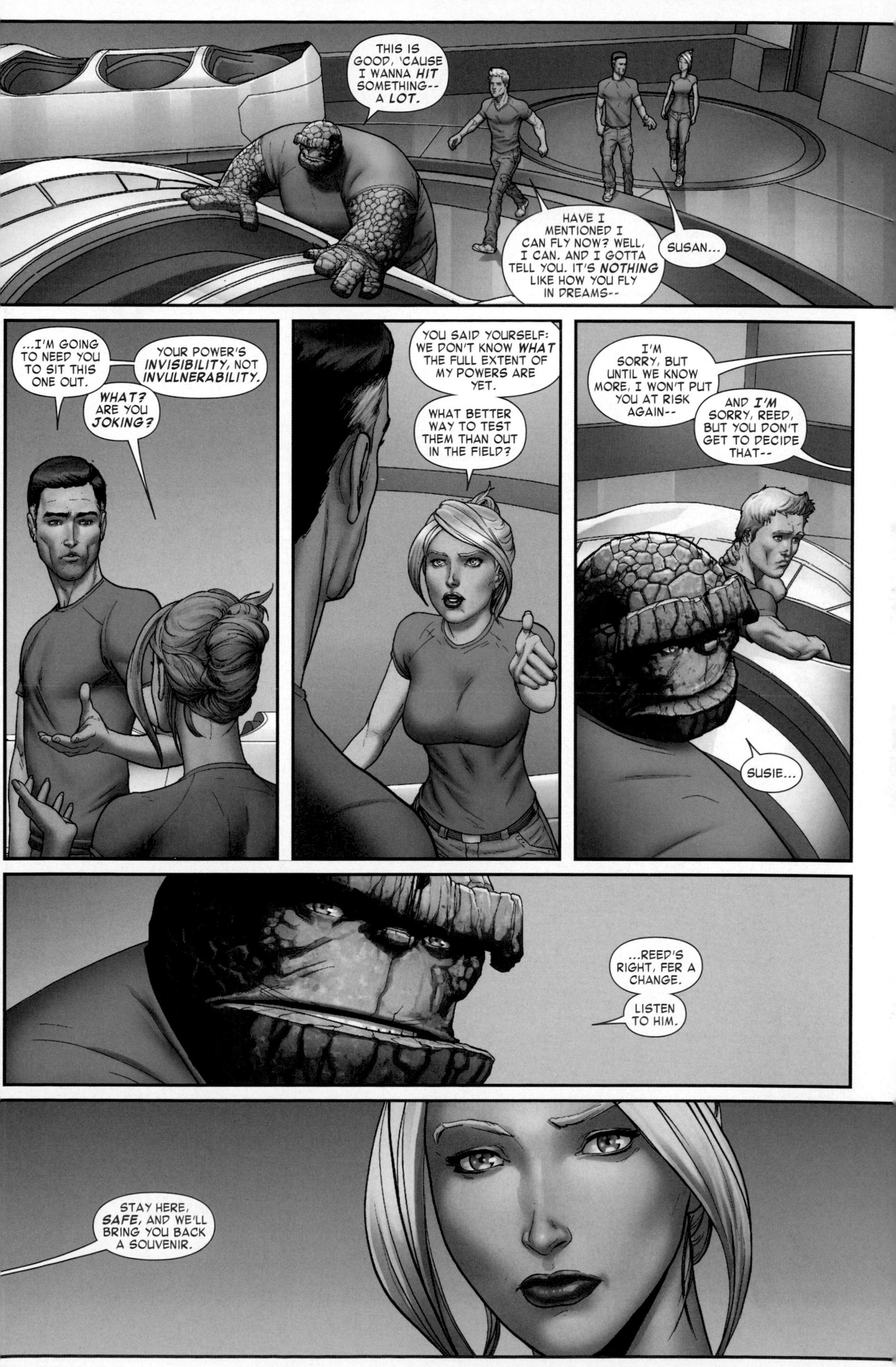
THIS IS GOOD, 'CAUSE I WANNA HIT SOMETHING-- A LOT.
HAVE I MENTIONED I CAN FLY NOW? WELL, I CAN. AND I GOTTA TELL YOU. IT'S NOTHING LIKE HOW YOU FLY IN DREAMS--
SUSAN...
...I'M GOING TO NEED YOU TO SIT THIS ONE OUT.
YOUR POWER'S INVISIBILITY, NOT INVULNERABILITY.
WHAT? ARE YOU JOKING?
YOU SAID YOURSELF: WE DON'T KNOW WHAT THE FULL EXTENT OF MY POWERS ARE YET.
WHAT BETTER WAY TO TEST THEM THAN OUT IN THE FIELD?
I'M SORRY, BUT UNTIL WE KNOW MORE, I WON'T PUT YOU AT RISK AGAIN--
AND I'M SORRY, REED, BUT YOU DON'T GET TO DECIDE THAT--
SUSIE...
...REED'S RIGHT, FER A CHANGE.
LISTEN TO HIM.
STAY HERE, SAFE, AND WE'LL BRING YOU BACK A SOUVENIR.

Subsequently.

HEY, ABOUT THE SUE THING? I COMPLETELY AGREE, REED--BUT HOW COME YOU'RE NOT WORRIED ABOUT *US*? 'CAUSE WE'RE GUYS?

BEN'S INDESTRUCTIBLE, I'M INDESTRUCTIBLE, AND YOU SAID SOMETHING ABOUT FLYING, I BELIEVE?

OH, YEAH, THAT'S *RIGHT*, I'M ALL ABOUT THE FLY--

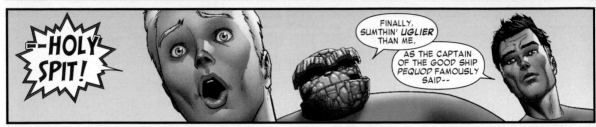

--HOLY SPIT!

FINALLY, SUMTHIN' *UGLIER* THAN ME.

AS THE CAPTAIN OF THE GOOD SHIP *PEQUOD* FAMOUSLY SAID--

THAR SHE BLOWS!

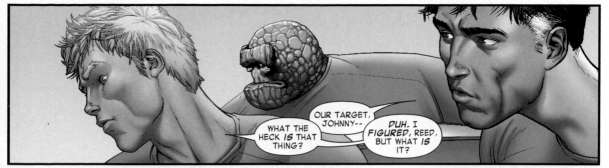

WHAT THE HECK **IS** THAT THING?

OUR TARGET, JOHNNY--

DUH. I **FIGURED,** REED, BUT WHAT **IS** IT?

WHO CARES? LIKE I SAID, I WANNA HIT IT.

GET ME IN CLOSE, STRETCH, AND I'LL **JUMP** ALL OVER ITS--

I THINK, BEN, WE NEED A **SLIGHTLY** MORE EVOLVED PLAN THAN THAT.

OH, YEAH? LIKE WHAT? INVITING IT OVER FOR COOKIES AND **PUNCH?**

NO, LIKE-- JOHNNY, DISTRACT IT. LEAD THE CREATURE AWAY FROM THE CROWDS TOWARDS CENTRAL PARK. WE'LL NEUTRALIZE IT THERE.

GREAT, BUT-- UHM--DISTRACT IT HOW?

FOR PETE'S SAKE, YOU'RE A HUMAN TORCH, JOHNNY, **USE YOUR IMAGINATION--**

RIGHT--

TORCH--

HUMAN--

ME--

GOTCHA--

BEN, I'M TAKING US DOWN. YOU AND I ARE **GROUND SUPPORT.**

CROWD-CONTROL AND BACKUP FOR JOHNNY.

BACKUP FOR JOHNNY? **SHEESH--**

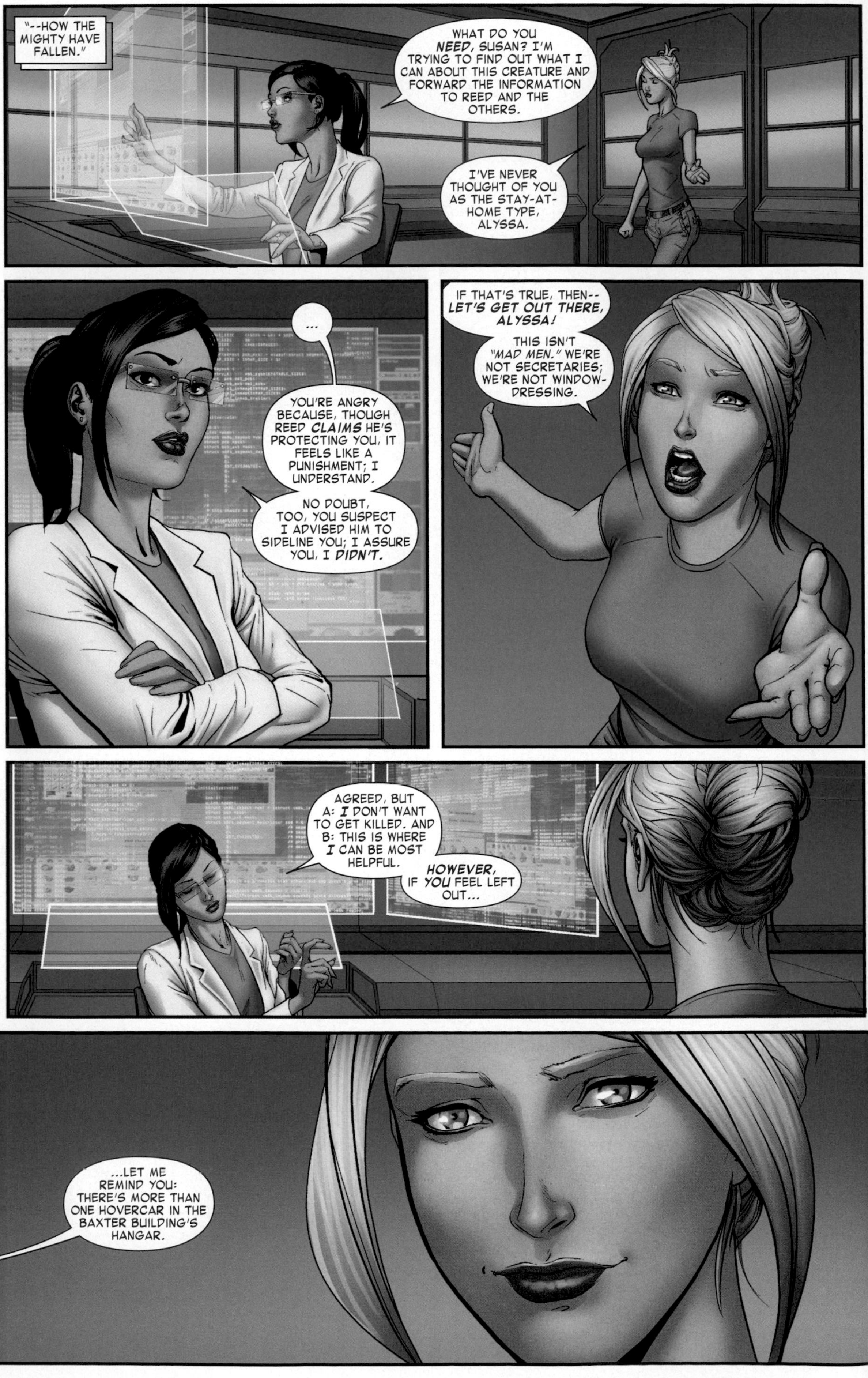
"--HOW THE MIGHTY HAVE FALLEN."
WHAT DO YOU NEED, SUSAN? I'M TRYING TO FIND OUT WHAT I CAN ABOUT THIS CREATURE AND FORWARD THE INFORMATION TO REED AND THE OTHERS.
I'VE NEVER THOUGHT OF YOU AS THE STAY-AT-HOME TYPE, ALYSSA.
...
YOU'RE ANGRY BECAUSE, THOUGH REED CLAIMS HE'S PROTECTING YOU, IT FEELS LIKE A PUNISHMENT; I UNDERSTAND.
NO DOUBT, TOO, YOU SUSPECT I ADVISED HIM TO SIDELINE YOU; I ASSURE YOU, I DIDN'T.
IF THAT'S TRUE, THEN-- LET'S GET OUT THERE, ALYSSA!
THIS ISN'T "MAD MEN." WE'RE NOT SECRETARIES; WE'RE NOT WINDOW-DRESSING.
AGREED, BUT A: I DON'T WANT TO GET KILLED. AND B: THIS IS WHERE I CAN BE MOST HELPFUL.
HOWEVER, IF YOU FEEL LEFT OUT...
...LET ME REMIND YOU: THERE'S MORE THAN ONE HOVERCAR IN THE BAXTER BUILDING'S HANGAR.

JOHNNY AND SUE STORM'S FATHER WAS A HUGE GODZILLA FAN. BY EXTENSION:

MOTHRA? NO. GIGAN? NOPE. MEGALON? UH-UH. GROTTU?

(HMMMM, MAYBE...)

HERE, GROTTU, THIS WAY!

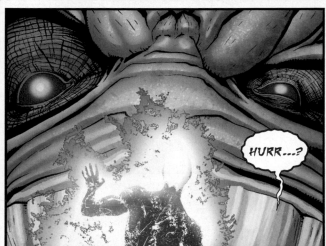

HURR...?

YEAH-- OKAY--GROTTU WORKS...

Street Level.

AHHHHH! IT'S ONE OF THE MONSTER'S BABIES! THE MONSTER HAS BABIES! IT'S A BABY MONSTER!

MOVE IT, PEOPLE, MOVE IT!

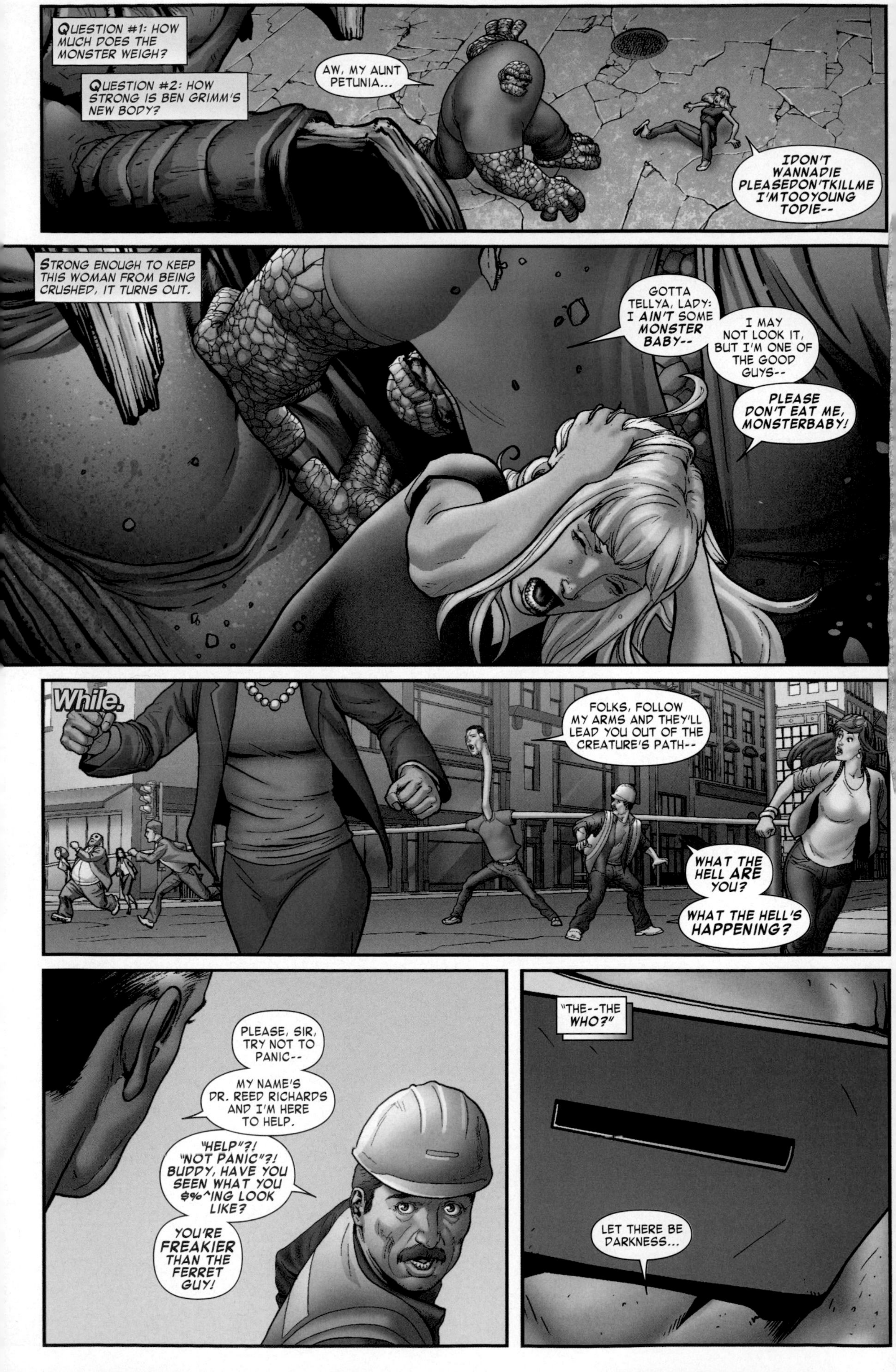
QUESTION #1: HOW MUCH DOES THE MONSTER WEIGH?
QUESTION #2: HOW STRONG IS BEN GRIMM'S NEW BODY?
AW, MY AUNT PETUNIA...
IDON'T WANNADIE PLEASEDON'TKILLME I'MTOOYOUNG TODIE--
STRONG ENOUGH TO KEEP THIS WOMAN FROM BEING CRUSHED, IT TURNS OUT.
GOTTA TELLYA, LADY: I AIN'T SOME MONSTER BABY--
I MAY NOT LOOK IT, BUT I'M ONE OF THE GOOD GUYS--
PLEASE DON'T EAT ME, MONSTERBABY!
While.
FOLKS, FOLLOW MY ARMS AND THEY'LL LEAD YOU OUT OF THE CREATURE'S PATH--
WHAT THE HELL ARE YOU?
WHAT THE HELL'S HAPPENING?
PLEASE, SIR, TRY NOT TO PANIC--
MY NAME'S DR. REED RICHARDS AND I'M HERE TO HELP.
"HELP"?! "NOT PANIC"?! BUDDY, HAVE YOU SEEN WHAT YOU $%^ING LOOK LIKE?
YOU'RE FREAKIER THAN THE FERRET GUY!
"THE--THE WHO?"
LET THERE BE DARKNESS...

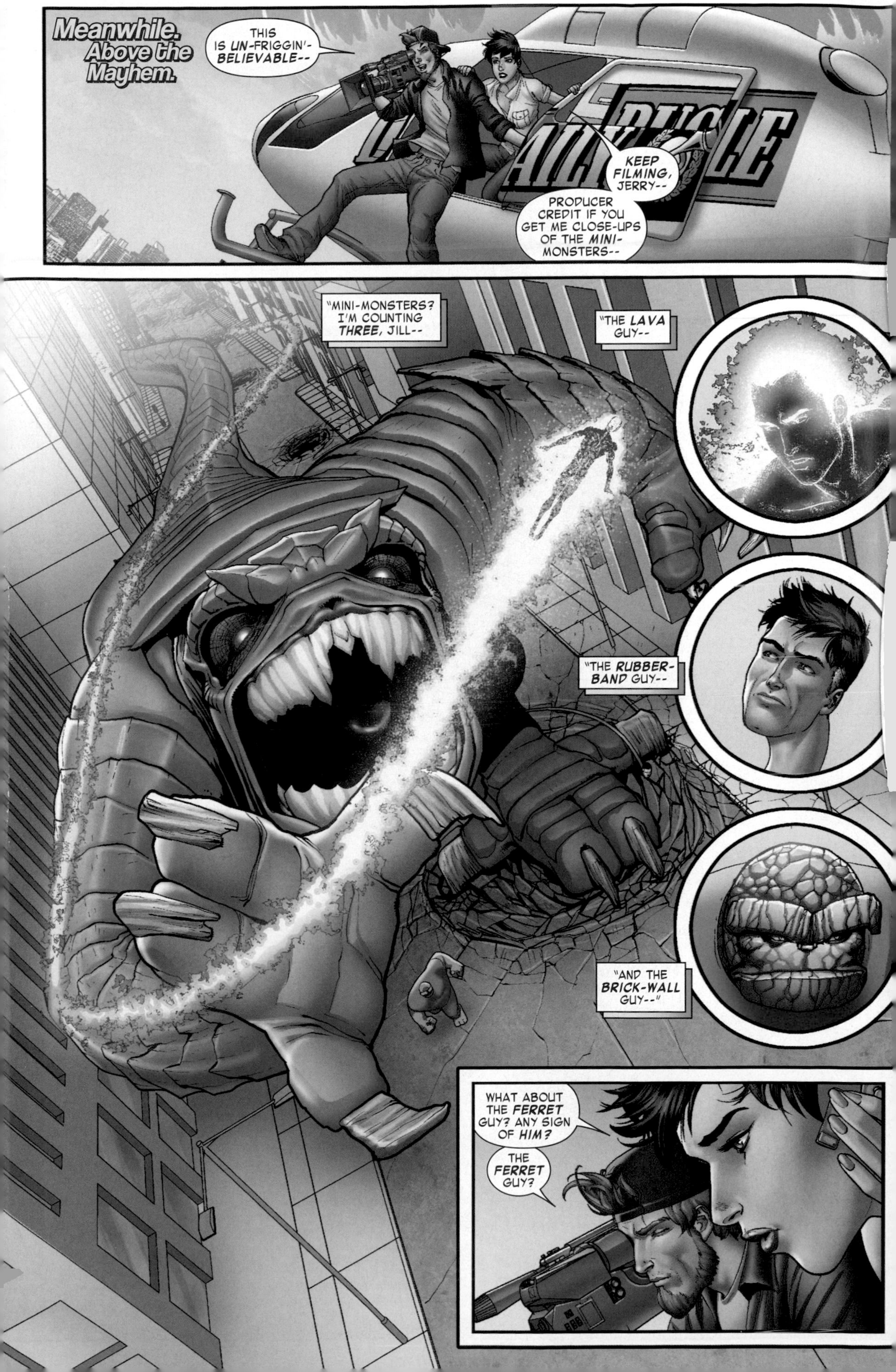
Meanwhile. Above the Mayhem.
THIS IS UN-FRIGGIN'-BELIEVABLE--
KEEP FILMING, JERRY--
PRODUCER CREDIT IF YOU GET ME CLOSE-UPS OF THE MINI-MONSTERS--
"MINI-MONSTERS? I'M COUNTING THREE, JILL--
"THE LAVA GUY--
"THE RUBBER-BAND GUY--
"AND THE BRICK-WALL GUY--"
WHAT ABOUT THE FERRET GUY? ANY SIGN OF HIM?
THE FERRET GUY?

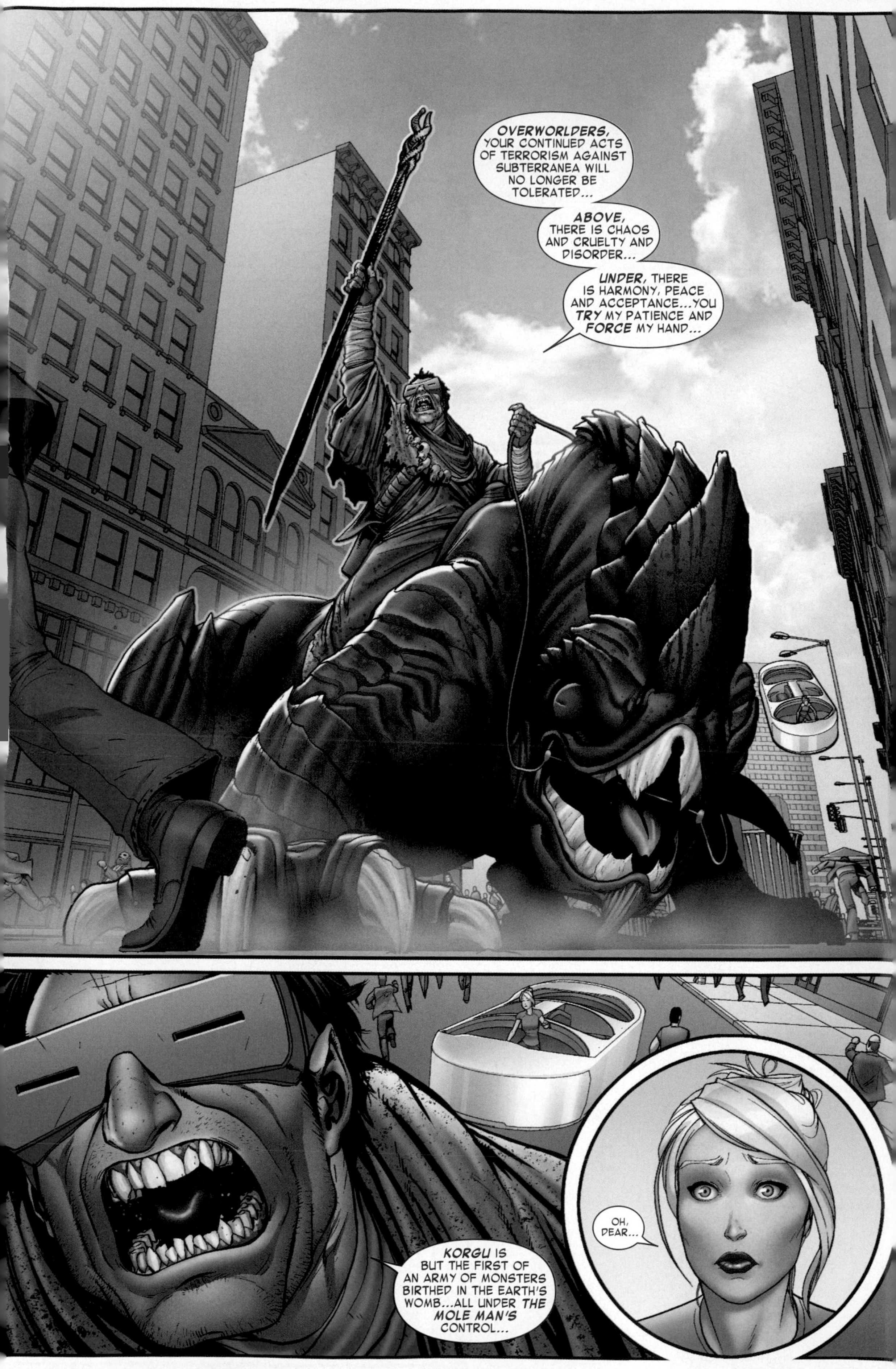
OVERWORLDERS, YOUR CONTINUED ACTS OF TERRORISM AGAINST SUBTERRANEA WILL NO LONGER BE TOLERATED...
ABOVE, THERE IS CHAOS AND CRUELTY AND DISORDER...
UNDER, THERE IS HARMONY, PEACE AND ACCEPTANCE...YOU TRY MY PATIENCE AND FORCE MY HAND...
KORGU IS BUT THE FIRST OF AN ARMY OF MONSTERS BIRTHED IN THE EARTH'S WOMB...ALL UNDER THE MOLE MAN'S CONTROL...
OH, DEAR...

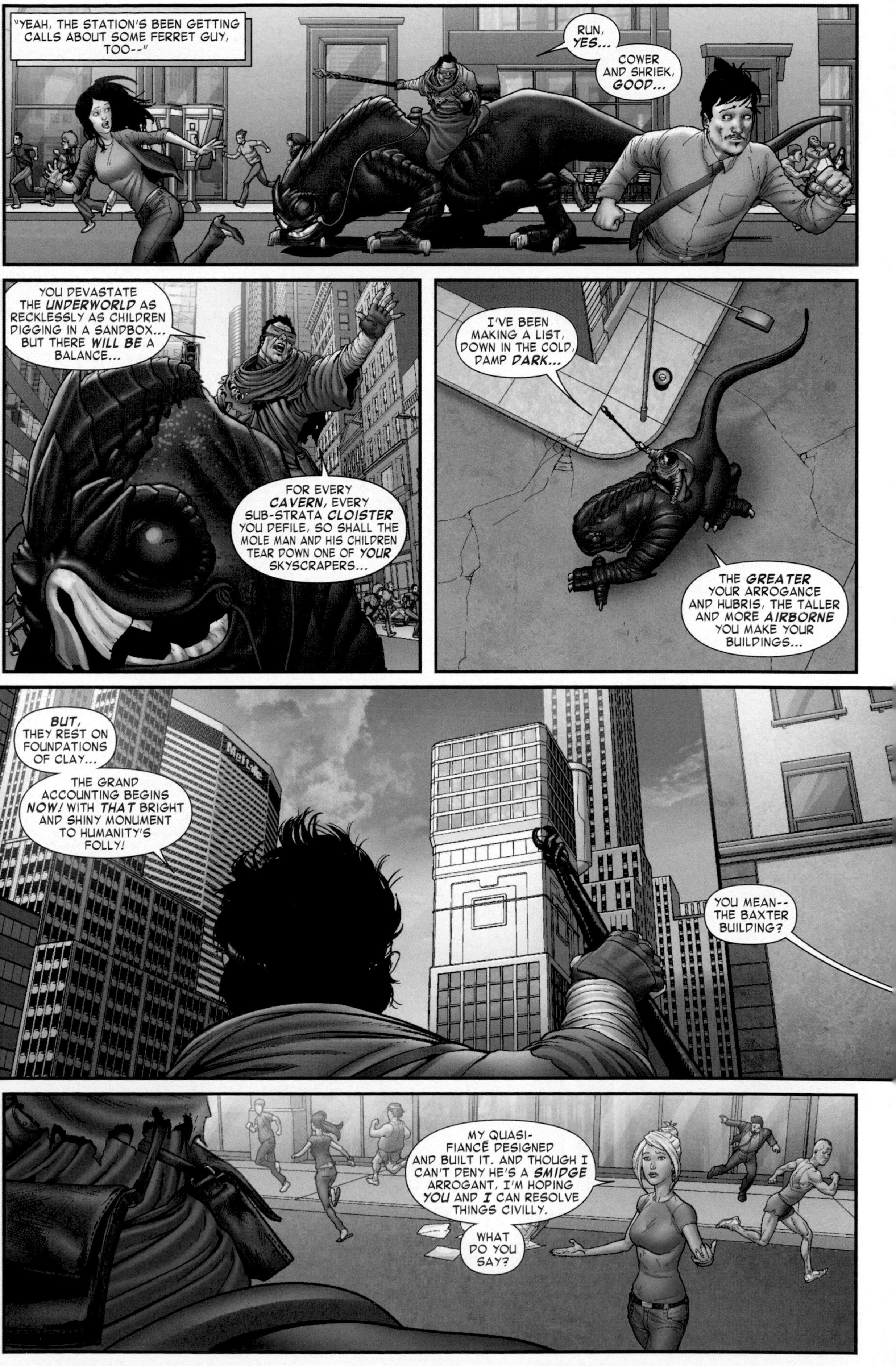
"YEAH, THE STATION'S BEEN GETTING CALLS ABOUT SOME FERRET GUY, TOO--"
RUN, YES...
COWER AND SHRIEK, GOOD...
YOU DEVASTATE THE UNDERWORLD AS RECKLESSLY AS CHILDREN DIGGING IN A SANDBOX... BUT THERE WILL BE A BALANCE...
FOR EVERY CAVERN, EVERY SUB-STRATA CLOISTER YOU DEFILE, SO SHALL THE MOLE MAN AND HIS CHILDREN TEAR DOWN ONE OF YOUR SKYSCRAPERS...
I'VE BEEN MAKING A LIST, DOWN IN THE COLD, DAMP DARK...
THE GREATER YOUR ARROGANCE AND HUBRIS, THE TALLER AND MORE AIRBORNE YOU MAKE YOUR BUILDINGS...
BUT, THEY REST ON FOUNDATIONS OF CLAY...
THE GRAND ACCOUNTING BEGINS NOW! WITH THAT BRIGHT AND SHINY MONUMENT TO HUMANITY'S FOLLY!
YOU MEAN-- THE BAXTER BUILDING?
MY QUASI-FIANCÉ DESIGNED AND BUILT IT. AND THOUGH I CAN'T DENY HE'S A SMIDGE ARROGANT, I'M HOPING YOU AND I CAN RESOLVE THINGS CIVILLY.
WHAT DO YOU SAY?

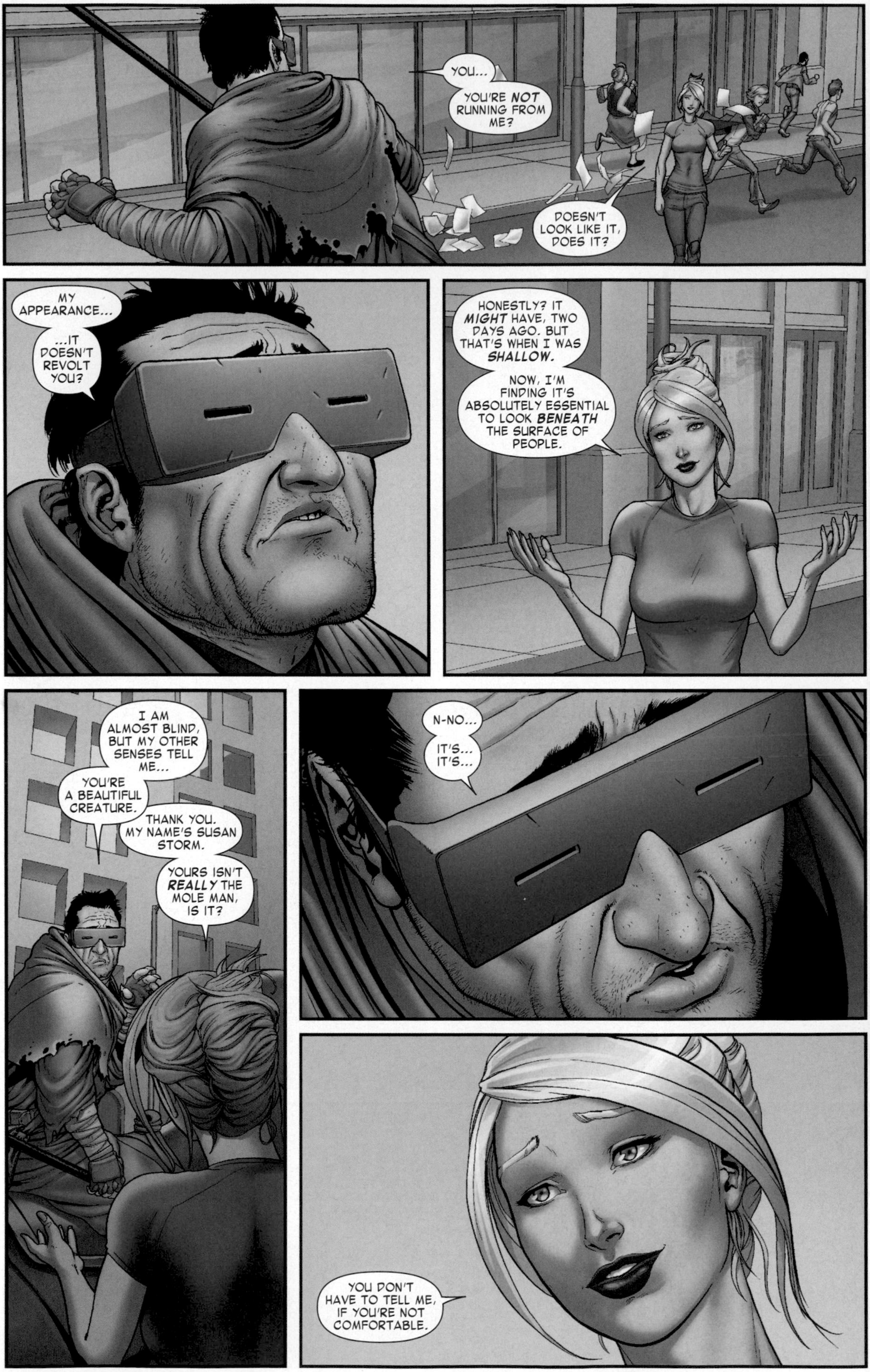
YOU...
YOU'RE NOT RUNNING FROM ME?
DOESN'T LOOK LIKE IT, DOES IT?
MY APPEARANCE...
...IT DOESN'T REVOLT YOU?
HONESTLY? IT MIGHT HAVE, TWO DAYS AGO. BUT THAT'S WHEN I WAS SHALLOW.
NOW, I'M FINDING IT'S ABSOLUTELY ESSENTIAL TO LOOK BENEATH THE SURFACE OF PEOPLE.
I AM ALMOST BLIND, BUT MY OTHER SENSES TELL ME...
YOU'RE A BEAUTIFUL CREATURE.
THANK YOU. MY NAME'S SUSAN STORM.
YOURS ISN'T REALLY THE MOLE MAN, IS IT?
N-NO...
IT'S... IT'S...
YOU DON'T HAVE TO TELL ME, IF YOU'RE NOT COMFORTABLE.

"I-IT'S HARVEY..."

HERE, *GROTTU*--

FOLLOW THE FLAMING CARROT--

ALL THE WAY TO CENTRAL PARK, WHICH WE GET TO-- *HOW* AGAIN?

JOHNN?! CAREFUL!

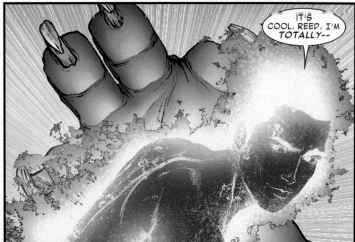

IT'S *COOL,* REED, I'M *TOTALLY*--

KSSSHHH

⟨GASP⟩

...DOUSED...

I WAS A STUDENT OF THE GEOLOGICAL SCIENCES...

THAT MAKES SENSE.

THE *SERENITY* OF THE UNDERWORLD PROVIDED REFUGE FROM THE *CACOPHONY* OF HATRED DIRECTED TOWARDS ME FOR MY UNIQUE PHYSIQUE...

MMM-HMMM.

ODDLY, SHE THINKS, HE REMINDS ME OF--

BEN! JOHNNY'S BEEN NEUTRALIZED!

WHA--?

YA DON'T MEAN LIKE IN A *PERMANENT* WAY, DO YA?

"NO, BUT HE'S STRUGGLING TO REIGNITE--"

COME ON, COME ON...

CONCENTRATE, STORM...RELAX... BURN...

SO IT'S THE *TWO* OF US--

WHEN I GIVE THE SIGNAL, CAN YOU PIN DOWN ONE OF THE CREATURE'S FEET?

OH, YEAH, SURE, NO PROBLEM--

WHILE YOU DO *WHAT?* HAVE A BON-BON?

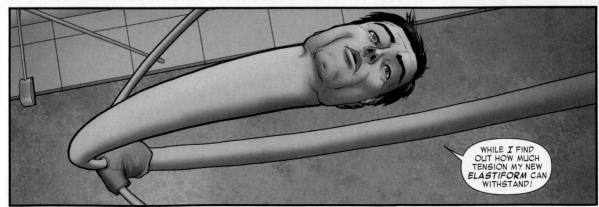

WHILE *I* FIND OUT HOW MUCH TENSION MY NEW *ELASTIFORM* CAN WITHSTAND!

ALL RIGHT, BEN, *NOW!* WE'RE CLOSE ENOUGH TO CENTRAL PARK THAT IF IT TRIPS--

WAIT--REED-- I'VE MADE CONTACT--

"NO, BEN, *DON'T!* YOU DON'T HAVE TO--"

TRIP, DAMMIT!

HHURR?

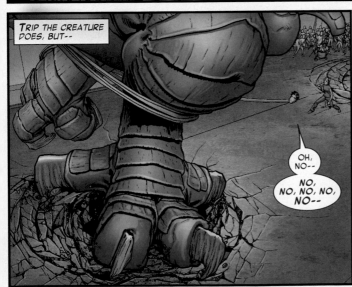

TRIP THE CREATURE DOES, BUT--

OH, NO--

NO, NO, NO, NO--

--IN THE WRONG DIRECTION.

OHMYGOD.

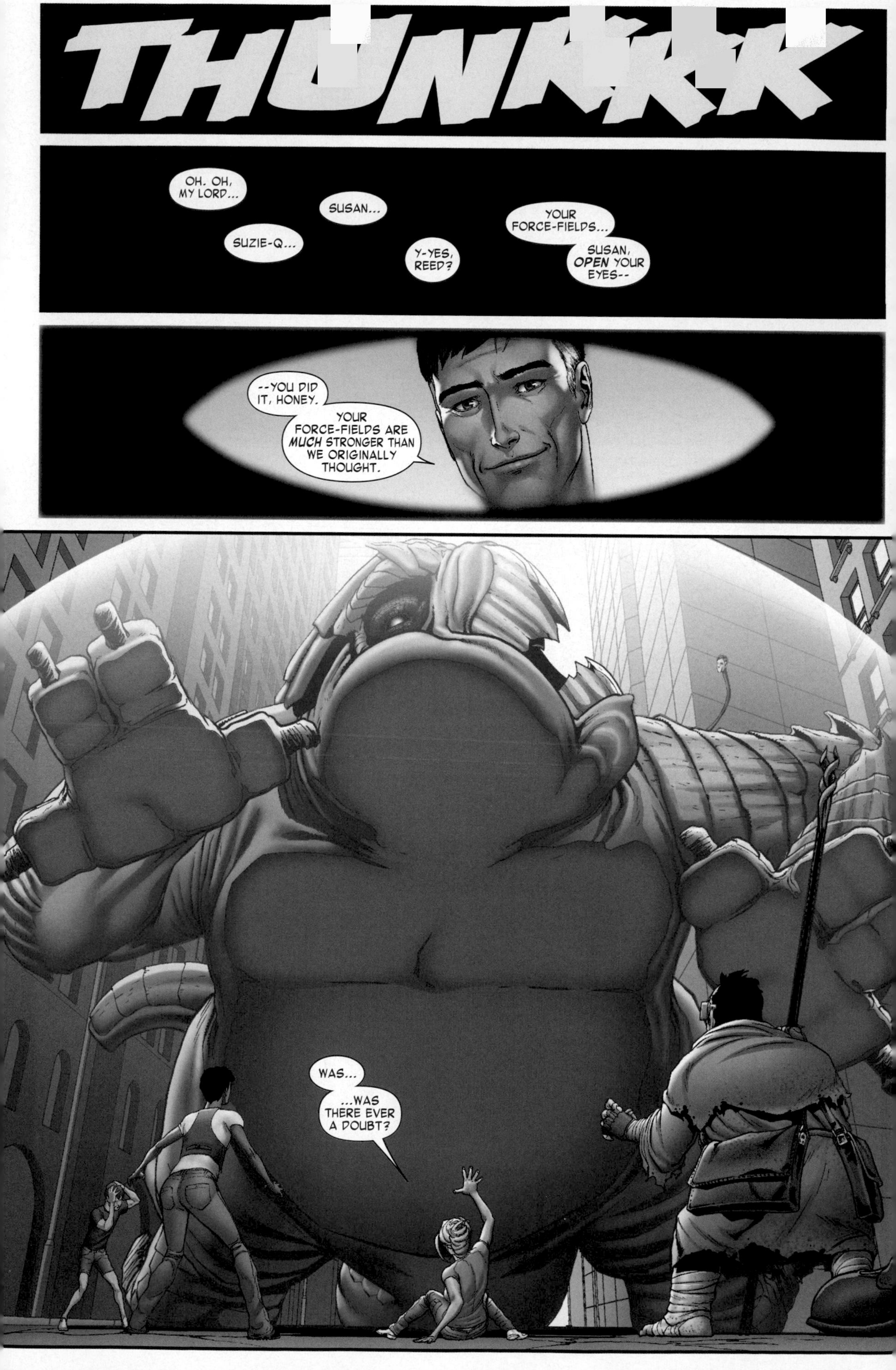
THUNKKK
OH. OH, MY LORD...
SUSAN...
SUZIE-Q...
Y-YES, REED?
YOUR FORCE-FIELDS...
SUSAN, OPEN YOUR EYES--
--YOU DID IT, HONEY.
YOUR FORCE-FIELDS ARE MUCH STRONGER THAN WE ORIGINALLY THOUGHT.
WAS...
...WAS THERE EVER A DOUBT?

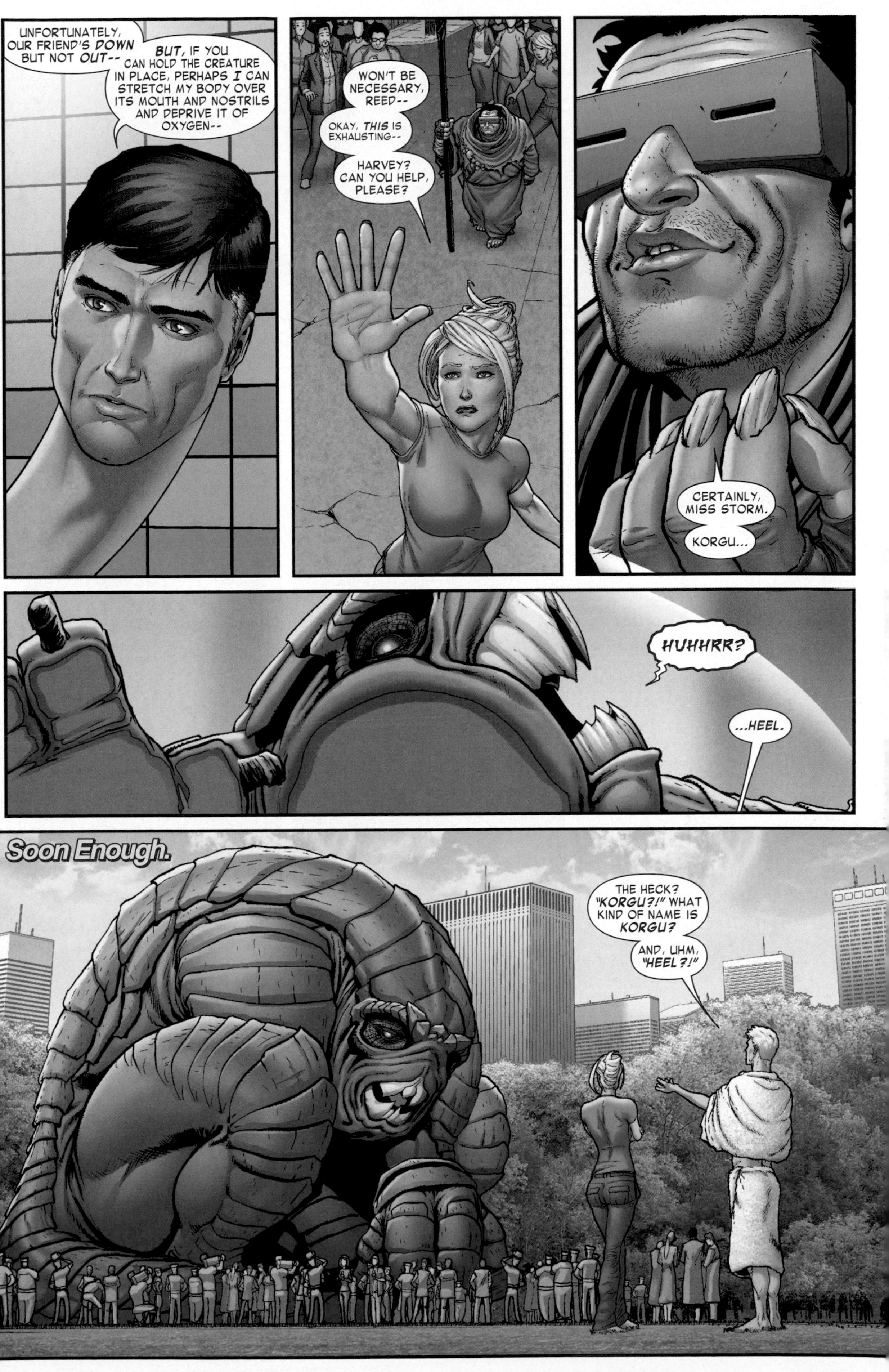
UNFORTUNATELY, OUR FRIEND'S DOWN BUT NOT OUT--
BUT, IF YOU CAN HOLD THE CREATURE IN PLACE, PERHAPS I CAN STRETCH MY BODY OVER ITS MOUTH AND NOSTRILS AND DEPRIVE IT OF OXYGEN--
WON'T BE NECESSARY, REED--
OKAY, THIS IS EXHAUSTING--
HARVEY? CAN YOU HELP, PLEASE?
CERTAINLY, MISS STORM.
KORGU...
HUHHRR?
...HEEL.
Soon Enough.
THE HECK? "KORGU?!" WHAT KIND OF NAME IS KORGU?
AND, UHM, "HEEL?!"

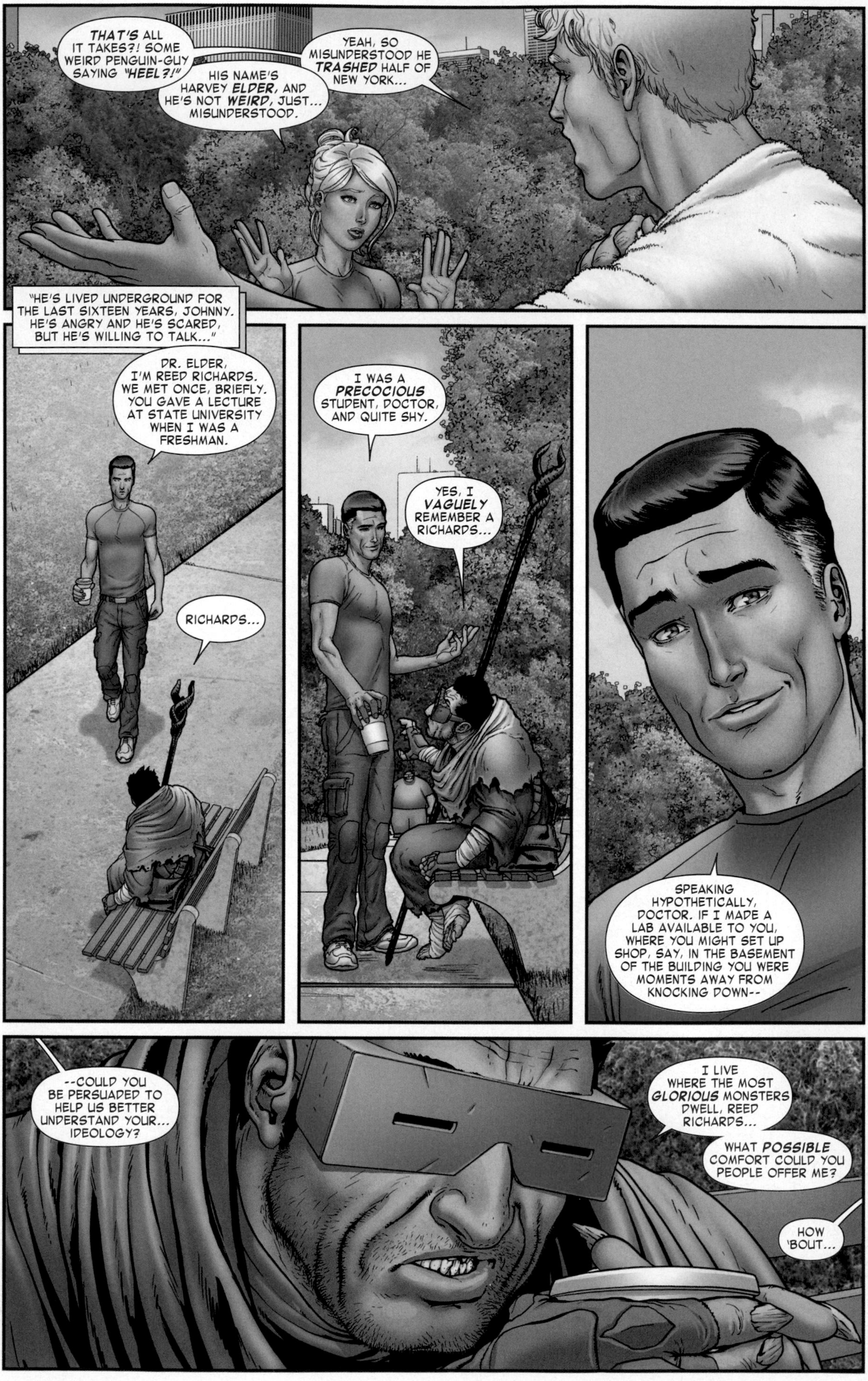
THAT'S ALL IT TAKES?! SOME WEIRD PENGUIN-GUY SAYING "HEEL?!"
HIS NAME'S HARVEY ELDER, AND HE'S NOT WEIRD, JUST... MISUNDERSTOOD.
YEAH, SO MISUNDERSTOOD HE TRASHED HALF OF NEW YORK...
"HE'S LIVED UNDERGROUND FOR THE LAST SIXTEEN YEARS, JOHNNY. HE'S ANGRY AND HE'S SCARED, BUT HE'S WILLING TO TALK..."
DR. ELDER, I'M REED RICHARDS. WE MET ONCE, BRIEFLY. YOU GAVE A LECTURE AT STATE UNIVERSITY WHEN I WAS A FRESHMAN.
RICHARDS...
I WAS A PRECOCIOUS STUDENT, DOCTOR, AND QUITE SHY.
YES, I VAGUELY REMEMBER A RICHARDS...
SPEAKING HYPOTHETICALLY, DOCTOR. IF I MADE A LAB AVAILABLE TO YOU, WHERE YOU MIGHT SET UP SHOP, SAY, IN THE BASEMENT OF THE BUILDING YOU WERE MOMENTS AWAY FROM KNOCKING DOWN--
--COULD YOU BE PERSUADED TO HELP US BETTER UNDERSTAND YOUR... IDEOLOGY?
I LIVE WHERE THE MOST GLORIOUS MONSTERS DWELL, REED RICHARDS...
WHAT POSSIBLE COMFORT COULD YOU PEOPLE OFFER ME?
HOW 'BOUT...

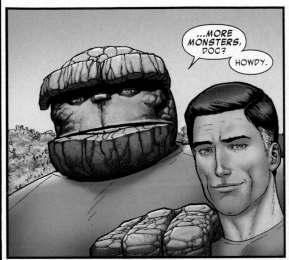

...MORE MONSTERS, DOC?

HOWDY.

WE'LL BROKER A PEACE BETWEEN OUR WORLDS, HARVEY.

AND MAKE YOU COMFORTABLE, ON *YOUR* TERMS.

THERE WOULD BE CERTAIN REQUIREMENTS...

And So.

...I DON'T KNOW, WE'LL SEE WHAT HAPPENS. FINGERS CROSSED, THOUGH.

IF THE CREATURES *BENEATH* GROUND TRULY DECIDED TO RISE UP AND ATTACK THE CREATURES *ABOVE* GROUND, I DON'T THINK WE'D STAND MUCH OF A CHANCE.

EXCUSE ME--HI--HELLO THERE--

JILLIAN JONES, *SPOTLIGHT ON NEW YORK*--

THIS IS MY NEWLY PROMOTED *PRODUCER,* JERRY COHEN--

CAN WE STEAL *FIVE* MINUTES OF YOUR TIME?

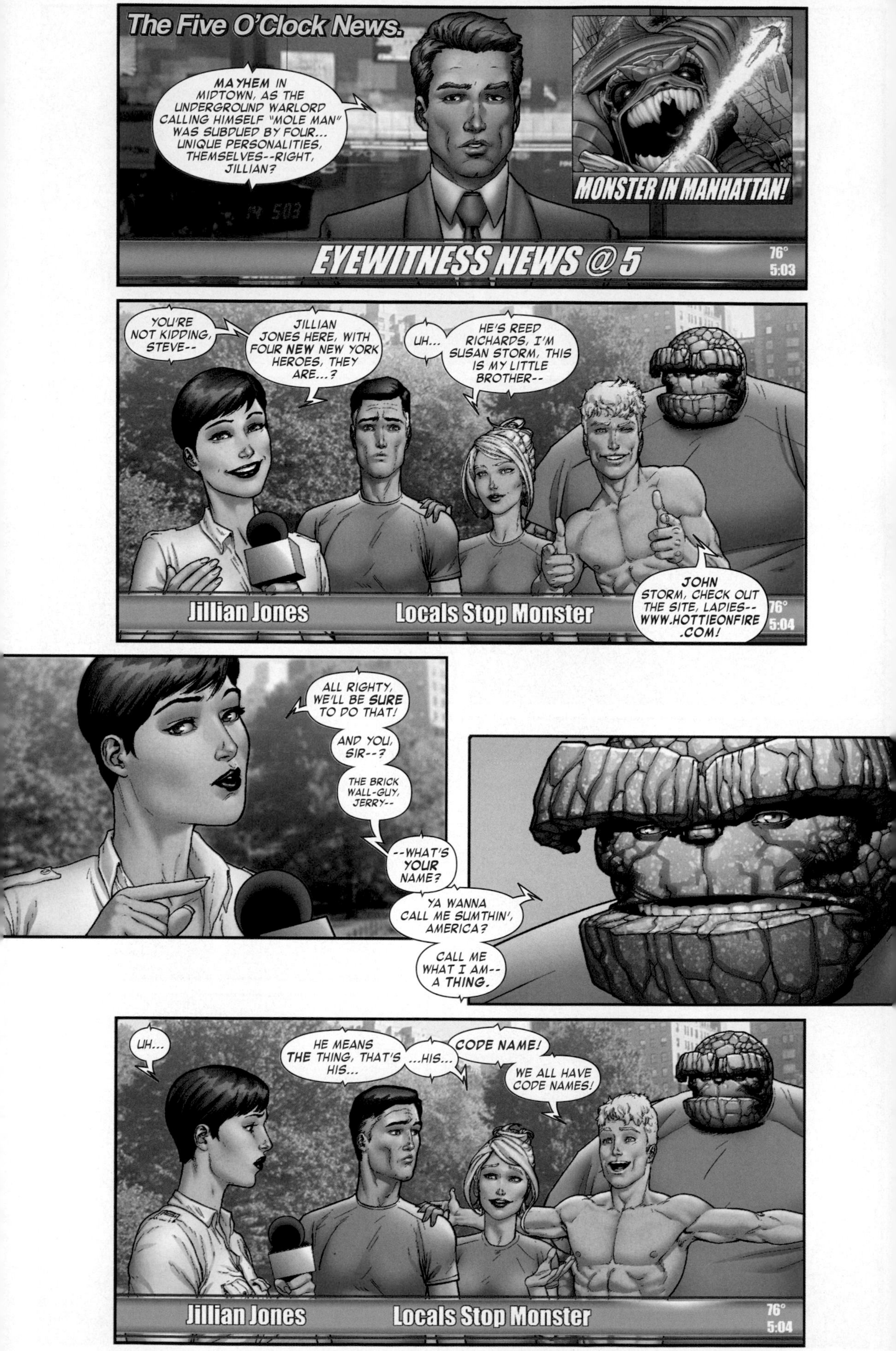
The Five O'Clock News.
MAYHEM IN MIDTOWN, AS THE UNDERGROUND WARLORD CALLING HIMSELF "MOLE MAN" WAS SUBDUED BY FOUR... UNIQUE PERSONALITIES, THEMSELVES--RIGHT, JILLIAN?
MONSTER IN MANHATTAN!
EYEWITNESS NEWS @ 5
76°
5:03
YOU'RE NOT KIDDING, STEVE--
JILLIAN JONES HERE, WITH FOUR NEW NEW YORK HEROES, THEY ARE...?
UH...
HE'S REED RICHARDS, I'M SUSAN STORM, THIS IS MY LITTLE BROTHER--
JOHN STORM, CHECK OUT THE SITE, LADIES-- WWW.HOTTIEONFIRE.COM!
Jillian Jones
Locals Stop Monster
76°
5:04
ALL RIGHTY, WE'LL BE SURE TO DO THAT!
AND YOU, SIR--?
THE BRICK WALL-GUY, JERRY--
--WHAT'S YOUR NAME?
YA WANNA CALL ME SUMTHIN', AMERICA?
CALL ME WHAT I AM-- A THING.
UH...
HE MEANS THE THING, THAT'S HIS...
...HIS...
CODE NAME!
WE ALL HAVE CODE NAMES!
Jillian Jones
Locals Stop Monster
76°
5:04

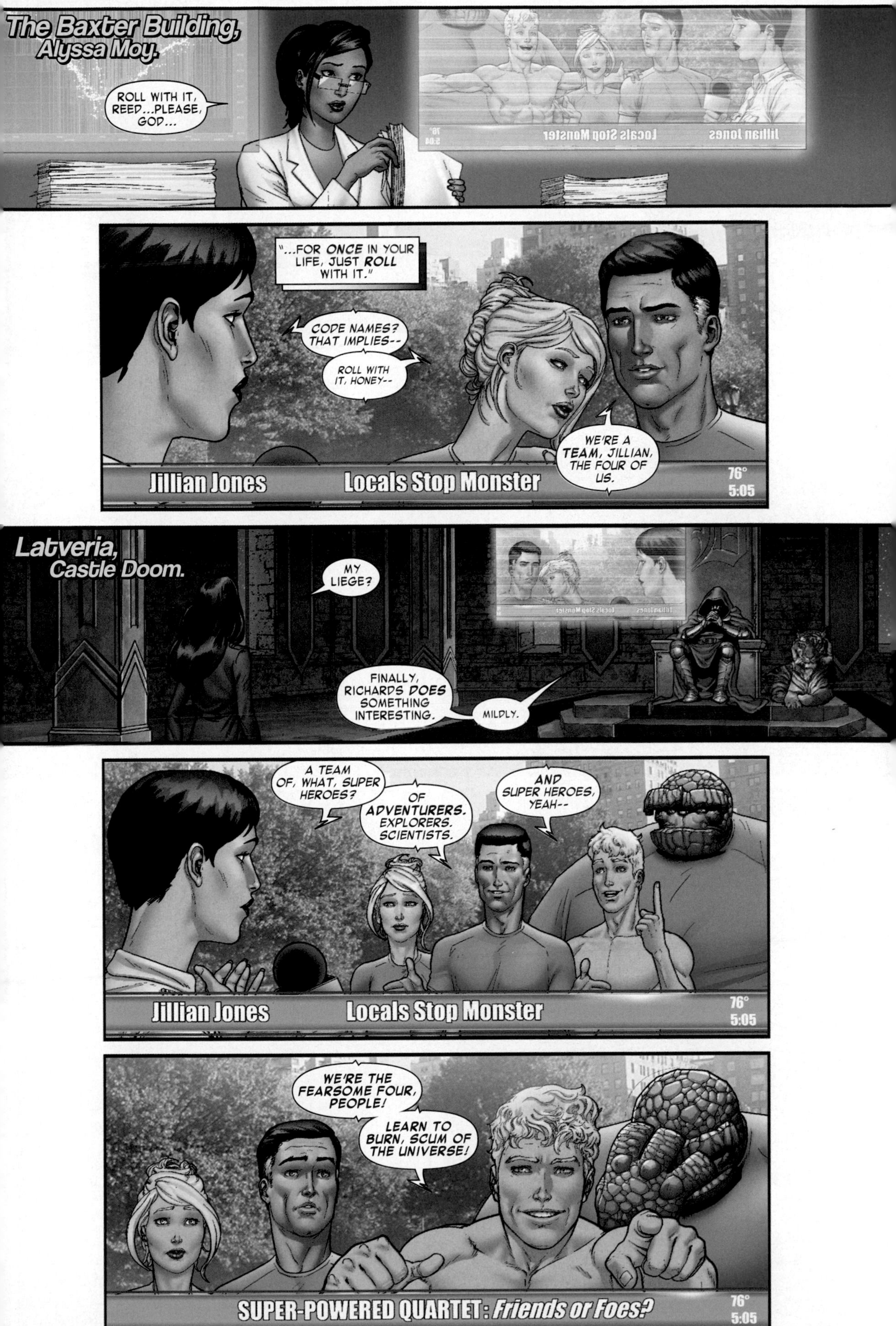

The Baxter Building, Alyssa Moy.
ROLL WITH IT, REED...PLEASE, GOD...
Jillian Jones
Locals Stop Monster
"...FOR ONCE IN YOUR LIFE, JUST ROLL WITH IT."
CODE NAMES? THAT IMPLIES--
ROLL WITH IT, HONEY--
WE'RE A TEAM, JILLIAN, THE FOUR OF US.
Jillian Jones
Locals Stop Monster
76°
5:05
Latveria, Castle Doom.
MY LIEGE?
FINALLY, RICHARDS DOES SOMETHING INTERESTING.
MILDLY.
A TEAM OF, WHAT, SUPER HEROES?
OF ADVENTURERS. EXPLORERS. SCIENTISTS.
AND SUPER HEROES, YEAH--
Jillian Jones
Locals Stop Monster
76°
5:05
WE'RE THE FEARSOME FOUR, PEOPLE!
LEARN TO BURN, SCUM OF THE UNIVERSE!
SUPER-POWERED QUARTET: Friends or Foes?
76°
5:05

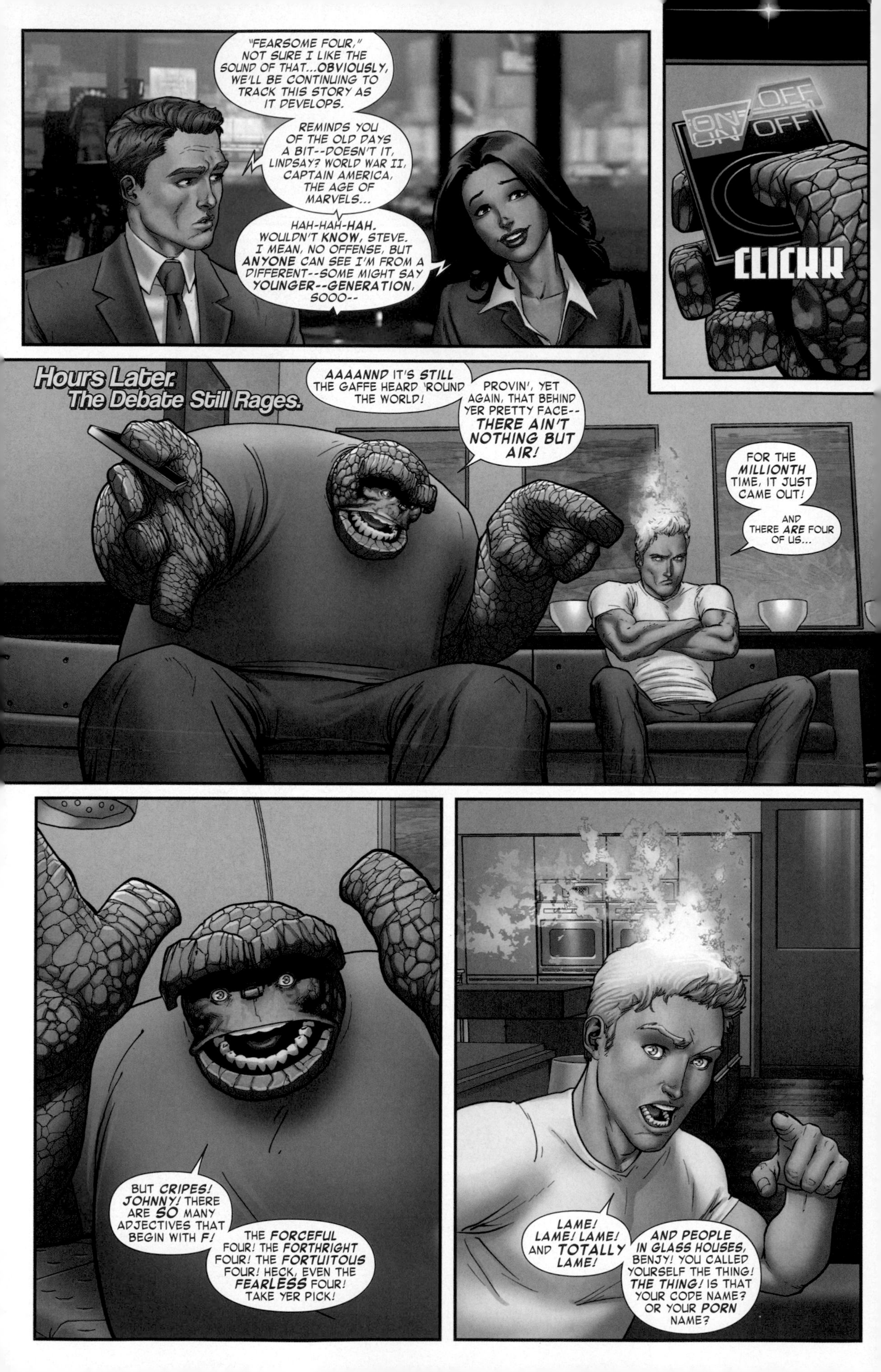
"FEARSOME FOUR," NOT SURE I LIKE THE SOUND OF THAT...OBVIOUSLY, WE'LL BE CONTINUING TO TRACK THIS STORY AS IT DEVELOPS.
REMINDS YOU OF THE OLD DAYS A BIT--DOESN'T IT, LINDSAY? WORLD WAR II, CAPTAIN AMERICA, THE AGE OF MARVELS...
HAH-HAH-HAH. WOULDN'T KNOW, STEVE. I MEAN, NO OFFENSE, BUT ANYONE CAN SEE I'M FROM A DIFFERENT--SOME MIGHT SAY YOUNGER--GENERATION, SOOO--
ON OFF
CLICKK
Hours Later. The Debate Still Rages.
AAAANND IT'S STILL THE GAFFE HEARD 'ROUND THE WORLD!
PROVIN', YET AGAIN, THAT BEHIND YER PRETTY FACE-- THERE AIN'T NOTHING BUT AIR!
FOR THE MILLIONTH TIME, IT JUST CAME OUT!
AND THERE ARE FOUR OF US...
BUT CRIPES! JOHNNY! THERE ARE SO MANY ADJECTIVES THAT BEGIN WITH F!
THE FORCEFUL FOUR! THE FORTHRIGHT FOUR! THE FORTUITOUS FOUR! HECK, EVEN THE FEARLESS FOUR! TAKE YER PICK!
LAME! LAME! LAME! AND TOTALLY LAME!
AND PEOPLE IN GLASS HOUSES, BENJY! YOU CALLED YOURSELF THE THING! THE THING! IS THAT YOUR CODE NAME? OR YOUR PORN NAME?

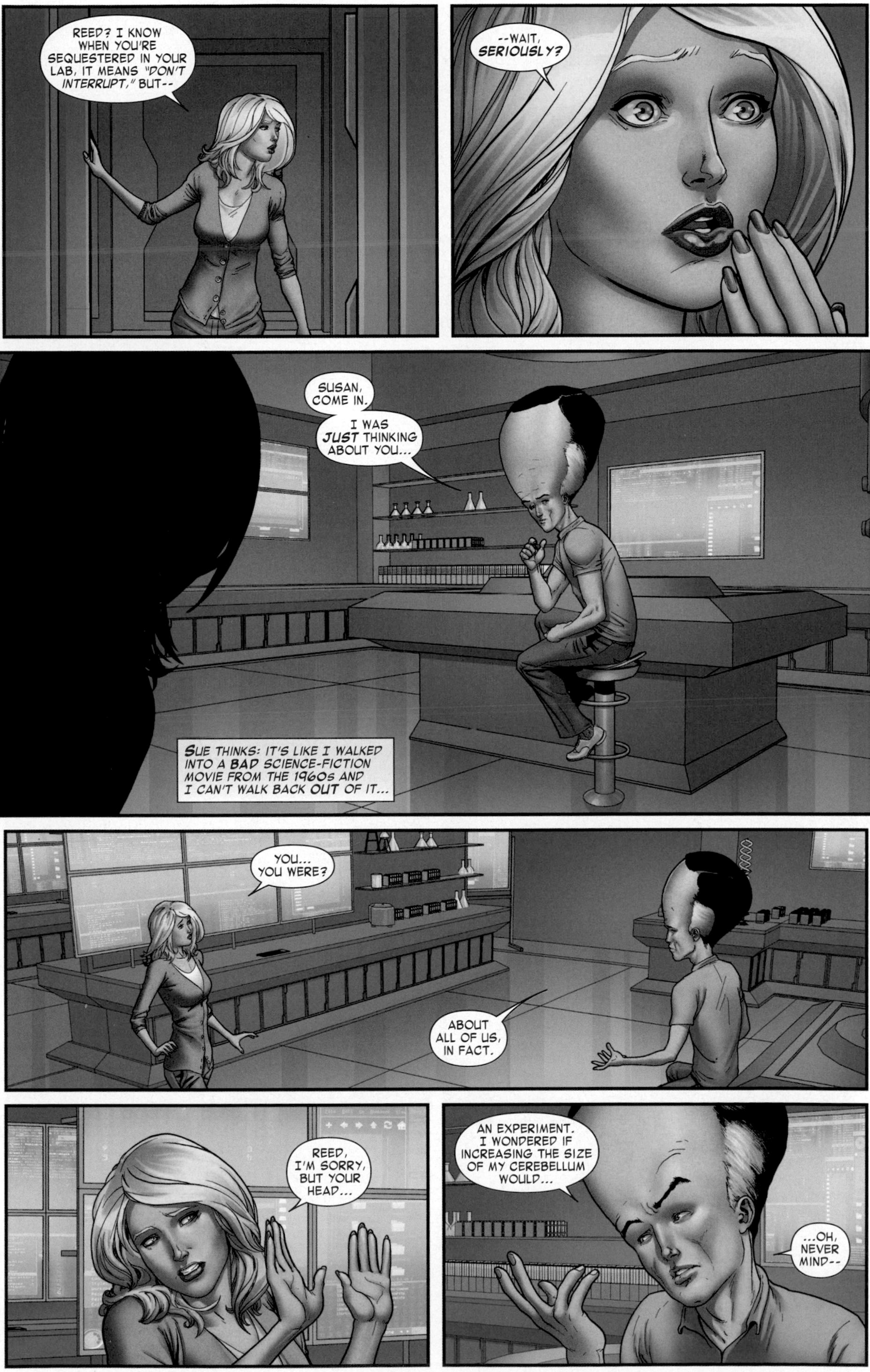
REED? I KNOW WHEN YOU'RE SEQUESTERED IN YOUR LAB, IT MEANS "DON'T INTERRUPT," BUT--
--WAIT, SERIOUSLY?
SUSAN, COME IN.
I WAS JUST THINKING ABOUT YOU...
SUE THINKS: IT'S LIKE I WALKED INTO A BAD SCIENCE-FICTION MOVIE FROM THE 1960s AND I CAN'T WALK BACK OUT OF IT...
YOU... YOU WERE?
ABOUT ALL OF US, IN FACT.
REED, I'M SORRY, BUT YOUR HEAD...
AN EXPERIMENT. I WONDERED IF INCREASING THE SIZE OF MY CEREBELLUM WOULD...
...OH, NEVER MIND--

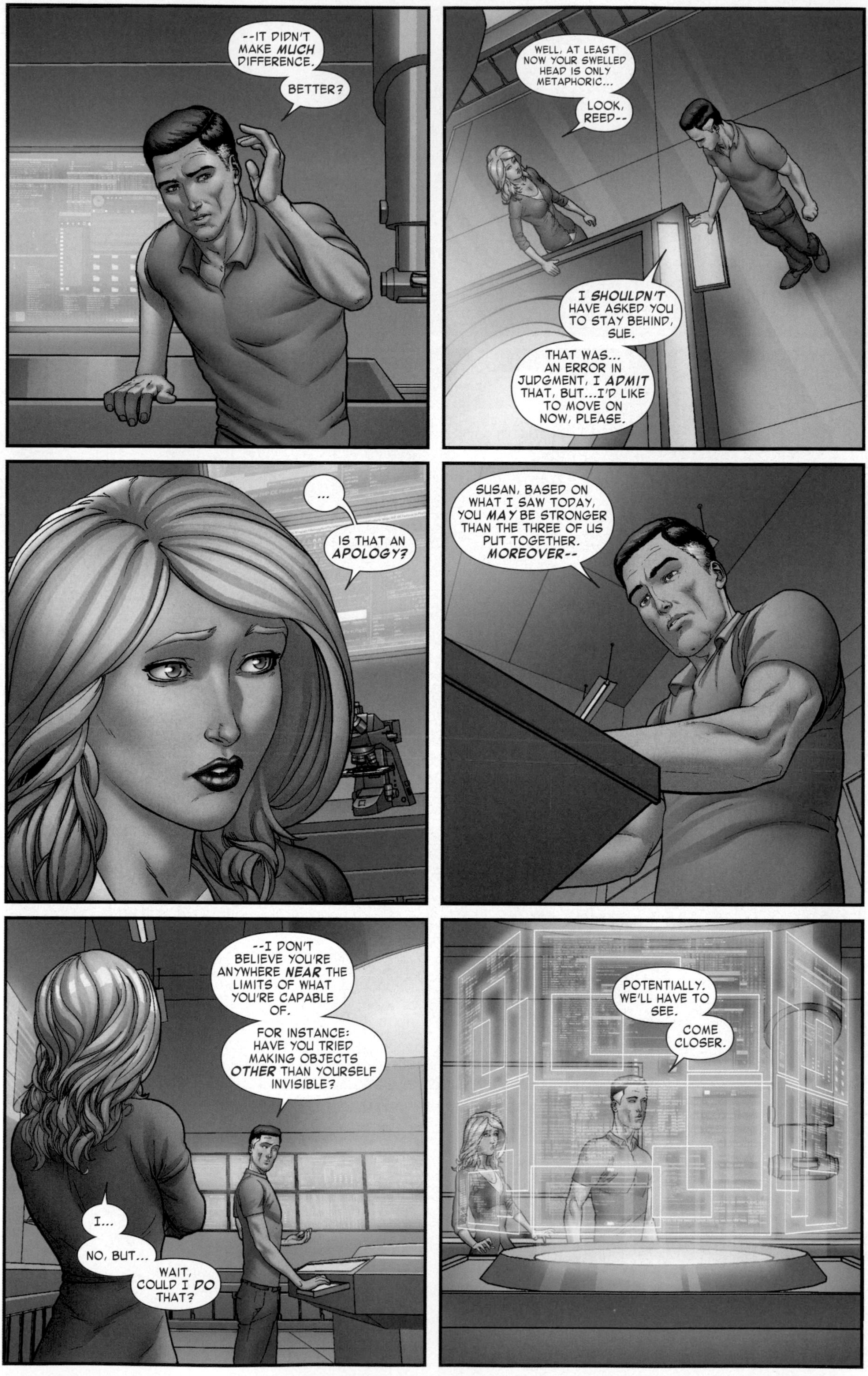
--IT DIDN'T MAKE MUCH DIFFERENCE.
BETTER?
WELL, AT LEAST NOW YOUR SWELLED HEAD IS ONLY METAPHORIC...
LOOK, REED--
I SHOULDN'T HAVE ASKED YOU TO STAY BEHIND, SUE.
THAT WAS... AN ERROR IN JUDGMENT, I ADMIT THAT, BUT...I'D LIKE TO MOVE ON NOW, PLEASE.
...
IS THAT AN APOLOGY?
SUSAN, BASED ON WHAT I SAW TODAY, YOU MAY BE STRONGER THAN THE THREE OF US PUT TOGETHER. MOREOVER--
--I DON'T BELIEVE YOU'RE ANYWHERE NEAR THE LIMITS OF WHAT YOU'RE CAPABLE OF.
FOR INSTANCE: HAVE YOU TRIED MAKING OBJECTS OTHER THAN YOURSELF INVISIBLE?
I...
NO, BUT...
WAIT, COULD I DO THAT?
POTENTIALLY. WE'LL HAVE TO SEE.
COME CLOSER.

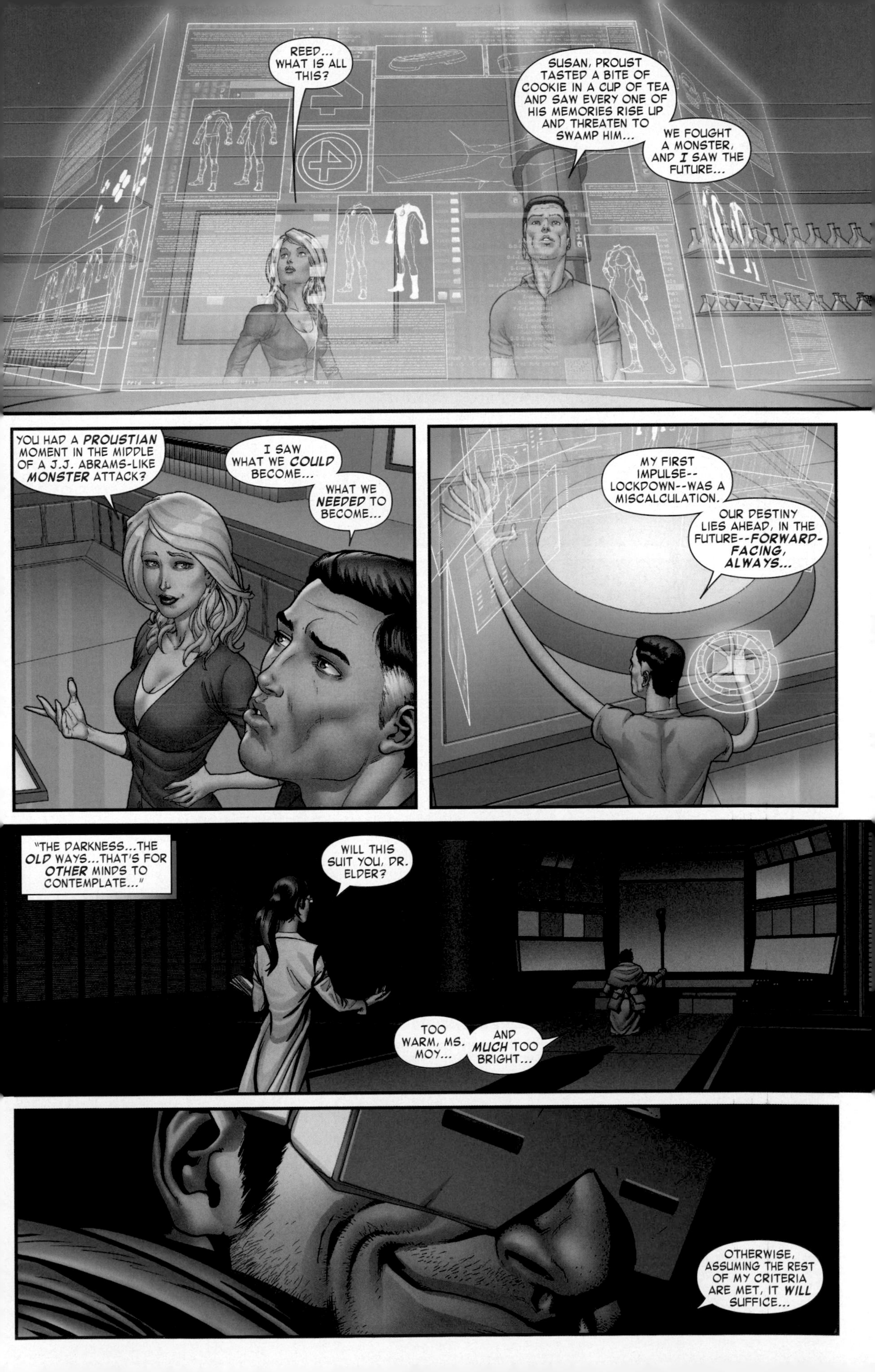
REED... WHAT IS ALL THIS?
SUSAN, PROUST TASTED A BITE OF COOKIE IN A CUP OF TEA AND SAW EVERY ONE OF HIS MEMORIES RISE UP AND THREATEN TO SWAMP HIM...
WE FOUGHT A MONSTER, AND *I* SAW THE FUTURE...
YOU HAD A *PROUSTIAN* MOMENT IN THE MIDDLE OF A J.J. ABRAMS-LIKE *MONSTER* ATTACK?
I SAW WHAT WE *COULD* BECOME...
WHAT WE *NEEDED* TO BECOME...
MY FIRST IMPULSE--LOCKDOWN--WAS A MISCALCULATION.
OUR DESTINY LIES AHEAD, IN THE FUTURE--*FORWARD-FACING, ALWAYS...*
"THE DARKNESS...THE *OLD* WAYS...THAT'S FOR *OTHER* MINDS TO CONTEMPLATE..."
WILL THIS SUIT YOU, DR. ELDER?
TOO WARM, MS. MOY...
AND *MUCH* TOO BRIGHT...
OTHERWISE, ASSUMING THE REST OF MY CRITERIA ARE MET, IT *WILL* SUFFICE...

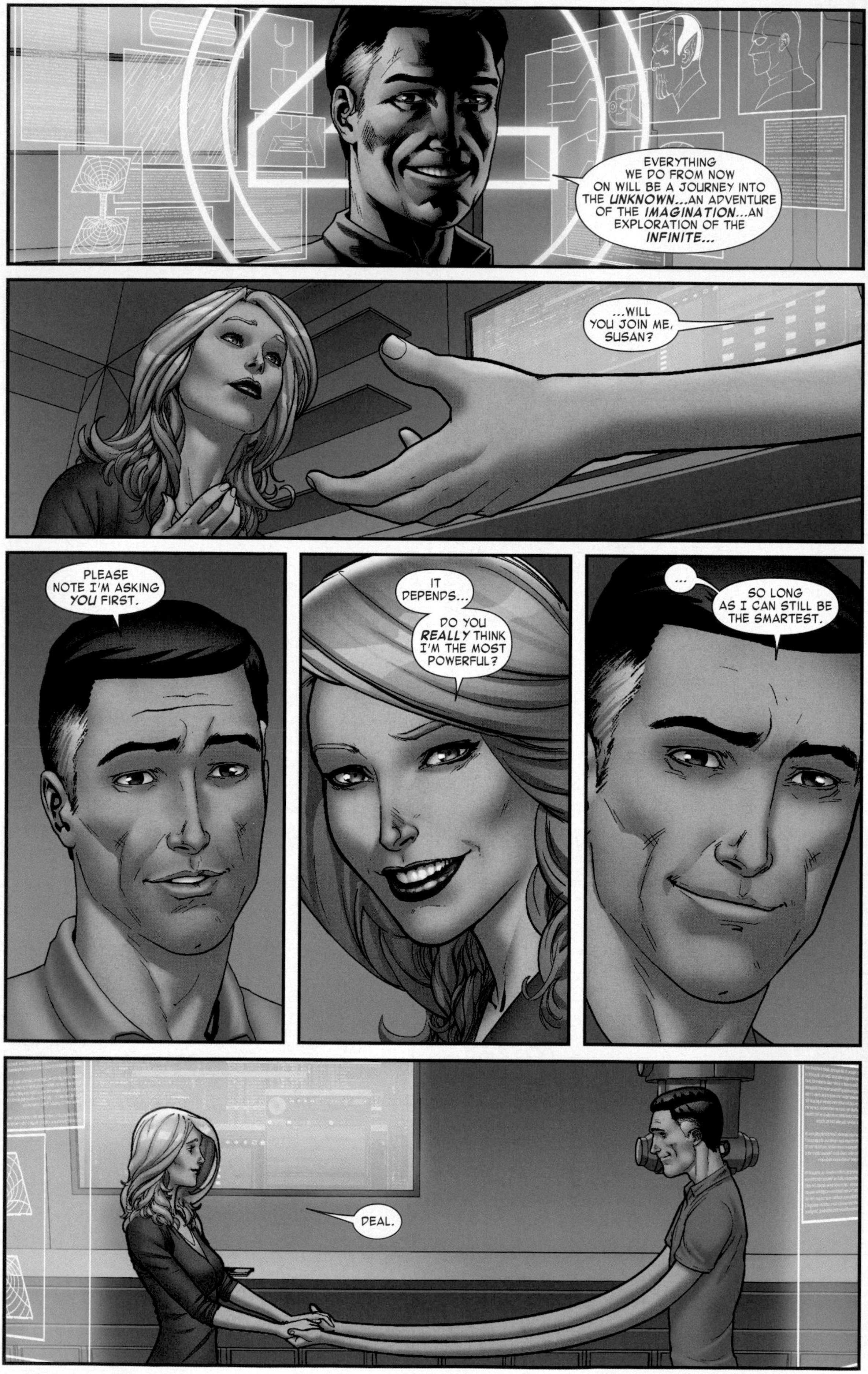
EVERYTHING WE DO FROM NOW ON WILL BE A JOURNEY INTO THE UNKNOWN...AN ADVENTURE OF THE IMAGINATION...AN EXPLORATION OF THE INFINITE...
...WILL YOU JOIN ME, SUSAN?
PLEASE NOTE I'M ASKING YOU FIRST.
IT DEPENDS...
DO YOU REALLY THINK I'M THE MOST POWERFUL?
...
SO LONG AS I CAN STILL BE THE SMARTEST.
DEAL.

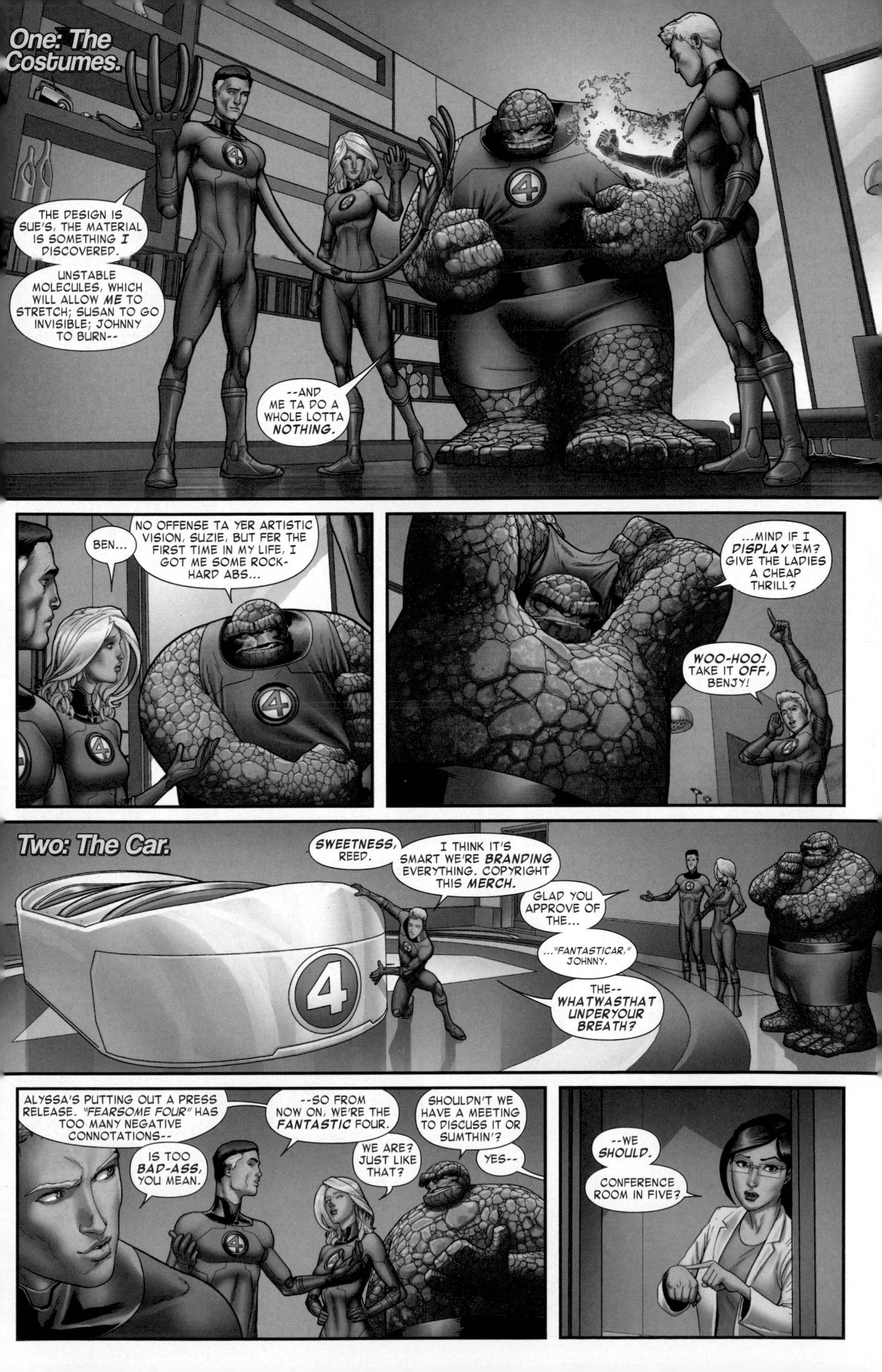

One: The Costumes.
THE DESIGN IS SUE'S, THE MATERIAL IS SOMETHING I DISCOVERED.
UNSTABLE MOLECULES, WHICH WILL ALLOW ME TO STRETCH; SUSAN TO GO INVISIBLE; JOHNNY TO BURN--
--AND ME TA DO A WHOLE LOTTA NOTHING.
BEN...
NO OFFENSE TA YER ARTISTIC VISION, SUZIE, BUT FER THE FIRST TIME IN MY LIFE, I GOT ME SOME ROCK-HARD ABS...
...MIND IF I DISPLAY 'EM? GIVE THE LADIES A CHEAP THRILL?
WOO-HOO! TAKE IT OFF, BENJY!
Two: The Car.
SWEETNESS, REED.
I THINK IT'S SMART WE'RE BRANDING EVERYTHING. COPYRIGHT THIS MERCH.
GLAD YOU APPROVE OF THE...
..."FANTASTICAR," JOHNNY.
THE--
WHATWASTHAT UNDERYOUR BREATH?
ALYSSA'S PUTTING OUT A PRESS RELEASE. "FEARSOME FOUR" HAS TOO MANY NEGATIVE CONNOTATIONS--
IS TOO BAD-ASS, YOU MEAN.
--SO FROM NOW ON, WE'RE THE FANTASTIC FOUR.
WE ARE? JUST LIKE THAT?
SHOULDN'T WE HAVE A MEETING TO DISCUSS IT OR SUMTHIN'?
YES--
--WE SHOULD.
CONFERENCE ROOM IN FIVE?

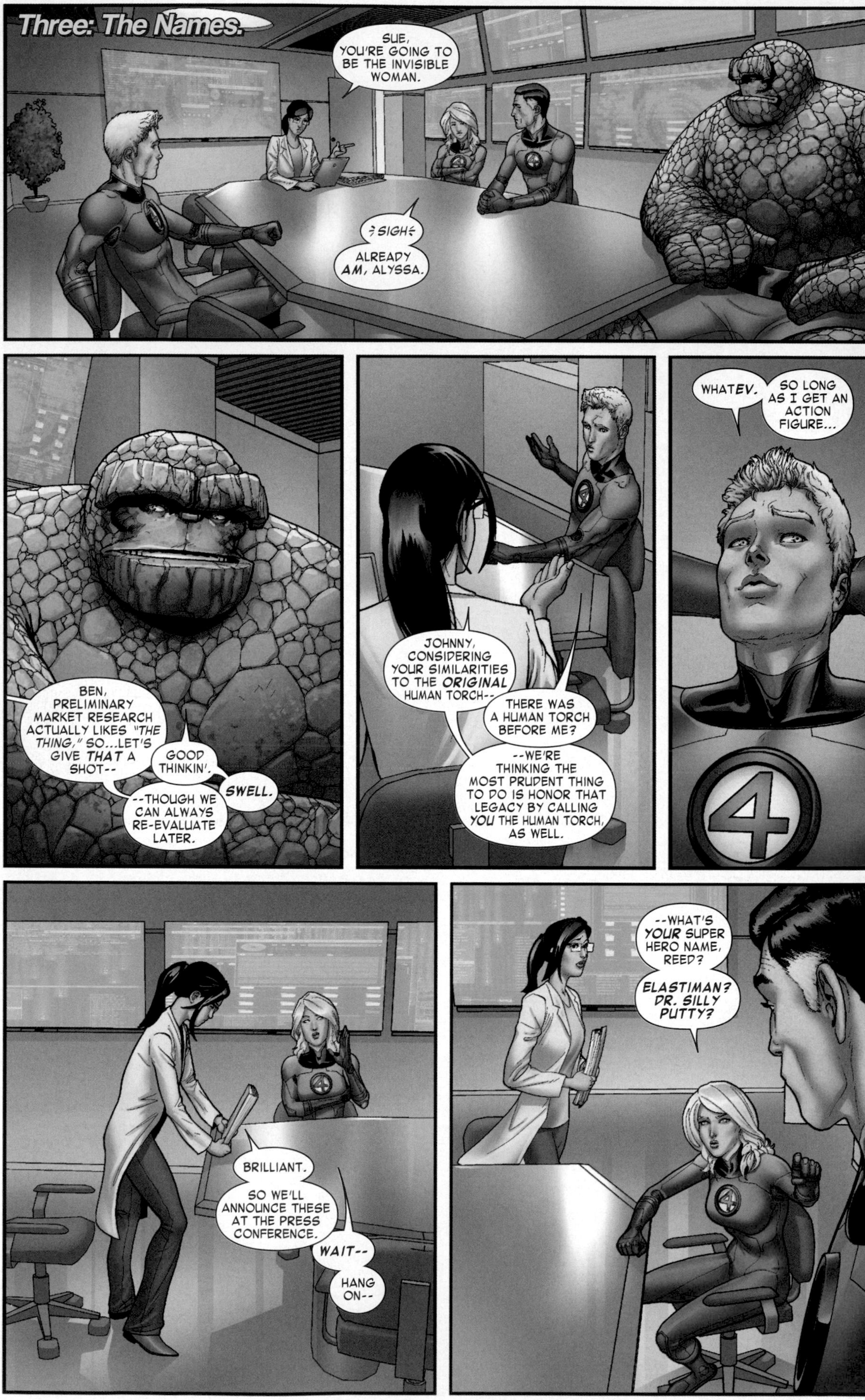
Three: The Names.
SUE, YOU'RE GOING TO BE THE INVISIBLE WOMAN.
⇢SIGH⇠ ALREADY AM, ALYSSA.
BEN, PRELIMINARY MARKET RESEARCH ACTUALLY LIKES "THE THING," SO...LET'S GIVE THAT A SHOT--
GOOD THINKIN'.
SWELL.
--THOUGH WE CAN ALWAYS RE-EVALUATE LATER.
JOHNNY, CONSIDERING YOUR SIMILARITIES TO THE ORIGINAL HUMAN TORCH--
THERE WAS A HUMAN TORCH BEFORE ME?
--WE'RE THINKING THE MOST PRUDENT THING TO DO IS HONOR THAT LEGACY BY CALLING YOU THE HUMAN TORCH, AS WELL.
WHATEV.
SO LONG AS I GET AN ACTION FIGURE...
BRILLIANT.
SO WE'LL ANNOUNCE THESE AT THE PRESS CONFERENCE.
WAIT--
HANG ON--
--WHAT'S YOUR SUPER HERO NAME, REED?
ELASTIMAN? DR. SILLY PUTTY?

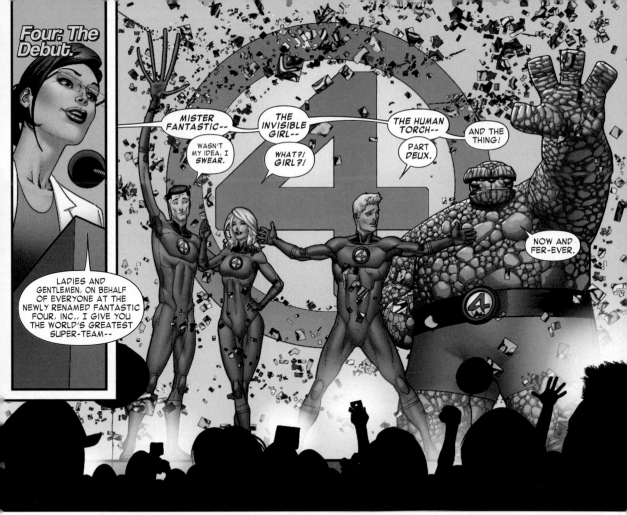

Four: The Debut.

MISTER FANTASTIC--

WASN'T MY IDEA, I SWEAR.

THE INVISIBLE GIRL--

WHAT?! GIRL?!

THE HUMAN TORCH--

PART DEUX.

AND THE THING!

NOW AND FER-EVER.

LADIES AND GENTLEMEN, ON BEHALF OF EVERYONE AT THE NEWLY RENAMED FANTASTIC FOUR, INC., I GIVE YOU THE WORLD'S GREATEST SUPER-TEAM--

"TOGETHER, THEY ARE-- THE FANTASTIC FOUR!"

WOO-HOO! YEAHHH!

THE HUMAN TORCH...

"...MY GREATEST ENEMY..."

...ALIVE?

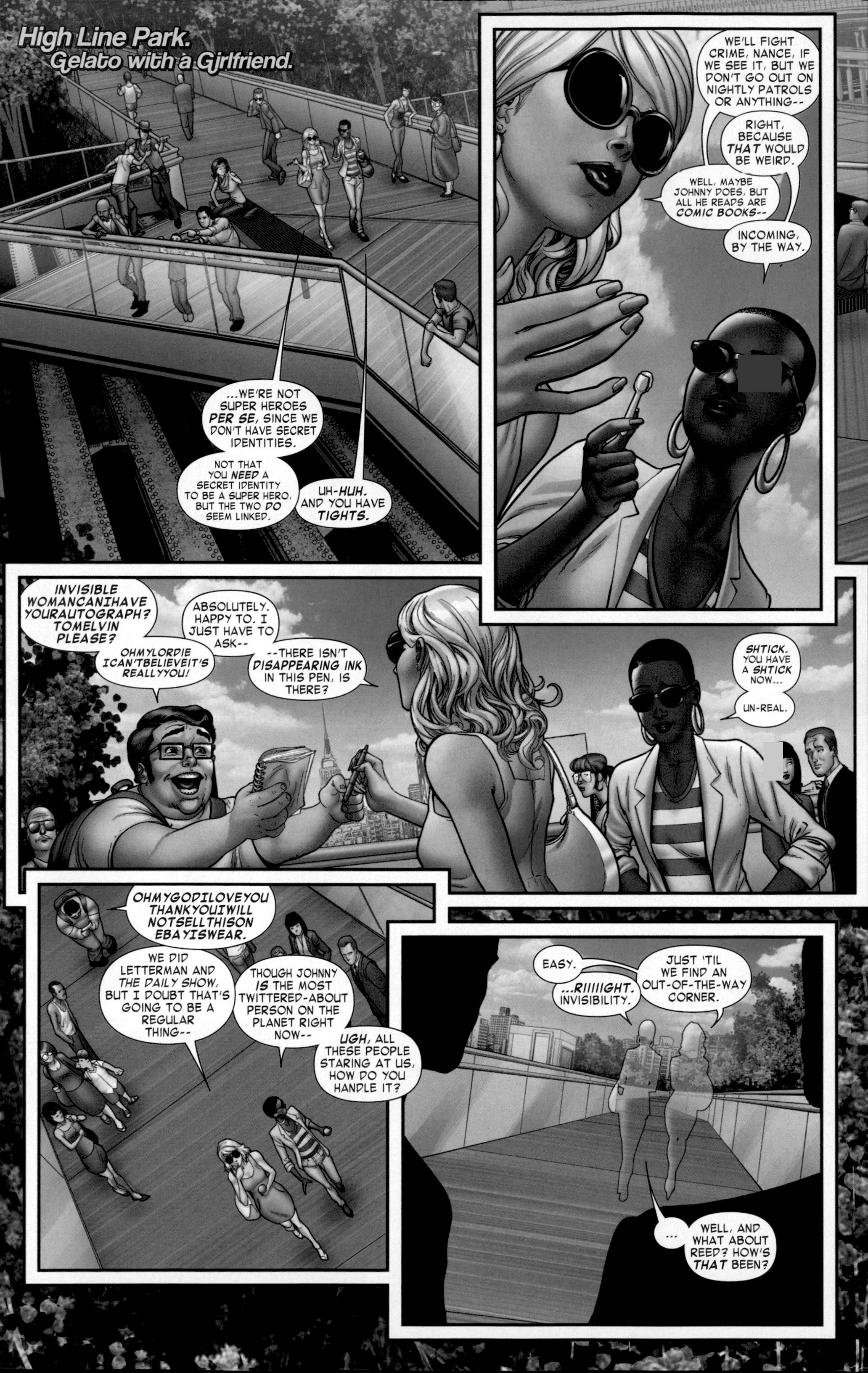
High Line Park.
Gelato with a Girlfriend.
...WE'RE NOT SUPER HEROES PER SE, SINCE WE DON'T HAVE SECRET IDENTITIES.
NOT THAT YOU NEED A SECRET IDENTITY TO BE A SUPER HERO, BUT THE TWO DO SEEM LINKED.
UH-HUH. AND YOU HAVE TIGHTS.
WE'LL FIGHT CRIME, NANCE, IF WE SEE IT, BUT WE DON'T GO OUT ON NIGHTLY PATROLS OR ANYTHING--
RIGHT, BECAUSE THAT WOULD BE WEIRD.
WELL, MAYBE JOHNNY DOES, BUT ALL HE READS ARE COMIC BOOKS--
INCOMING, BY THE WAY.
INVISIBLE WOMANCANIHAVE YOURAUTOGRAPH? TOMELVIN PLEASE?
OHMYLORDIE ICAN'TBELIEVEIT'S REALLYYOU!
ABSOLUTELY. HAPPY TO. I JUST HAVE TO ASK--
--THERE ISN'T DISAPPEARING INK IN THIS PEN, IS THERE?
SHTICK. YOU HAVE A SHTICK NOW...
UN-REAL.
OHMYGODILOVEYOU THANKYOUIWILL NOTSELLTHISON EBAYISWEAR.
WE DID LETTERMAN AND THE DAILY SHOW, BUT I DOUBT THAT'S GOING TO BE A REGULAR THING--
THOUGH JOHNNY IS THE MOST TWITTERED-ABOUT PERSON ON THE PLANET RIGHT NOW--
UGH, ALL THESE PEOPLE STARING AT US, HOW DO YOU HANDLE IT?
EASY.
...RIIIIIGHT. INVISIBILITY.
JUST 'TIL WE FIND AN OUT-OF-THE-WAY CORNER.
...
WELL, AND WHAT ABOUT REED? HOW'S THAT BEEN?

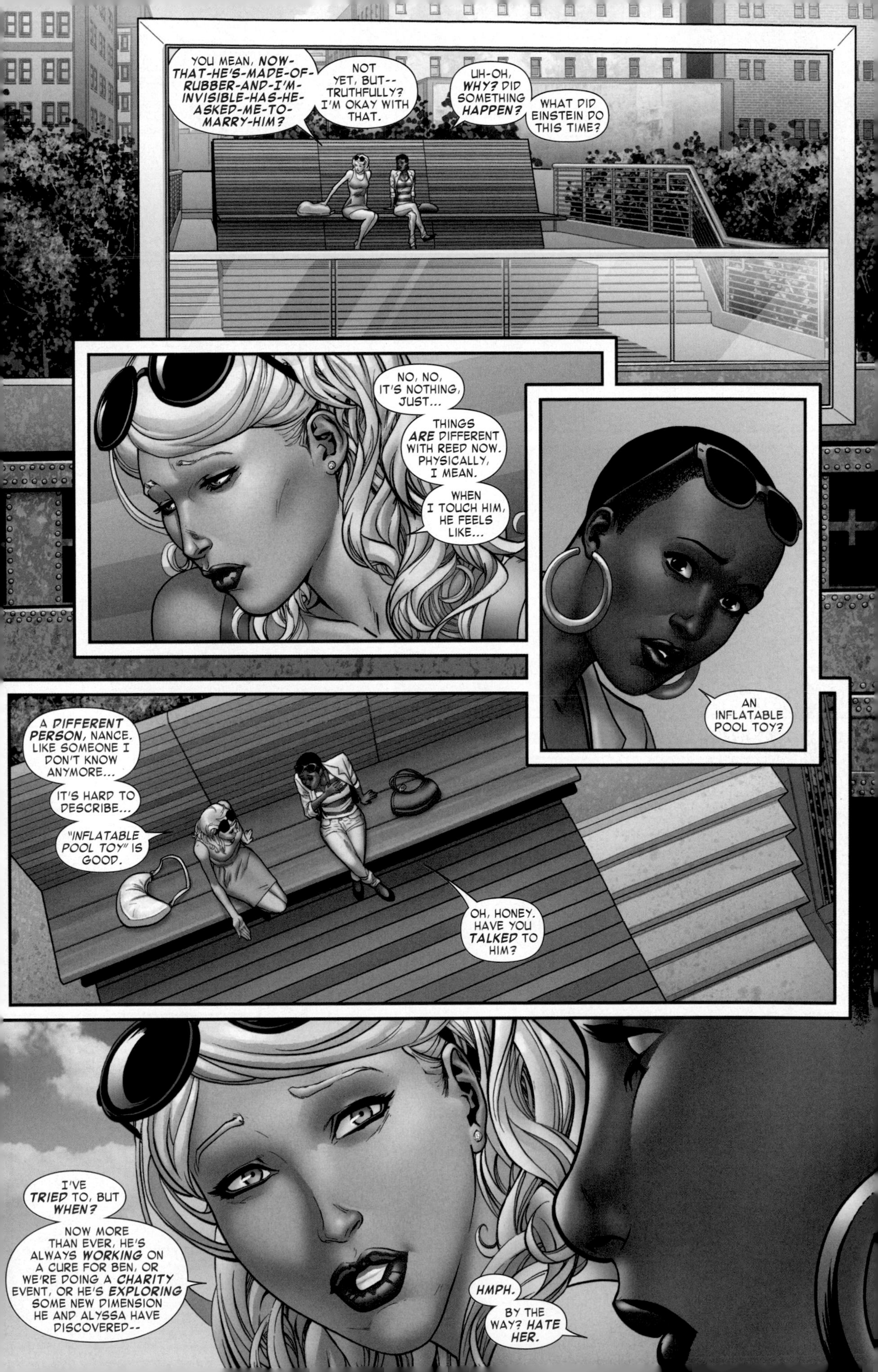

YOU MEAN, NOW-THAT-HE'S-MADE-OF-RUBBER-AND-I'M-INVISIBLE-HAS-HE-ASKED-ME-TO-MARRY-HIM?
NOT YET, BUT-- TRUTHFULLY? I'M OKAY WITH THAT.
UH-OH, WHY? DID SOMETHING HAPPEN?
WHAT DID EINSTEIN DO THIS TIME?
NO, NO, IT'S NOTHING, JUST...
THINGS ARE DIFFERENT WITH REED NOW. PHYSICALLY, I MEAN.
WHEN I TOUCH HIM, HE FEELS LIKE...
AN INFLATABLE POOL TOY?
A DIFFERENT PERSON, NANCE. LIKE SOMEONE I DON'T KNOW ANYMORE...
IT'S HARD TO DESCRIBE...
"INFLATABLE POOL TOY" IS GOOD.
OH, HONEY. HAVE YOU TALKED TO HIM?
I'VE TRIED TO, BUT WHEN?
NOW MORE THAN EVER, HE'S ALWAYS WORKING ON A CURE FOR BEN, OR WE'RE DOING A CHARITY EVENT, OR HE'S EXPLORING SOME NEW DIMENSION HE AND ALYSSA HAVE DISCOVERED--
HMPH.
BY THE WAY? HATE HER.

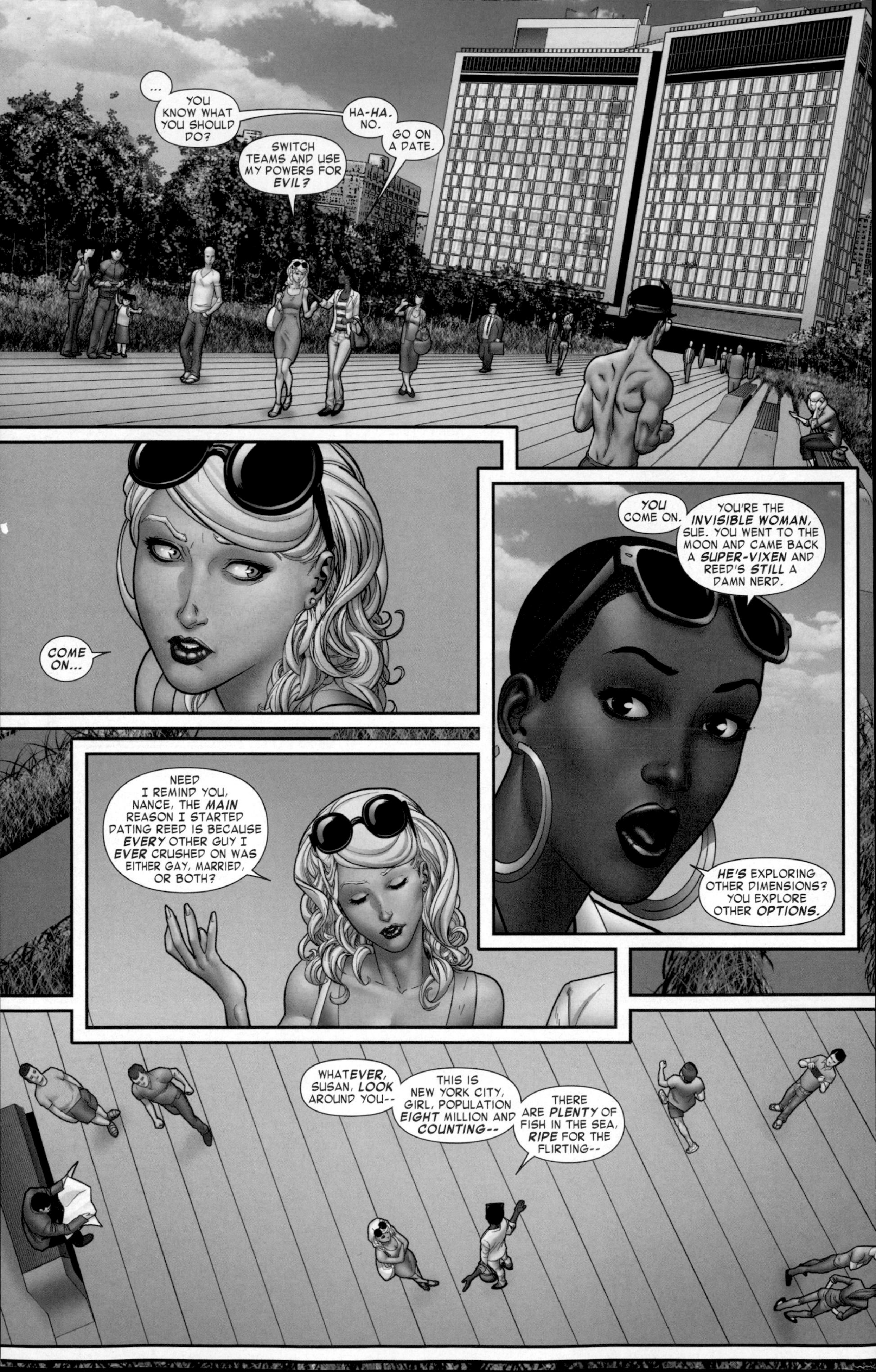
...
YOU KNOW WHAT YOU SHOULD DO?
HA-HA. NO.
SWITCH TEAMS AND USE MY POWERS FOR EVIL?
GO ON A DATE.
COME ON...
YOU COME ON.
YOU'RE THE INVISIBLE WOMAN, SUE. YOU WENT TO THE MOON AND CAME BACK A SUPER-VIXEN AND REED'S STILL A DAMN NERD.
NEED I REMIND YOU, NANCE, THE MAIN REASON I STARTED DATING REED IS BECAUSE EVERY OTHER GUY I EVER CRUSHED ON WAS EITHER GAY, MARRIED, OR BOTH?
HE'S EXPLORING OTHER DIMENSIONS? YOU EXPLORE OTHER OPTIONS.
WHATEVER, SUSAN, LOOK AROUND YOU--
THIS IS NEW YORK CITY, GIRL, POPULATION EIGHT MILLION AND COUNTING--
THERE ARE PLENTY OF FISH IN THE SEA, RIPE FOR THE FLIRTING--

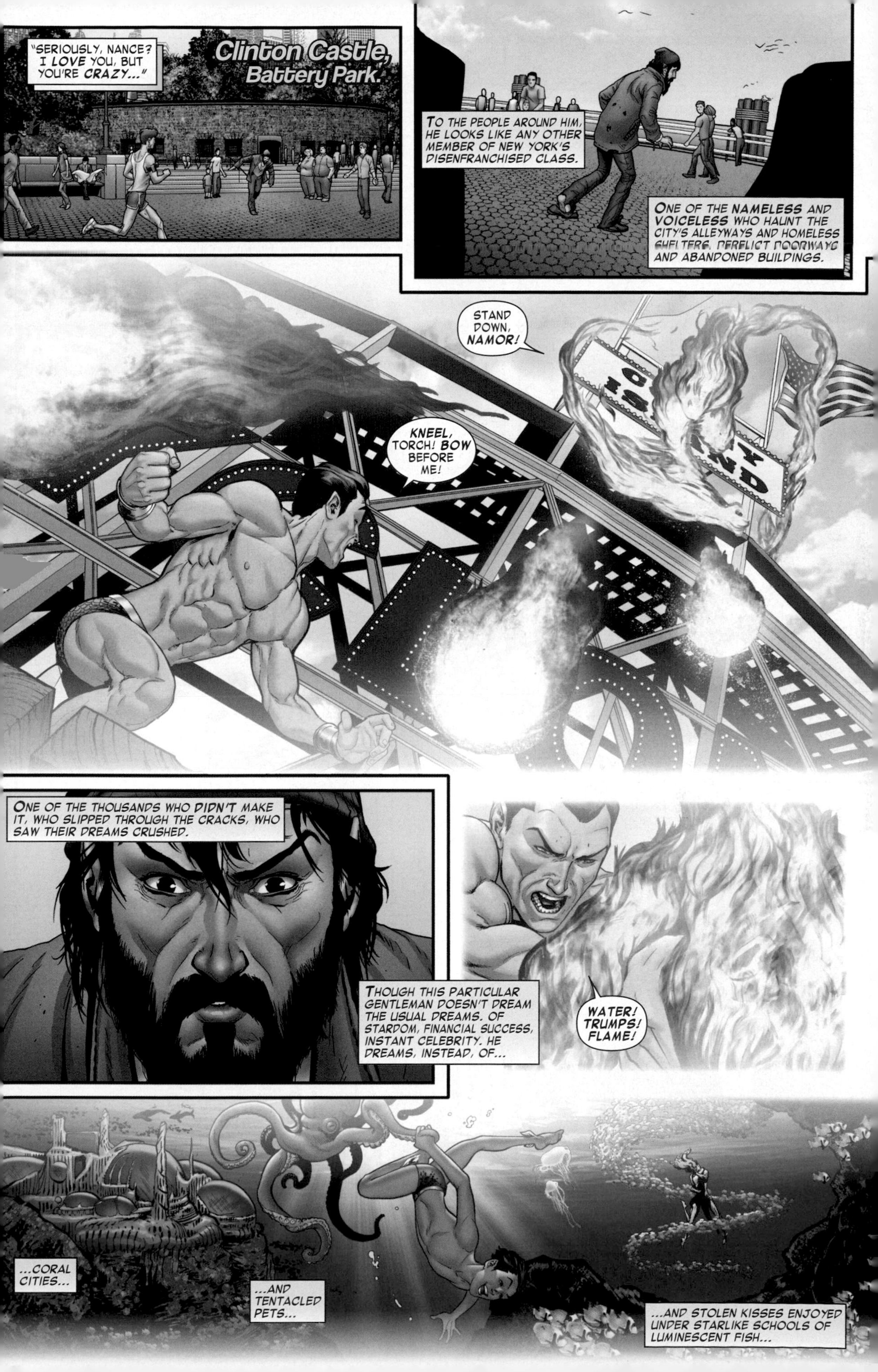
"SERIOUSLY, NANCE? I LOVE YOU, BUT YOU'RE CRAZY..."
Clinton Castle, Battery Park.
TO THE PEOPLE AROUND HIM, HE LOOKS LIKE ANY OTHER MEMBER OF NEW YORK'S DISENFRANCHISED CLASS.
ONE OF THE NAMELESS AND VOICELESS WHO HAUNT THE CITY'S ALLEYWAYS AND HOMELESS SHELTERS, DERELICT DOORWAYS AND ABANDONED BUILDINGS.
STAND DOWN, NAMOR!
KNEEL, TORCH! BOW BEFORE ME!
ONE OF THE THOUSANDS WHO DIDN'T MAKE IT, WHO SLIPPED THROUGH THE CRACKS, WHO SAW THEIR DREAMS CRUSHED.
THOUGH THIS PARTICULAR GENTLEMAN DOESN'T DREAM THE USUAL DREAMS. OF STARDOM, FINANCIAL SUCCESS, INSTANT CELEBRITY. HE DREAMS, INSTEAD, OF...
WATER! TRUMPS! FLAME!
...CORAL CITIES...
...AND TENTACLED PETS...
...AND STOLEN KISSES ENJOYED UNDER STARLIKE SCHOOLS OF LUMINESCENT FISH...

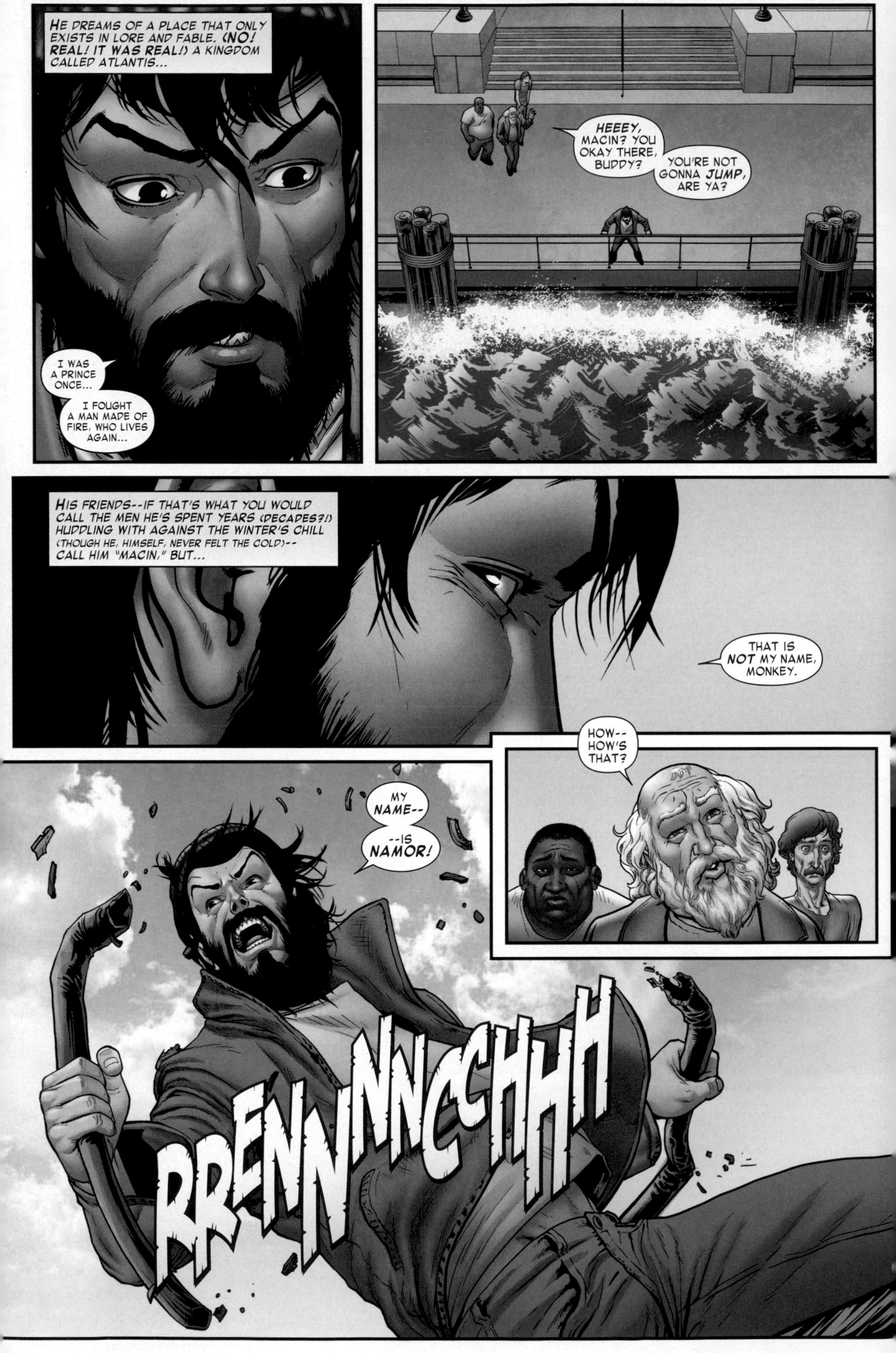
HE DREAMS OF A PLACE THAT ONLY EXISTS IN LORE AND FABLE. (NO! REAL! IT WAS REAL!) A KINGDOM CALLED ATLANTIS...
I WAS A PRINCE ONCE...
I FOUGHT A MAN MADE OF FIRE, WHO LIVES AGAIN...
HEEEY, MACIN? YOU OKAY THERE, BUDDY?
YOU'RE NOT GONNA JUMP, ARE YA?
HIS FRIENDS--IF THAT'S WHAT YOU WOULD CALL THE MEN HE'S SPENT YEARS (DECADES?!) HUDDLING WITH AGAINST THE WINTER'S CHILL (THOUGH HE, HIMSELF, NEVER FELT THE COLD)--CALL HIM "MACIN," BUT...
THAT IS NOT MY NAME, MONKEY.
HOW--HOW'S THAT?
MY NAME--
--IS NAMOR!
BRENNNNCHHH

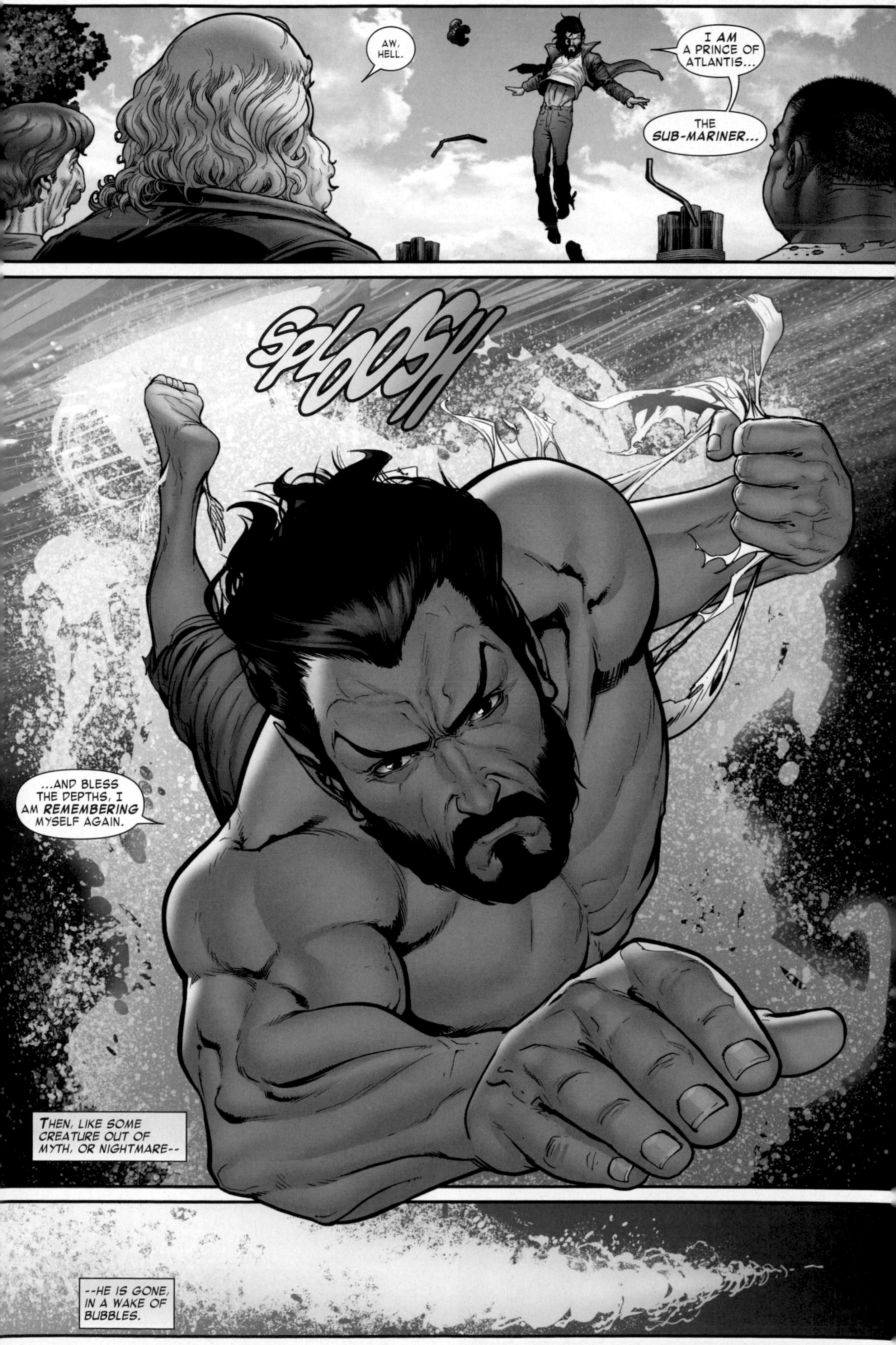
AW, HELL.
I AM A PRINCE OF ATLANTIS...
THE SUB-MARINER...
SPLOOSH
...AND BLESS THE DEPTHS, I AM REMEMBERING MYSELF AGAIN.
THEN, LIKE SOME CREATURE OUT OF MYTH, OR NIGHTMARE--
--HE IS GONE, IN A WAKE OF BUBBLES.

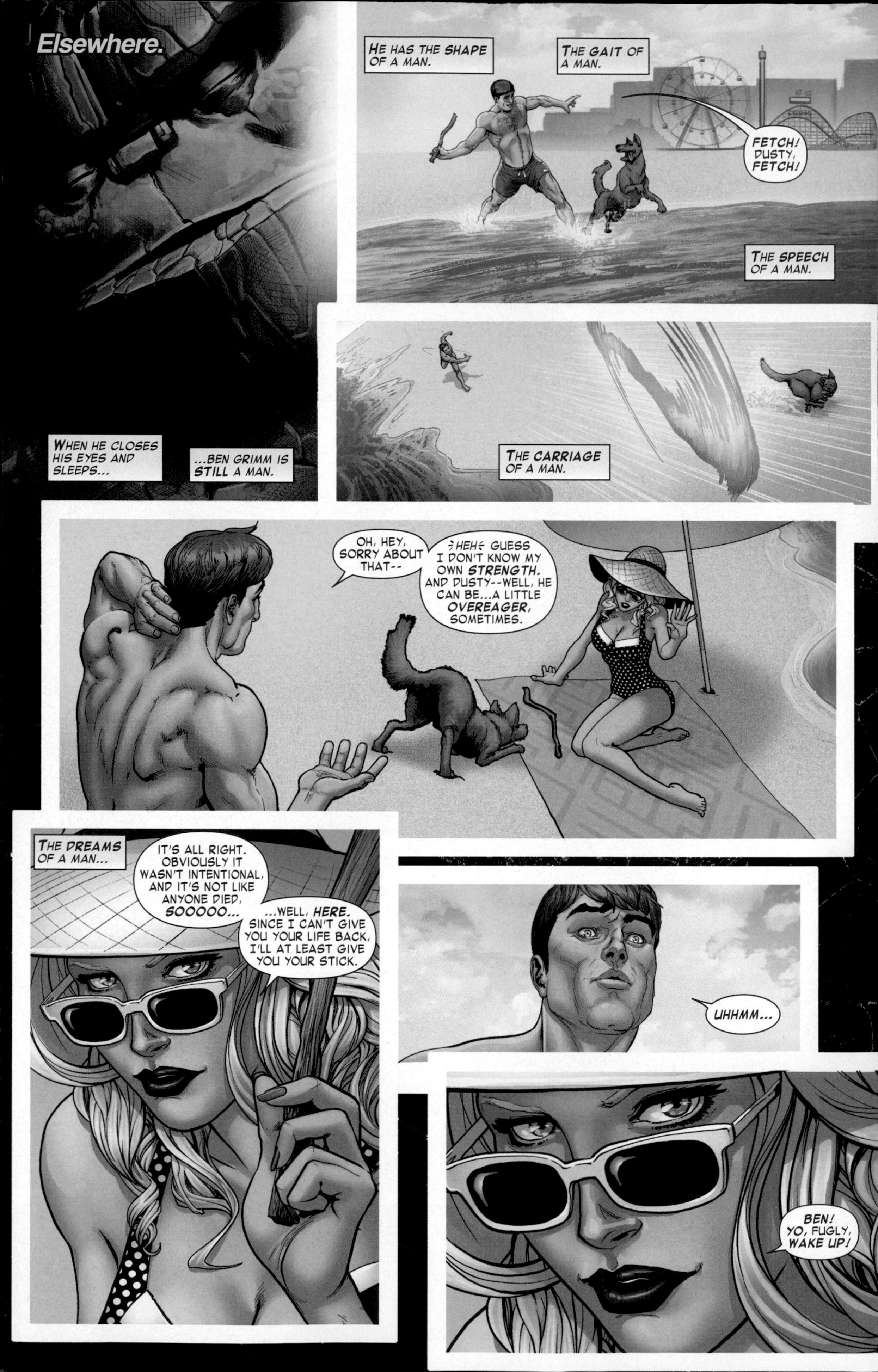
Elsewhere.
WHEN HE CLOSES HIS EYES AND SLEEPS...
...BEN GRIMM IS STILL A MAN.
HE HAS THE SHAPE OF A MAN.
THE GAIT OF A MAN.
FETCH! DUSTY, FETCH!
THE SPEECH OF A MAN.
THE CARRIAGE OF A MAN.
OH, HEY, SORRY ABOUT THAT--
HEH GUESS I DON'T KNOW MY OWN STRENGTH. AND DUSTY--WELL, HE CAN BE...A LITTLE OVEREAGER, SOMETIMES.
THE DREAMS OF A MAN...
IT'S ALL RIGHT. OBVIOUSLY IT WASN'T INTENTIONAL, AND IT'S NOT LIKE ANYONE DIED, SOOOOO...
...WELL, HERE. SINCE I CAN'T GIVE YOU YOUR LIFE BACK, I'LL AT LEAST GIVE YOU YOUR STICK.
UHHMM...
BEN! YO, FUGLY, WAKE UP!

THE HECK?! SUZIE--?

UHHH, GUESS AGAIN, ROCK-FER-BRAINS.

CRIMINIES, JOHNNY, FER A SECOND I THOUGHT--

UGHHH, NEVERMIND...

OH, MY GOD, WERE YOU DREAMING ABOUT MY SISTER?

IF SO, YOU ARE A PERV. IF NOT, YOU STILL ARE.

AND YOUR EXCLAMATIONS OF SURPRISE? NEED UPDATING. "CRIMINIES"? WHO SAYS "CRIMINIES" ANYMORE?

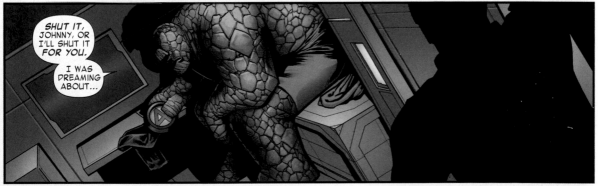

SHUT IT, JOHNNY, OR I'LL SHUT IT FOR YOU.

I WAS DREAMING ABOUT...

CONEY ISLAND, WHERE I SPENT MY SUMMERS, LIFEGUARDING AND HITTING ON GIRLS--

DUSTY, THE DOG I HAD GROWING UP ON YANCY STREET, WHO DIED WHEN A CAR HIT 'IM, WHEN I WAS FRIGGIN' TWELVE--

AND YEAH, JUNIOR, YOUR SISTER SUE. THE ONE GAL I DIDN'T MESS WITH IN COLLEGE, 'CAUSE MY BEST FRIEND LOVED HER--

...EHHHHH, SKIP IT. WHATTYA WANT?

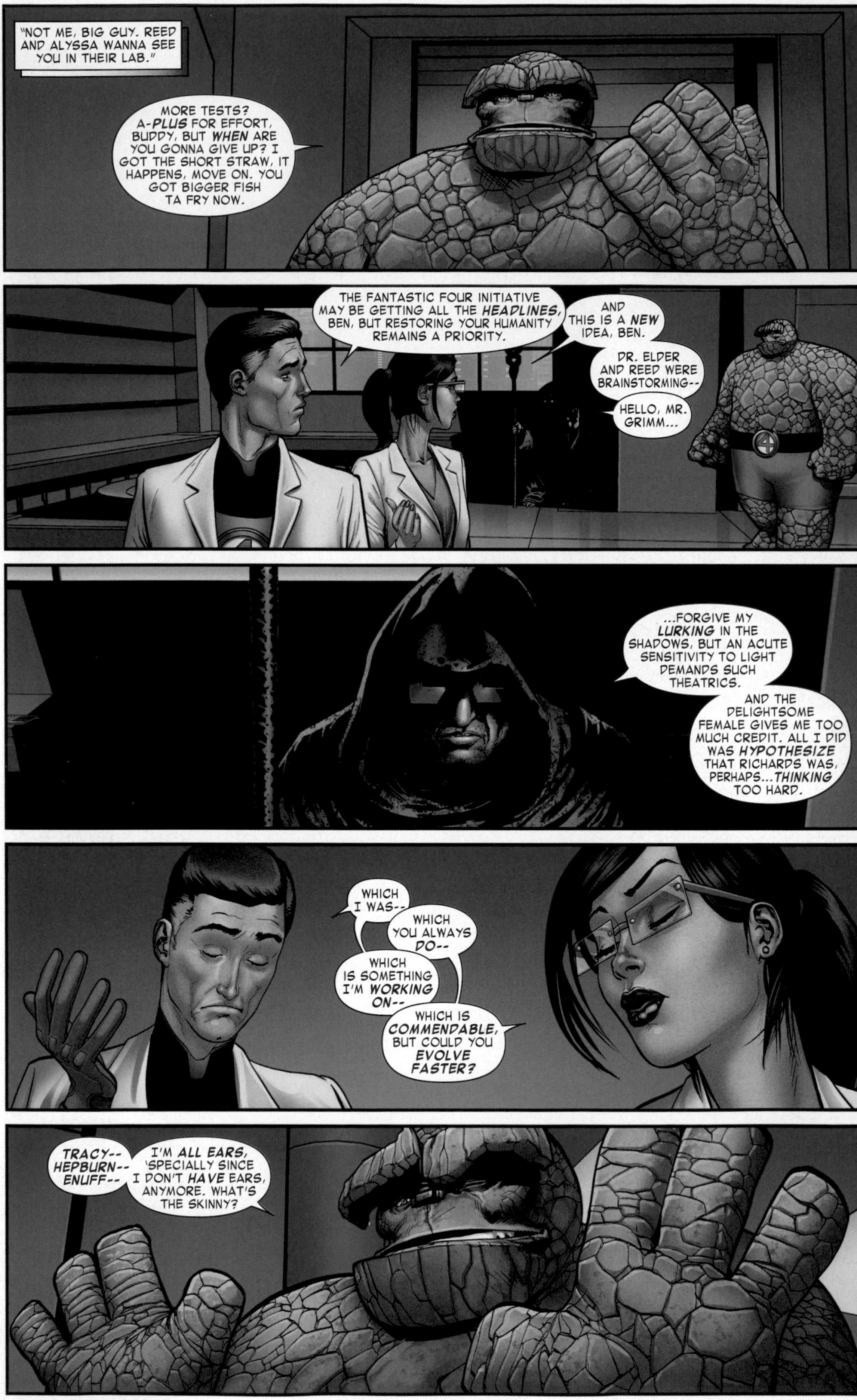
"NOT ME, BIG GUY. REED AND ALYSSA WANNA SEE YOU IN THEIR LAB."
MORE TESTS? A-PLUS FOR EFFORT, BUDDY, BUT WHEN ARE YOU GONNA GIVE UP? I GOT THE SHORT STRAW, IT HAPPENS, MOVE ON. YOU GOT BIGGER FISH TA FRY NOW.
THE FANTASTIC FOUR INITIATIVE MAY BE GETTING ALL THE HEADLINES, BEN, BUT RESTORING YOUR HUMANITY REMAINS A PRIORITY.
AND THIS IS A NEW IDEA, BEN.
DR. ELDER AND REED WERE BRAINSTORMING--
HELLO, MR. GRIMM...
...FORGIVE MY LURKING IN THE SHADOWS, BUT AN ACUTE SENSITIVITY TO LIGHT DEMANDS SUCH THEATRICS.
AND THE DELIGHTSOME FEMALE GIVES ME TOO MUCH CREDIT. ALL I DID WAS HYPOTHESIZE THAT RICHARDS WAS, PERHAPS...THINKING TOO HARD.
WHICH I WAS--
WHICH YOU ALWAYS DO--
WHICH IS SOMETHING I'M WORKING ON--
WHICH IS COMMENDABLE, BUT COULD YOU EVOLVE FASTER?
TRACY-- HEPBURN-- ENUFF--
I'M ALL EARS, 'SPECIALLY SINCE I DON'T HAVE EARS ANYMORE. WHAT'S THE SKINNY?

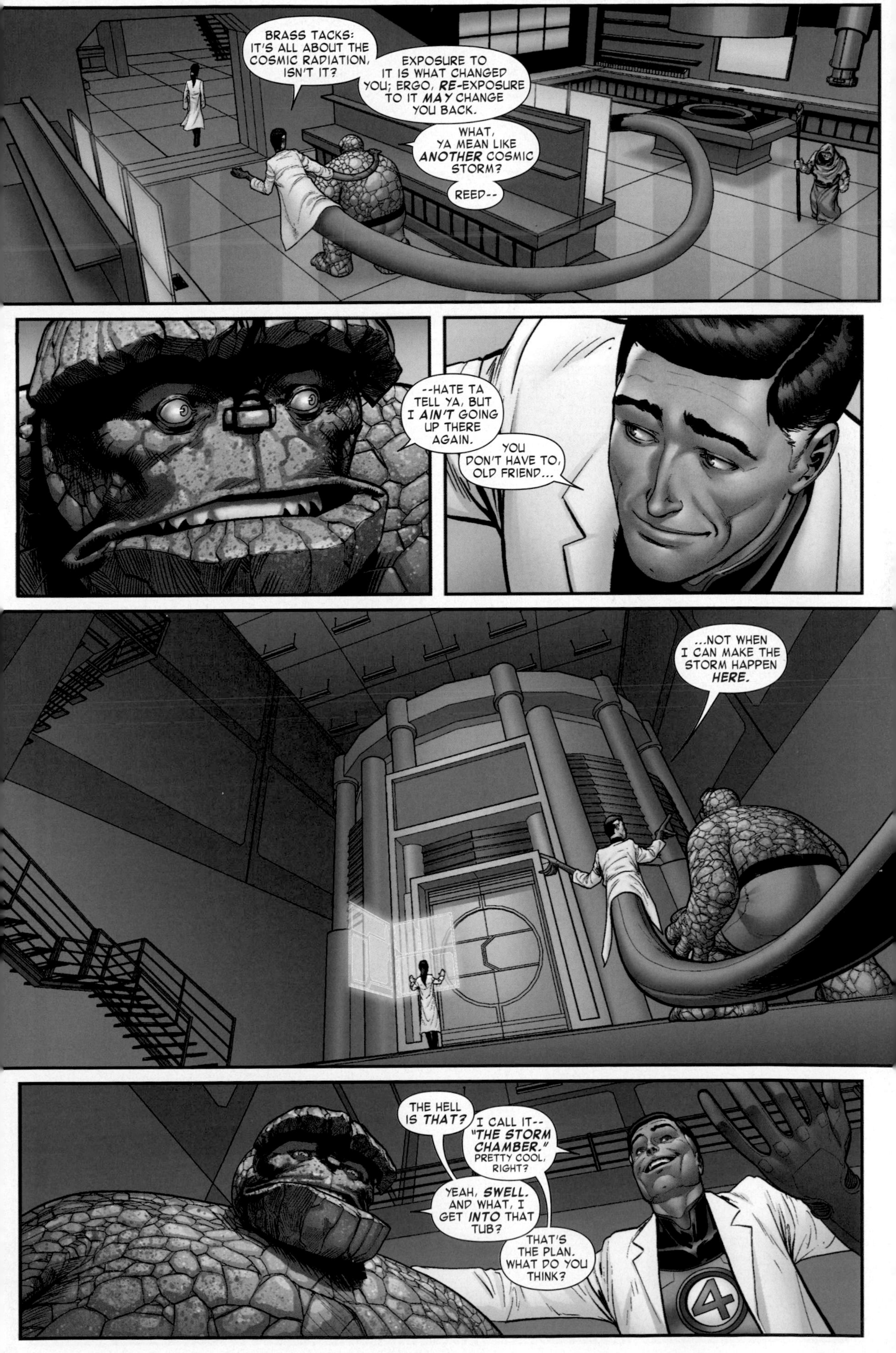
BRASS TACKS: IT'S ALL ABOUT THE COSMIC RADIATION, ISN'T IT?
EXPOSURE TO IT IS WHAT CHANGED YOU; ERGO, RE-EXPOSURE TO IT MAY CHANGE YOU BACK.
WHAT, YA MEAN LIKE ANOTHER COSMIC STORM?
REED--
--HATE TA TELL YA, BUT I AIN'T GOING UP THERE AGAIN.
YOU DON'T HAVE TO, OLD FRIEND...
...NOT WHEN I CAN MAKE THE STORM HAPPEN HERE.
THE HELL IS THAT?
I CALL IT-- "THE STORM CHAMBER." PRETTY COOL, RIGHT?
YEAH, SWELL. AND WHAT, I GET INTO THAT TUB?
THAT'S THE PLAN. WHAT DO YOU THINK?

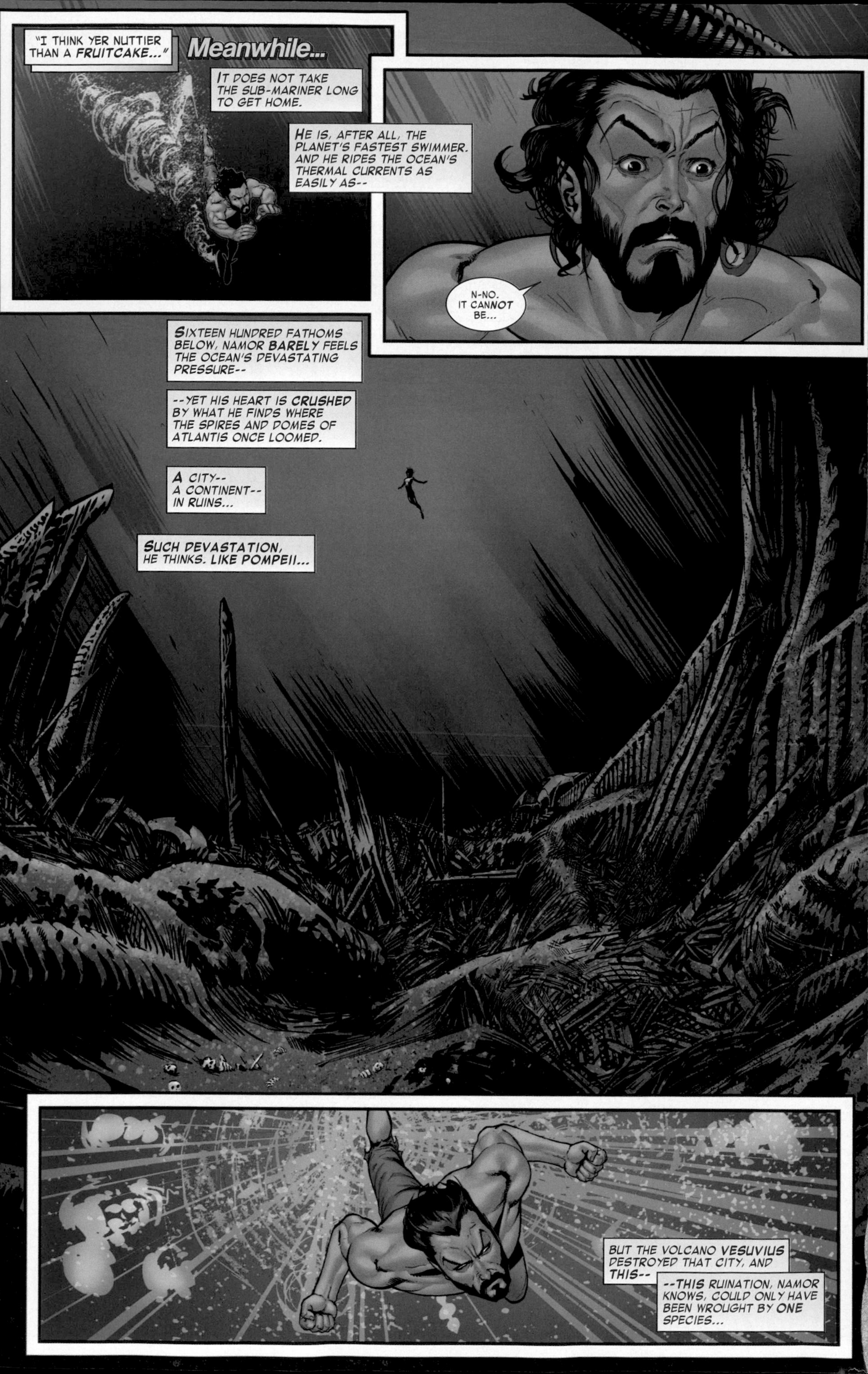
"I THINK YER NUTTIER THAN A FRUITCAKE..."
Meanwhile...
IT DOES NOT TAKE THE SUB-MARINER LONG TO GET HOME.
HE IS, AFTER ALL, THE PLANET'S FASTEST SWIMMER. AND HE RIDES THE OCEAN'S THERMAL CURRENTS AS EASILY AS--
N-NO. IT CANNOT BE...
SIXTEEN HUNDRED FATHOMS BELOW, NAMOR BARELY FEELS THE OCEAN'S DEVASTATING PRESSURE--
--YET HIS HEART IS CRUSHED BY WHAT HE FINDS WHERE THE SPIRES AND DOMES OF ATLANTIS ONCE LOOMED.
A CITY-- A CONTINENT-- IN RUINS...
SUCH DEVASTATION, HE THINKS. LIKE POMPEII...
BUT THE VOLCANO VESUVIUS DESTROYED THAT CITY, AND THIS--
--THIS RUINATION, NAMOR KNOWS, COULD ONLY HAVE BEEN WROUGHT BY ONE SPECIES...

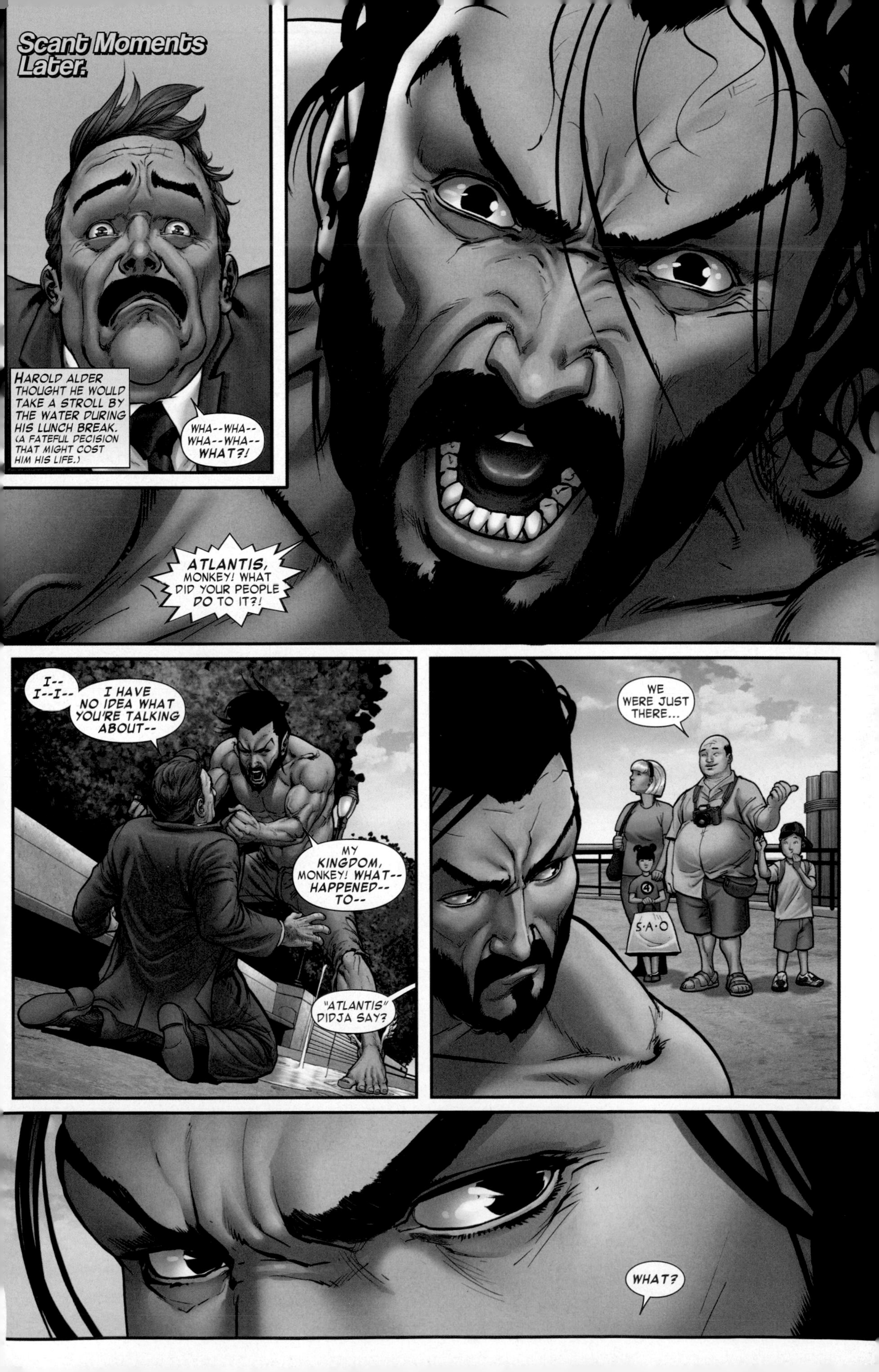
Scant Moments Later.
HAROLD ALDER THOUGHT HE WOULD TAKE A STROLL BY THE WATER DURING HIS LUNCH BREAK. (A FATEFUL DECISION THAT MIGHT COST HIM HIS LIFE.)
WHA--WHA--WHA--WHA--WHAT?!
ATLANTIS, MONKEY! WHAT DID YOUR PEOPLE DO TO IT?!
I--I--I--
I HAVE NO IDEA WHAT YOU'RE TALKING ABOUT--
MY KINGDOM, MONKEY! WHAT--HAPPENED--TO--
"ATLANTIS" DIDJA SAY?
WE WERE JUST THERE...
S.A.O
WHAT?

AFTER WE CRASHED IN ITHACA, ALYSSA RECOVERED THE REMAINS OF OUR SHIP. EVEN MORE THAN US, *ITS* HULL ABSORBED THE WORST OF THE STORM'S RAYS.

EXHIBIT-A, BEN. WE HYPER-COMPRESSED THE DEBRIS INTO A CUBE OF METAL *TEEMING* WITH COSMIC ENERGY. LIKE A... SYNTHETIC METEOR, ALMOST.

IN THIS FORM, WE CAN HARNESS AND MANIPULATE THE METAL'S RADIATION. SLIDE IT ALONG A SCALE, IF YOU WILL--

IMAGINE TUNING A RADIO...

--AND *RE*-IRRADIATE YOU, BEN--

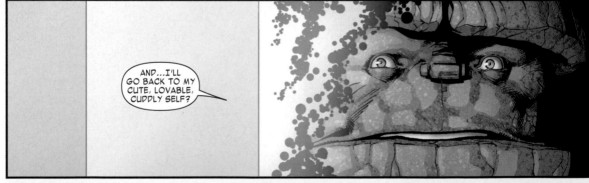

AND...I'LL GO BACK TO MY CUTE, LOVABLE, CUDDLY SELF?

HARD TO PREDICT, BUT THERE'S A CHANCE OF THAT, YES.

THAT *IS* THE HOPE.

CONVERSELY--

CONVERSELY, COSMIC ENERGY IS... DIFFICULT TO PREDICT. (UNDERSTATEMENT OF THE MILLENNIUM.) RE-EXPOSURE MAY "CURE" YOU, BEN, OR HAVE ZERO EFFECT, OR...

...MAYBE MAKE ME WORSE.

THE ETERNAL CONUNDRUM, MR. GRIMM. THE LADY OR THE TIGER, WHICH SHALL IT BE?

THE CHOICE IS YOURS, BEN.

OF COURSE WE'LL DO WHATEVER YOU WANT.

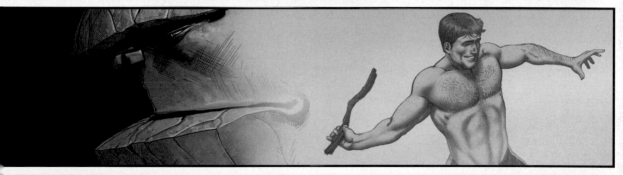

WHAT C'N I SAY? MRS. GRIMM'S BOY'S FEELING LUCKY.

CRANK THIS TUB UP--

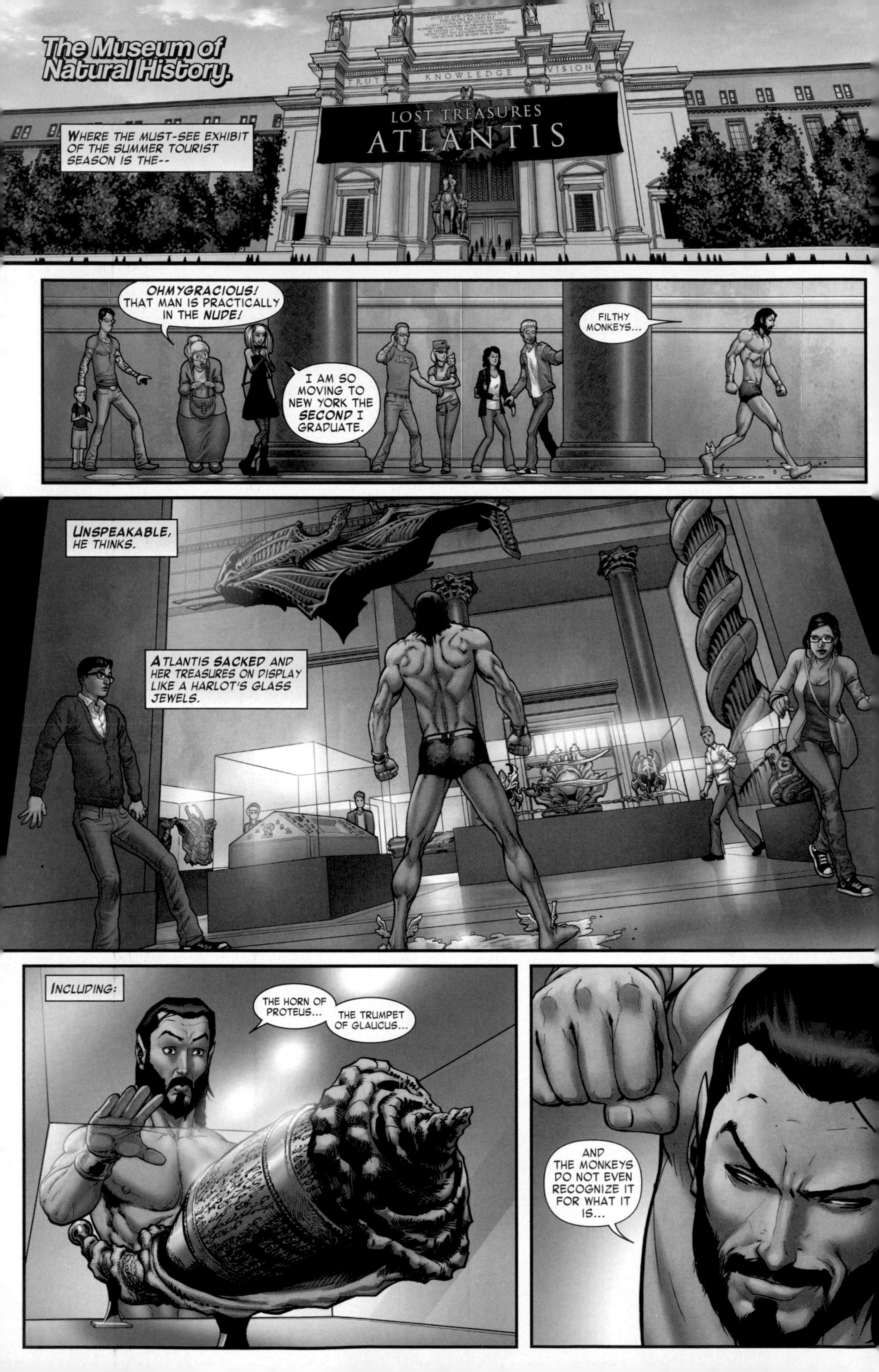
The Museum of Natural History.
WHERE THE MUST-SEE EXHIBIT OF THE SUMMER TOURIST SEASON IS THE--
LOST TREASURES ATLANTIS
TRUTH KNOWLEDGE VISION
OHMYGRACIOUS! THAT MAN IS PRACTICALLY IN THE NUDE!
I AM SO MOVING TO NEW YORK THE SECOND I GRADUATE.
FILTHY MONKEYS...
UNSPEAKABLE, HE THINKS.
ATLANTIS SACKED AND HER TREASURES ON DISPLAY LIKE A HARLOT'S GLASS JEWELS.
INCLUDING:
THE HORN OF PROTEUS...
THE TRUMPET OF GLAUCUS...
AND THE MONKEYS DO NOT EVEN RECOGNIZE IT FOR WHAT IT IS...

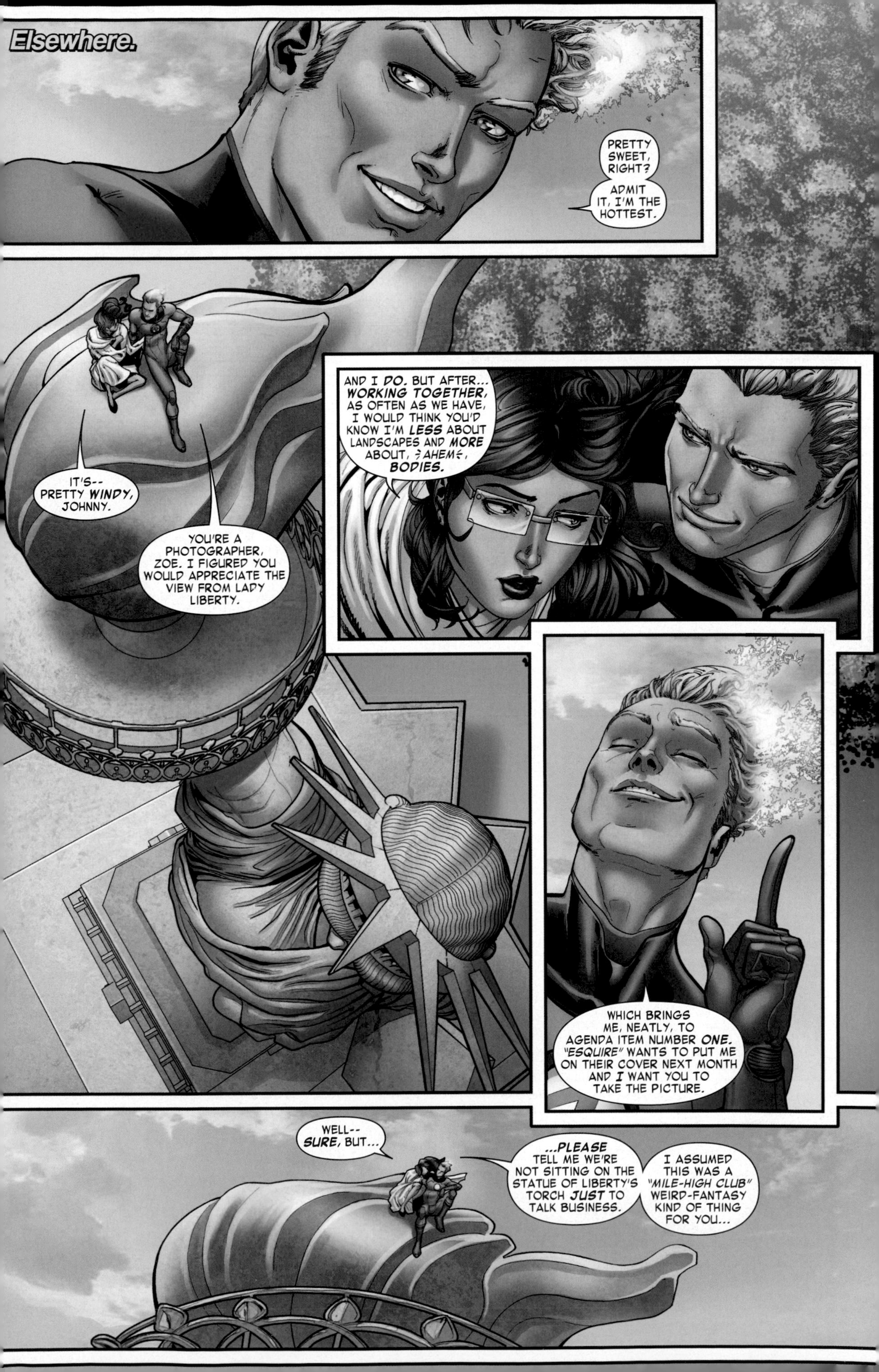
Elsewhere.
PRETTY SWEET, RIGHT?
ADMIT IT, I'M THE HOTTEST.
IT'S-- PRETTY WINDY, JOHNNY.
YOU'RE A PHOTOGRAPHER, ZOE. I FIGURED YOU WOULD APPRECIATE THE VIEW FROM LADY LIBERTY.
AND I DO. BUT AFTER... WORKING TOGETHER, AS OFTEN AS WE HAVE, I WOULD THINK YOU'D KNOW I'M LESS ABOUT LANDSCAPES AND MORE ABOUT, AHEM, BODIES.
WHICH BRINGS ME, NEATLY, TO AGENDA ITEM NUMBER ONE. "ESQUIRE" WANTS TO PUT ME ON THEIR COVER NEXT MONTH AND I WANT YOU TO TAKE THE PICTURE.
WELL-- SURE, BUT...
...PLEASE TELL ME WE'RE NOT SITTING ON THE STATUE OF LIBERTY'S TORCH JUST TO TALK BUSINESS.
I ASSUMED THIS WAS A "MILE-HIGH CLUB" WEIRD-FANTASY KIND OF THING FOR YOU...

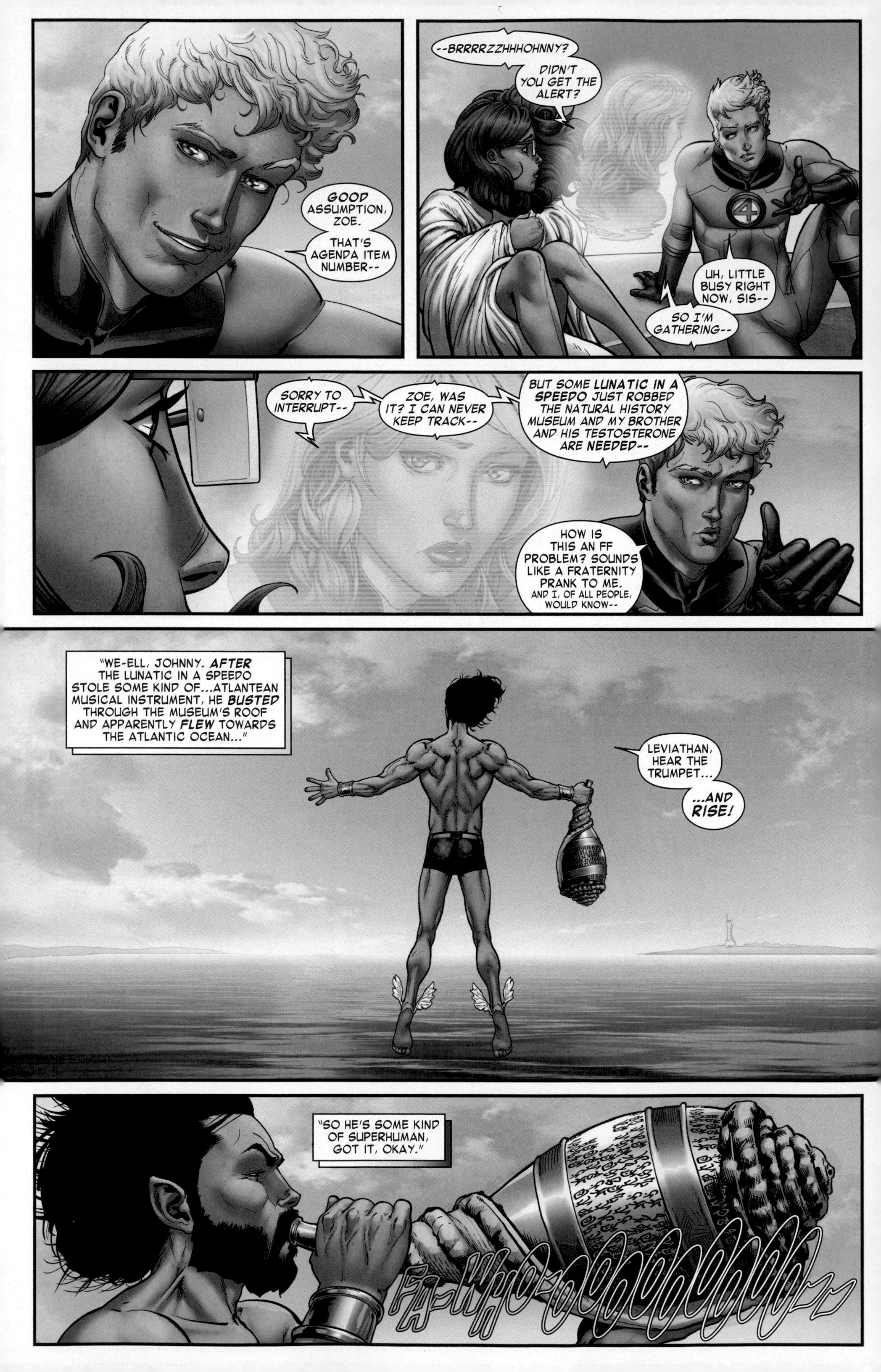
GOOD ASSUMPTION, ZOE.
THAT'S AGENDA ITEM NUMBER--
--BRRRRZZHHHOHNNY?
DIDN'T YOU GET THE ALERT?
UH, LITTLE BUSY RIGHT NOW, SIS--
SO I'M GATHERING--
SORRY TO INTERRUPT--
ZOE, WAS IT? I CAN NEVER KEEP TRACK--
BUT SOME LUNATIC IN A SPEEDO JUST ROBBED THE NATURAL HISTORY MUSEUM AND MY BROTHER AND HIS TESTOSTERONE ARE NEEDED--
HOW IS THIS AN FF PROBLEM? SOUNDS LIKE A FRATERNITY PRANK TO ME.
AND I, OF ALL PEOPLE, WOULD KNOW--
"WE-ELL, JOHNNY. AFTER THE LUNATIC IN A SPEEDO STOLE SOME KIND OF...ATLANTEAN MUSICAL INSTRUMENT, HE BUSTED THROUGH THE MUSEUM'S ROOF AND APPARENTLY FLEW TOWARDS THE ATLANTIC OCEAN..."
LEVIATHAN, HEAR THE TRUMPET...
...AND RISE!
"SO HE'S SOME KIND OF SUPERHUMAN, GOT IT, OKAY."

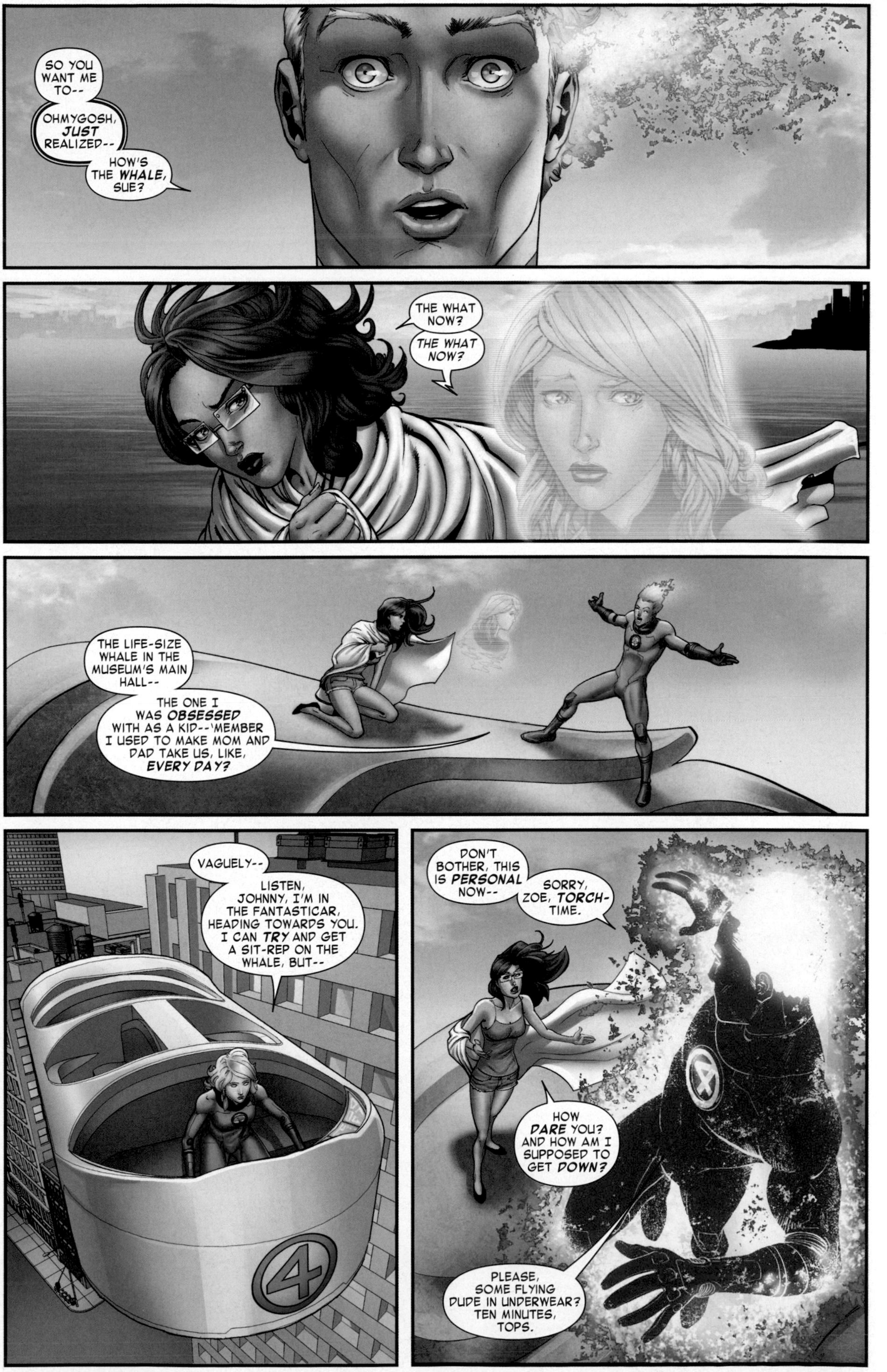
SO YOU WANT ME TO--
OHMYGOSH, JUST REALIZED--
HOW'S THE WHALE, SUE?
THE WHAT NOW?
THE WHAT NOW?
THE LIFE-SIZE WHALE IN THE MUSEUM'S MAIN HALL--
THE ONE I WAS OBSESSED WITH AS A KID--'MEMBER I USED TO MAKE MOM AND DAD TAKE US, LIKE, EVERY DAY?
VAGUELY--
LISTEN, JOHNNY, I'M IN THE FANTASTICAR, HEADING TOWARDS YOU. I CAN TRY AND GET A SIT-REP ON THE WHALE, BUT--
DON'T BOTHER, THIS IS PERSONAL NOW--
SORRY, ZOE, TORCH-TIME.
HOW DARE YOU? AND HOW AM I SUPPOSED TO GET DOWN?
PLEASE, SOME FLYING DUDE IN UNDERWEAR? TEN MINUTES, TOPS.

"WHAT ABOUT STRETCH ARMSTRONG AND THE GREAT WALL OF CHINA, SUE?"

"I *TRIED* THEM, BUT THEY'RE HOLED-UP IN REED'S LAB. *AGAIN.* WORKING ON SOMETHING QUOTE/UNQUOTE *'EXTREMELY IMPORTANT.' AGAIN.* PROBABLY A NEW VERSION OF ROCKY ROAD ICE CREAM..."

THIS IS AGONY, ALYSSA.

THIS IS *SCIENCE,* REED.

IRRADIATION ALMOST COMPLETE, BY THE WAY.

TAC-TAC-TAC TAC-TAC-TAC-TAC TAC

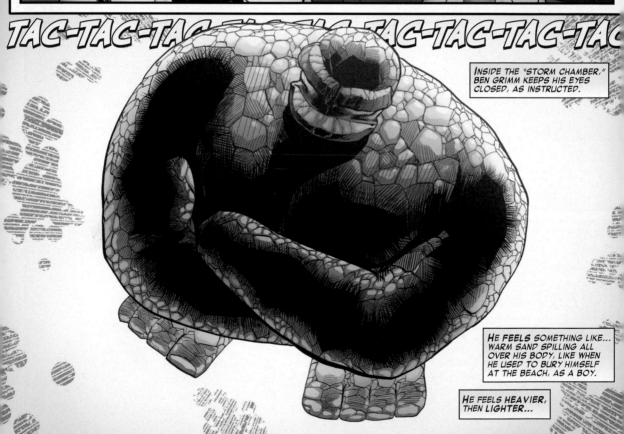

INSIDE THE "STORM CHAMBER," BEN GRIMM KEEPS HIS EYES CLOSED, AS INSTRUCTED.

HE FEELS SOMETHING LIKE... WARM SAND SPILLING ALL OVER HIS BODY, LIKE WHEN HE USED TO BURY HIMSELF AT THE BEACH, AS A BOY.

HE FEELS HEAVIER, THEN *LIGHTER...*

TIME SEEMS TO SLOW... STOP...REASSERT ITSELF...

TAC-TAC-TAC-TAC-TAC-TAC-TAC-TAC-TAC

IT GETS DARK BEHIND HIS EYELIDS, THEN...LESS DARK...

THAT SOUND--THAT DAMN, MISERABLE SOUND-- DWINDLES TO A TRICKLE...

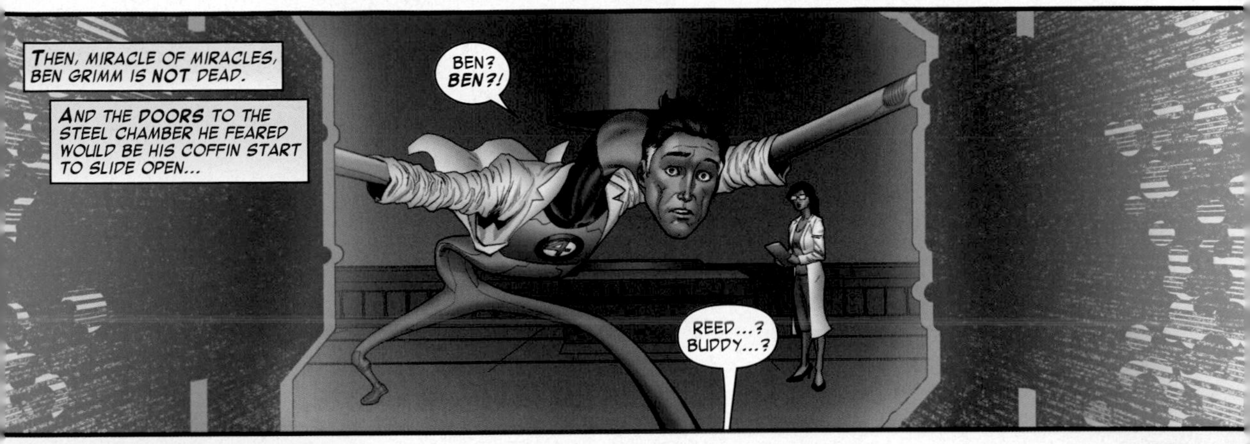
THEN, MIRACLE OF MIRACLES, BEN GRIMM IS NOT DEAD.
AND THE DOORS TO THE STEEL CHAMBER HE FEARED WOULD BE HIS COFFIN START TO SLIDE OPEN...
BEN? BEN?!
REED...? BUDDY...?

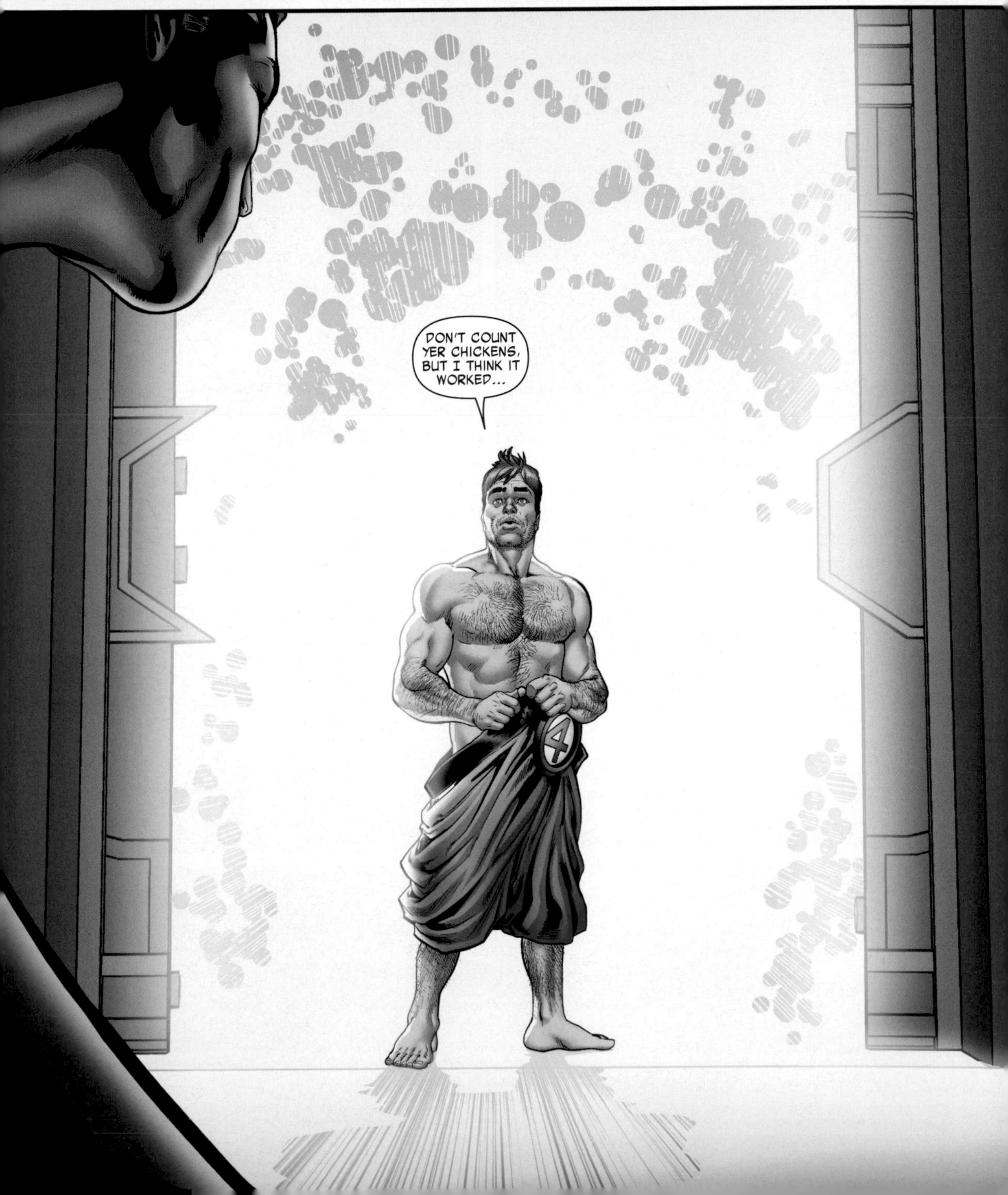
DON'T COUNT YER CHICKENS, BUT I THINK IT WORKED...

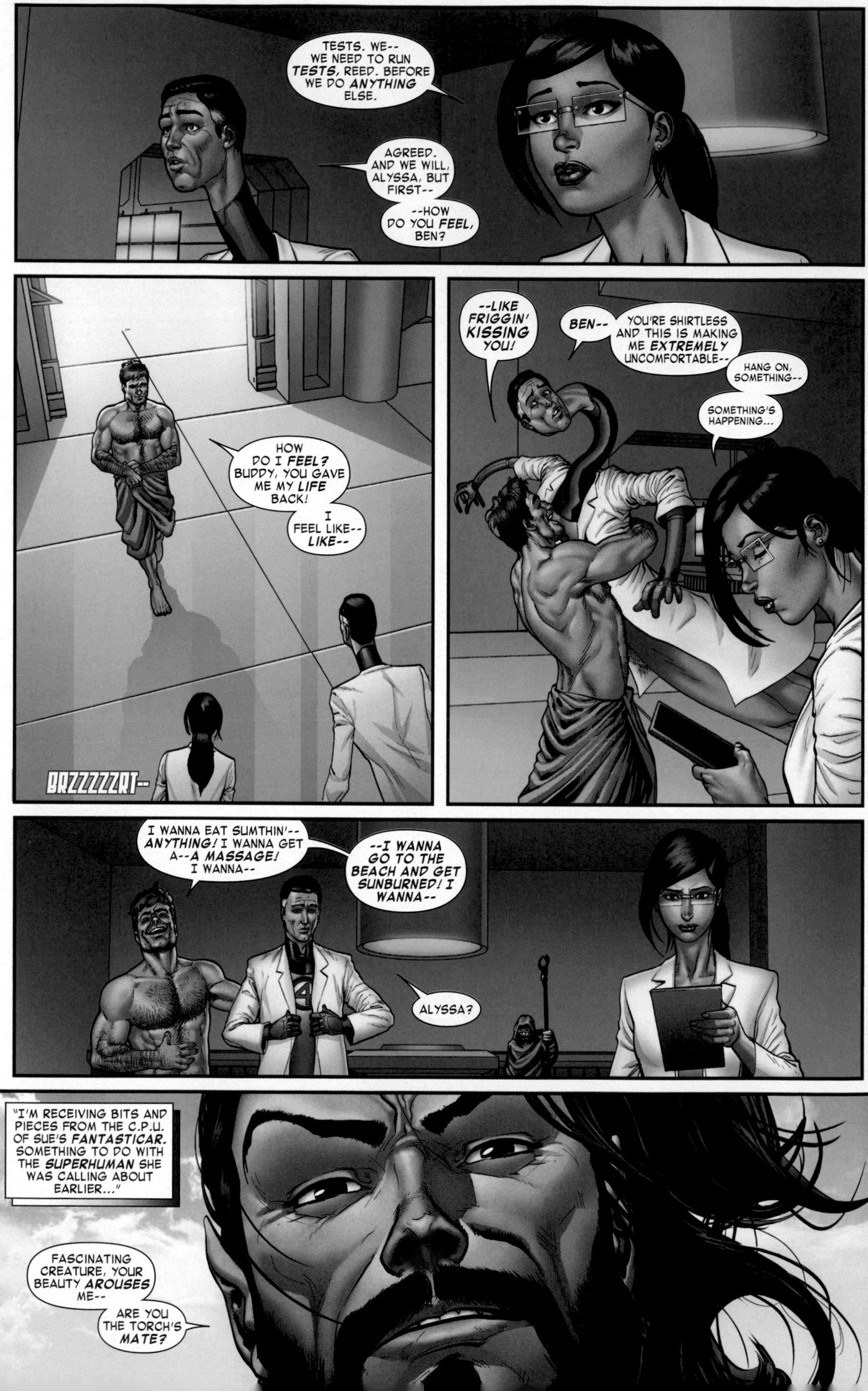
TESTS. WE-- WE NEED TO RUN TESTS, REED. BEFORE WE DO ANYTHING ELSE.
AGREED. AND WE WILL, ALYSSA, BUT FIRST--
--HOW DO YOU FEEL, BEN?
HOW DO I FEEL? BUDDY, YOU GAVE ME MY LIFE BACK!
I FEEL LIKE-- LIKE--
BRZZZZZRT--
--LIKE FRIGGIN' KISSING YOU!
BEN--
YOU'RE SHIRTLESS AND THIS IS MAKING ME EXTREMELY UNCOMFORTABLE--
HANG ON, SOMETHING--
SOMETHING'S HAPPENING...
I WANNA EAT SUMTHIN'-- ANYTHING! I WANNA GET A--A MASSAGE! I WANNA--
--I WANNA GO TO THE BEACH AND GET SUNBURNED! I WANNA--
ALYSSA?
"I'M RECEIVING BITS AND PIECES FROM THE C.P.U. OF SUE'S FANTASTICAR. SOMETHING TO DO WITH THE SUPERHUMAN SHE WAS CALLING ABOUT EARLIER..."
FASCINATING CREATURE, YOUR BEAUTY AROUSES ME--
ARE YOU THE TORCH'S MATE?

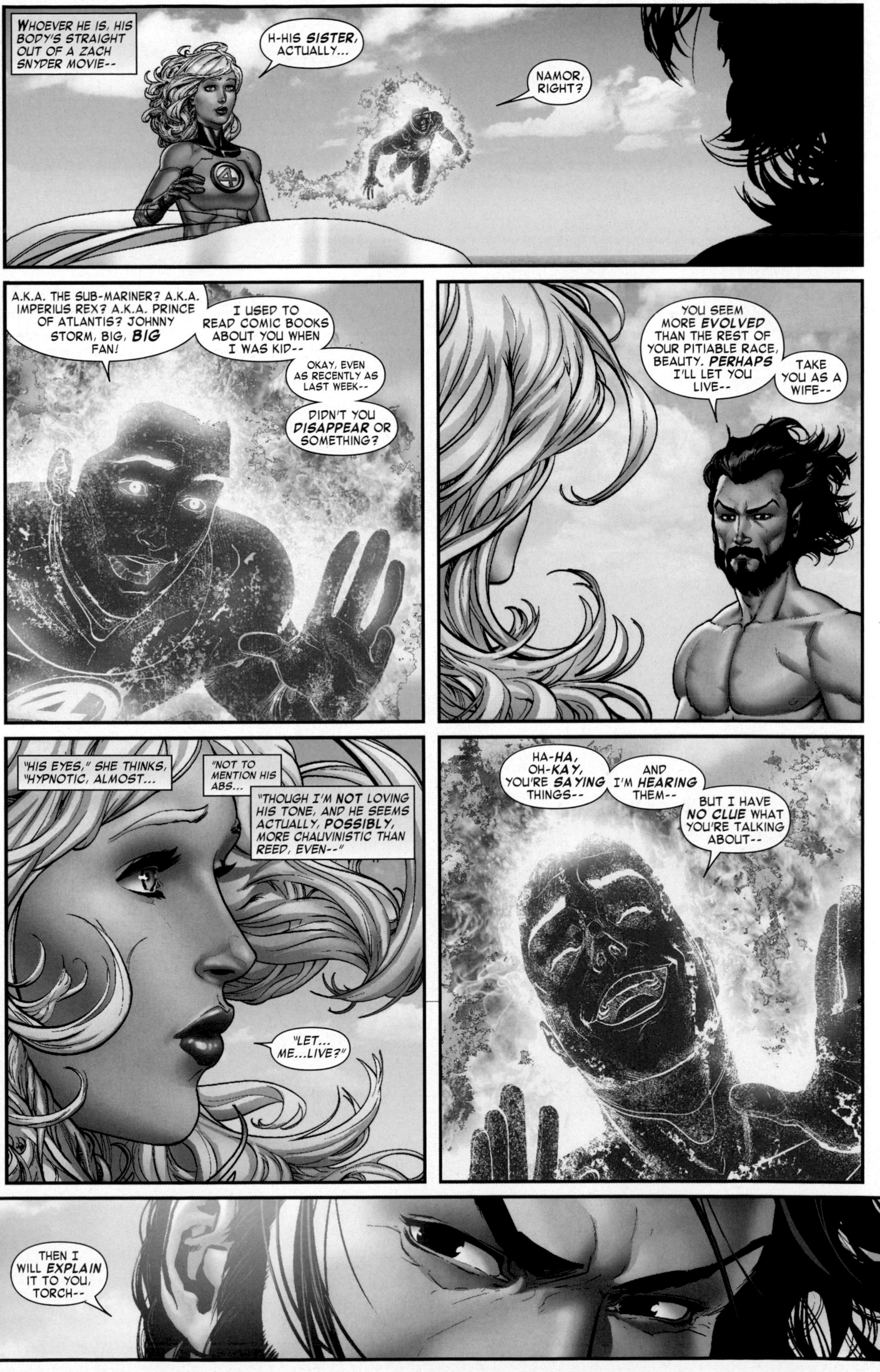
WHOEVER HE IS, HIS BODY'S STRAIGHT OUT OF A ZACH SNYDER MOVIE--
H-HIS SISTER, ACTUALLY...
NAMOR, RIGHT?
A.K.A. THE SUB-MARINER? A.K.A. IMPERIUS REX? A.K.A. PRINCE OF ATLANTIS? JOHNNY STORM, BIG, BIG FAN!
I USED TO READ COMIC BOOKS ABOUT YOU WHEN I WAS KID--
OKAY, EVEN AS RECENTLY AS LAST WEEK--
DIDN'T YOU DISAPPEAR OR SOMETHING?
YOU SEEM MORE EVOLVED THAN THE REST OF YOUR PITIABLE RACE, BEAUTY. PERHAPS I'LL LET YOU LIVE--
TAKE YOU AS A WIFE--
"HIS EYES," SHE THINKS, "HYPNOTIC, ALMOST...
"NOT TO MENTION HIS ABS...
"THOUGH I'M NOT LOVING HIS TONE, AND HE SEEMS ACTUALLY, POSSIBLY, MORE CHAUVINISTIC THAN REED, EVEN--"
"LET... ME...LIVE?"
HA-HA, OH-KAY, YOU'RE SAYING THINGS--
AND I'M HEARING THEM--
BUT I HAVE NO CLUE WHAT YOU'RE TALKING ABOUT--
THEN I WILL EXPLAIN IT TO YOU, TORCH--

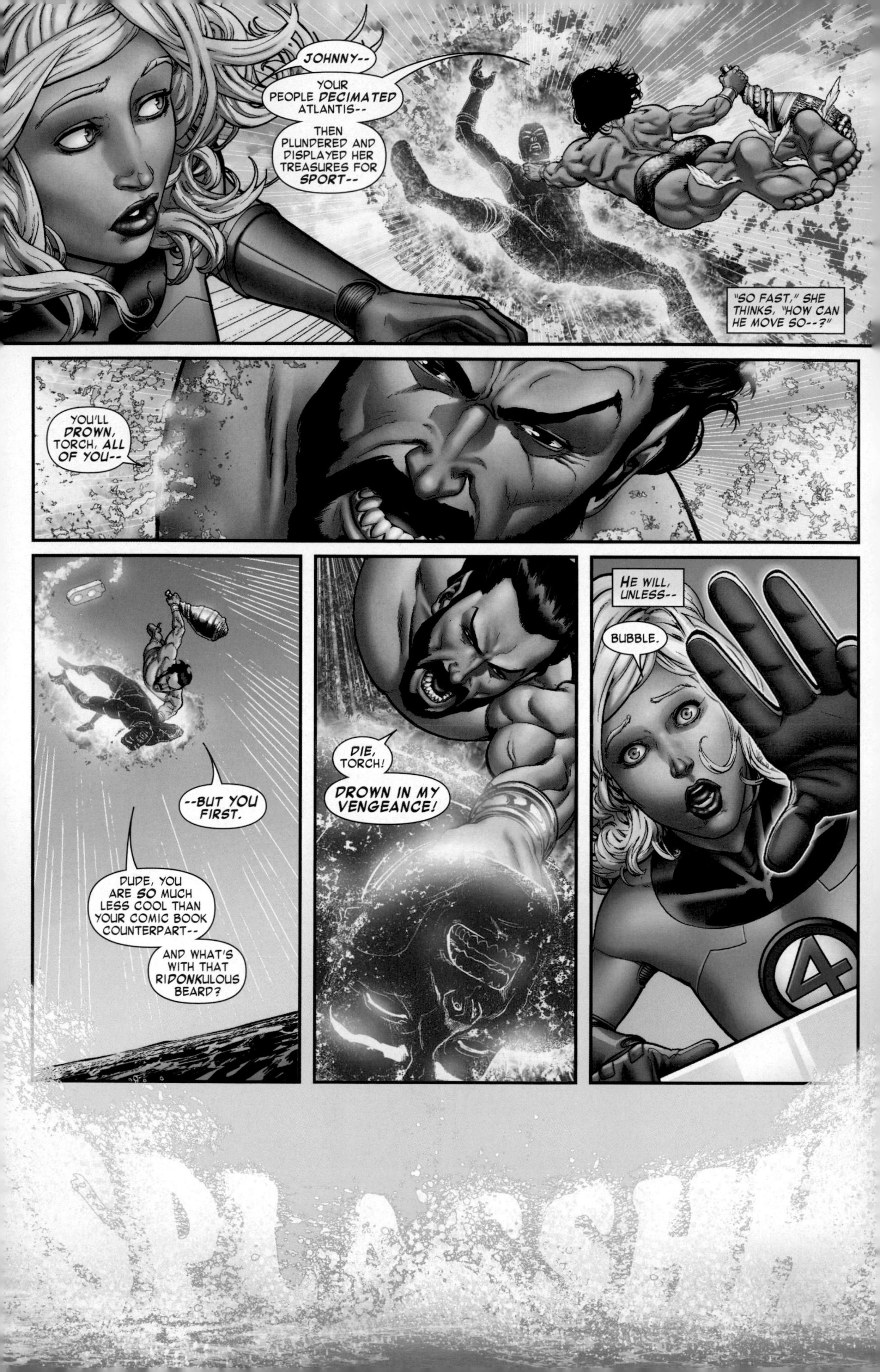
JOHNNY--
YOUR PEOPLE DECIMATED ATLANTIS--
THEN PLUNDERED AND DISPLAYED HER TREASURES FOR SPORT--
"SO FAST," SHE THINKS, "HOW CAN HE MOVE SO--?"
YOU'LL DROWN, TORCH, ALL OF YOU--
--BUT YOU FIRST.
DUDE, YOU ARE SO MUCH LESS COOL THAN YOUR COMIC BOOK COUNTERPART--
AND WHAT'S WITH THAT RIDONKULOUS BEARD?
DIE, TORCH!
DROWN IN MY VENGEANCE!
HE WILL, UNLESS--
BUBBLE.

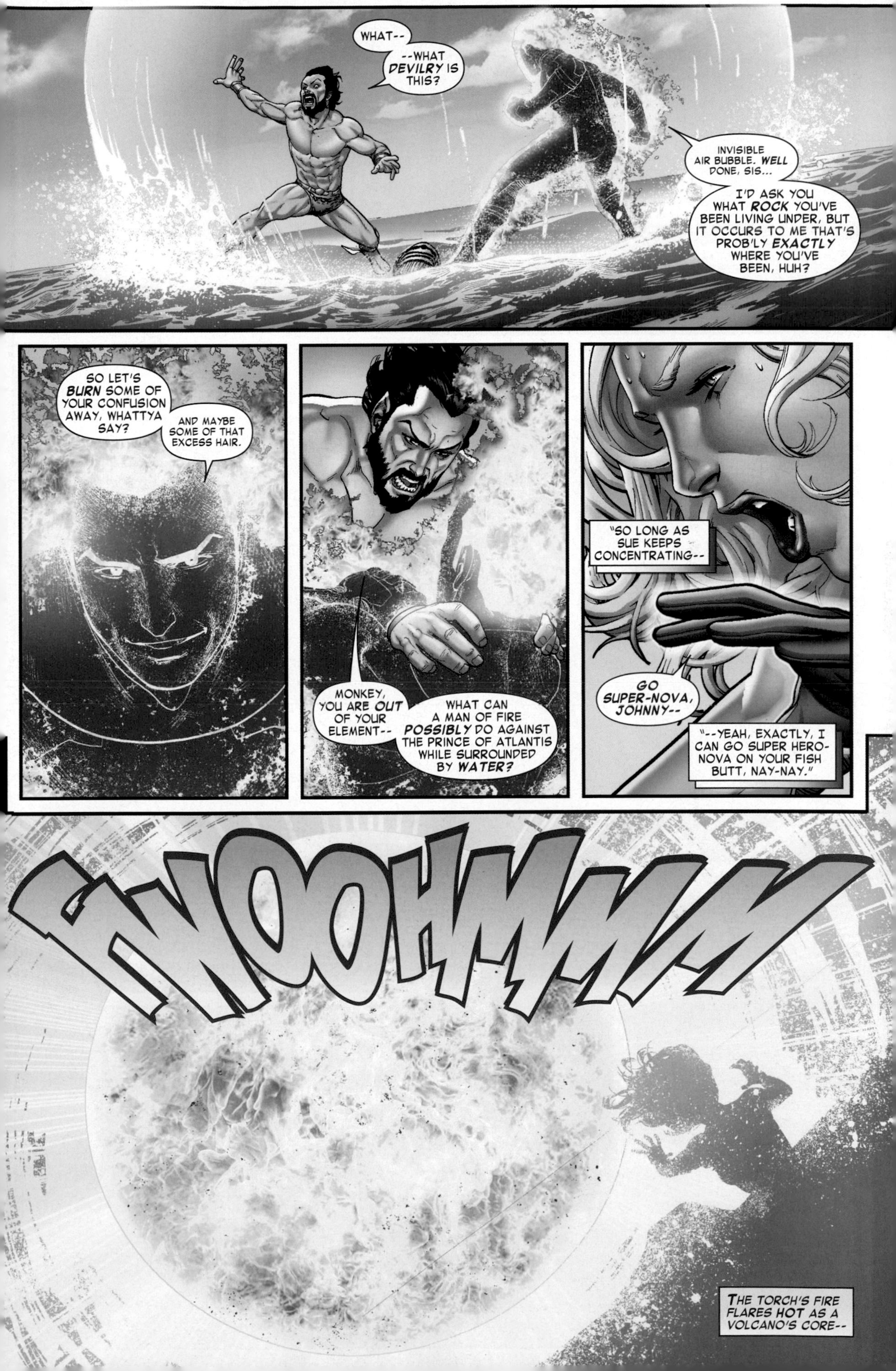
WHAT--
--WHAT DEVILRY IS THIS?
INVISIBLE AIR BUBBLE. WELL DONE, SIS...
I'D ASK YOU WHAT ROCK YOU'VE BEEN LIVING UNDER, BUT IT OCCURS TO ME THAT'S PROB'LY EXACTLY WHERE YOU'VE BEEN, HUH?
SO LET'S BURN SOME OF YOUR CONFUSION AWAY, WHATTYA SAY?
AND MAYBE SOME OF THAT EXCESS HAIR.
MONKEY, YOU ARE OUT OF YOUR ELEMENT--
WHAT CAN A MAN OF FIRE POSSIBLY DO AGAINST THE PRINCE OF ATLANTIS WHILE SURROUNDED BY WATER?
"SO LONG AS SUE KEEPS CONCENTRATING--
GO SUPER-NOVA, JOHNNY--
"--YEAH, EXACTLY, I CAN GO SUPER HERO-NOVA ON YOUR FISH BUTT, NAY-NAY."
FWOOHMMM
THE TORCH'S FIRE FLARES HOT AS A VOLCANO'S CORE--

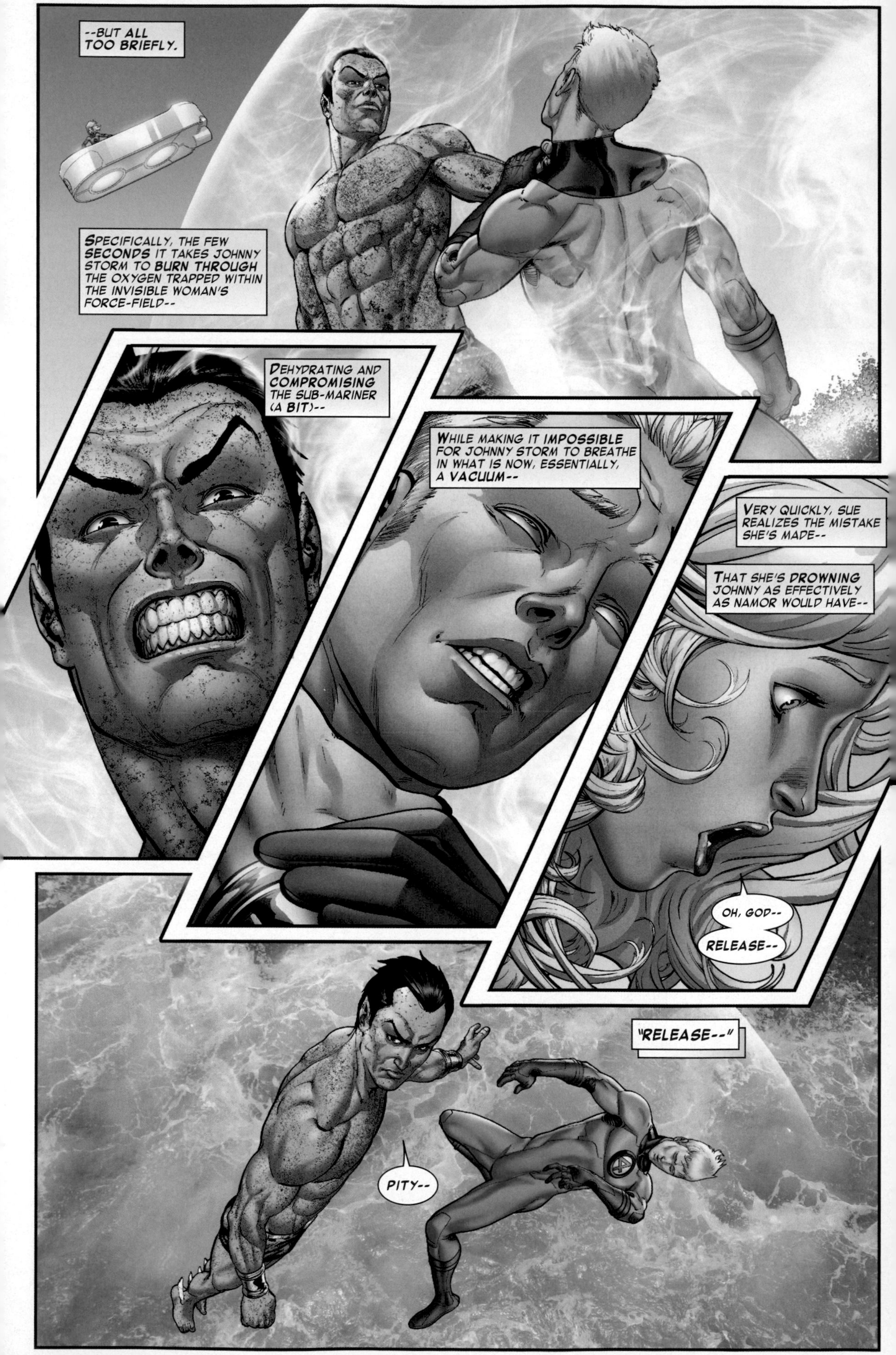

--BUT ALL TOO BRIEFLY.
SPECIFICALLY, THE FEW SECONDS IT TAKES JOHNNY STORM TO BURN THROUGH THE OXYGEN TRAPPED WITHIN THE INVISIBLE WOMAN'S FORCE-FIELD--
DEHYDRATING AND COMPROMISING THE SUB-MARINER (A BIT)--
WHILE MAKING IT IMPOSSIBLE FOR JOHNNY STORM TO BREATHE IN WHAT IS NOW, ESSENTIALLY, A VACUUM--
VERY QUICKLY, SUE REALIZES THE MISTAKE SHE'S MADE--
THAT SHE'S DROWNING JOHNNY AS EFFECTIVELY AS NAMOR WOULD HAVE--
OH, GOD--
RELEASE--
"RELEASE--"
PITY--

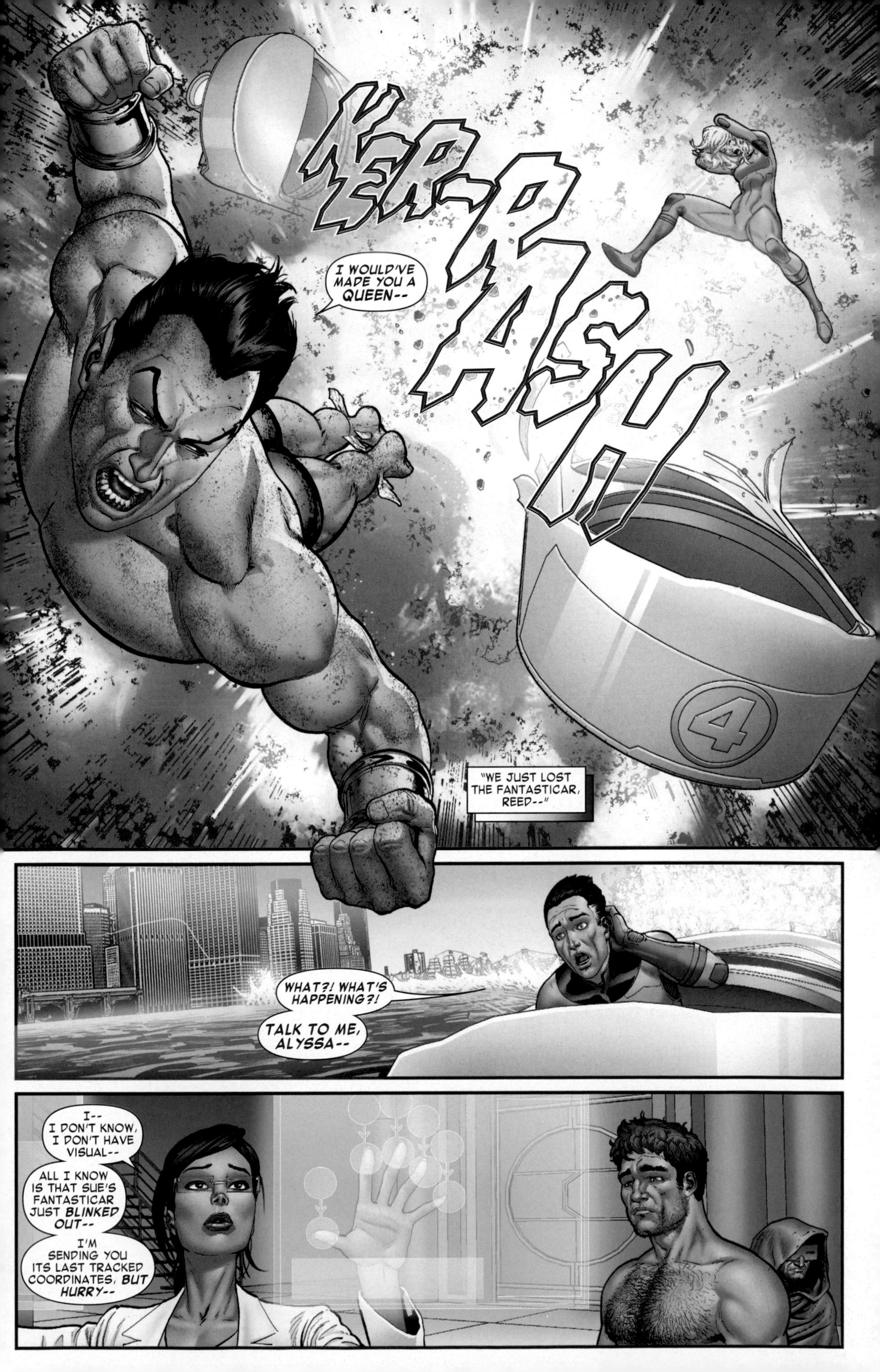
KER-RASH
I WOULD'VE MADE YOU A QUEEN--
"WE JUST LOST THE FANTASTICAR, REED--"
WHAT?! WHAT'S HAPPENING?!
TALK TO ME, ALYSSA--
I-- I DON'T KNOW, I DON'T HAVE VISUAL--
ALL I KNOW IS THAT SUE'S FANTASTICAR JUST BLINKED OUT--
I'M SENDING YOU ITS LAST TRACKED COORDINATES, BUT HURRY--

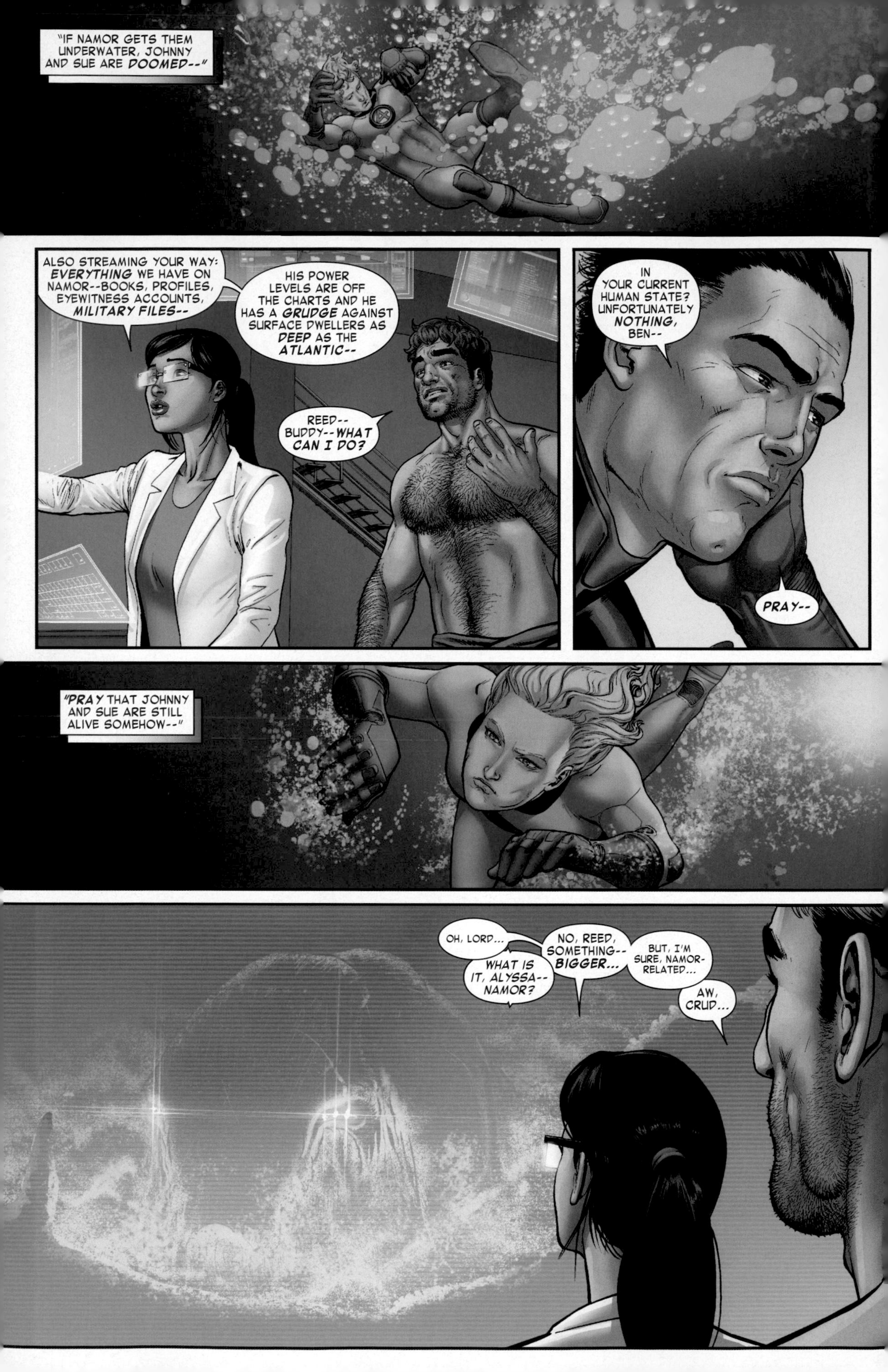
"IF NAMOR GETS THEM UNDERWATER, JOHNNY AND SUE ARE DOOMED--"
ALSO STREAMING YOUR WAY: EVERYTHING WE HAVE ON NAMOR--BOOKS, PROFILES, EYEWITNESS ACCOUNTS, MILITARY FILES--
HIS POWER LEVELS ARE OFF THE CHARTS AND HE HAS A GRUDGE AGAINST SURFACE DWELLERS AS DEEP AS THE ATLANTIC--
REED--BUDDY--WHAT CAN I DO?
IN YOUR CURRENT HUMAN STATE? UNFORTUNATELY NOTHING, BEN--
PRAY--
"PRAY THAT JOHNNY AND SUE ARE STILL ALIVE SOMEHOW--"
OH, LORD...
WHAT IS IT, ALYSSA--NAMOR?
NO, REED, SOMETHING--BIGGER...
BUT, I'M SURE, NAMOR-RELATED...
AW, CRUD...

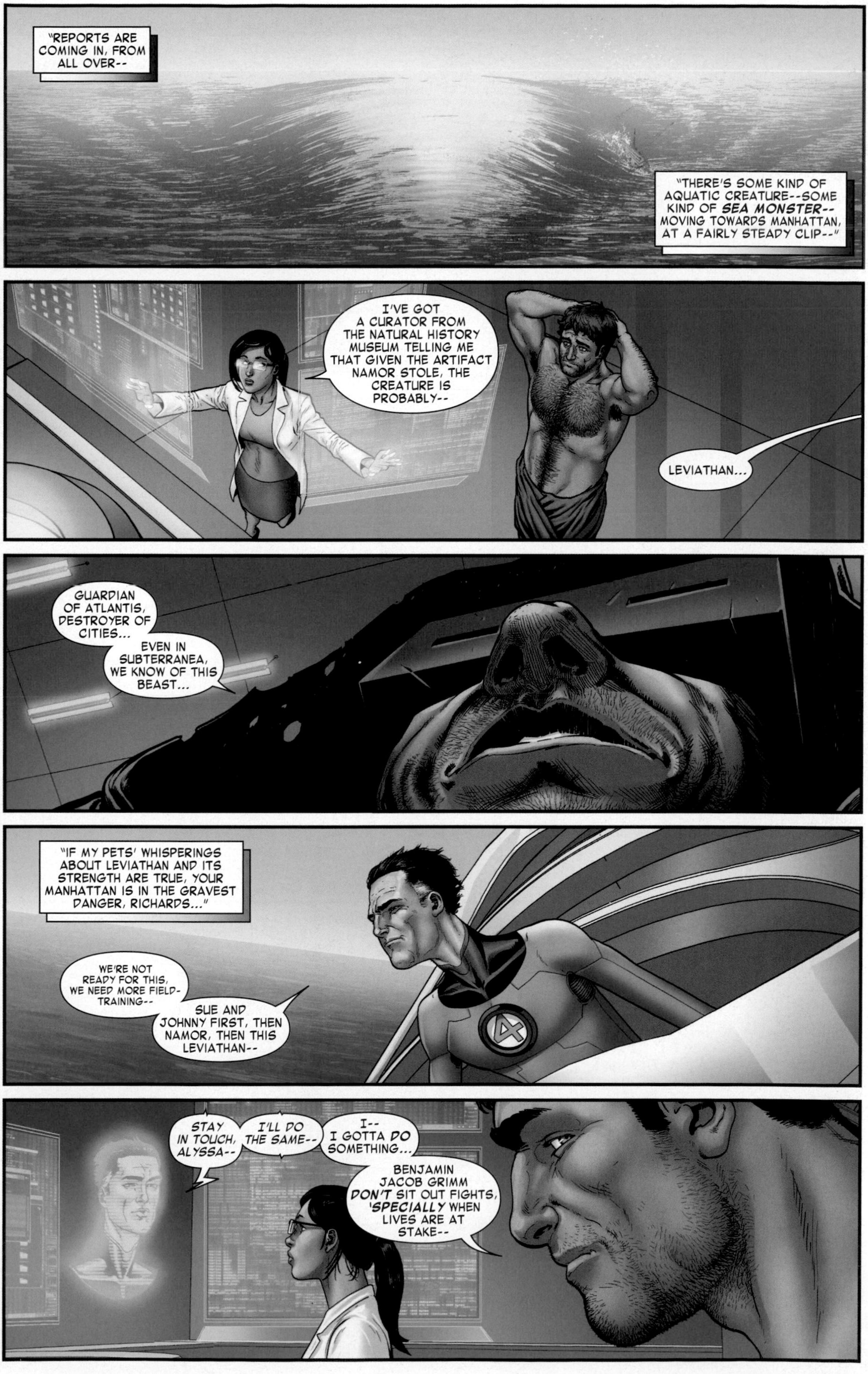
"REPORTS ARE COMING IN, FROM ALL OVER--
"THERE'S SOME KIND OF AQUATIC CREATURE--SOME KIND OF SEA MONSTER--MOVING TOWARDS MANHATTAN, AT A FAIRLY STEADY CLIP--"
I'VE GOT A CURATOR FROM THE NATURAL HISTORY MUSEUM TELLING ME THAT GIVEN THE ARTIFACT NAMOR STOLE, THE CREATURE IS PROBABLY--
LEVIATHAN...
GUARDIAN OF ATLANTIS, DESTROYER OF CITIES...
EVEN IN SUBTERRANEA, WE KNOW OF THIS BEAST...
"IF MY PETS' WHISPERINGS ABOUT LEVIATHAN AND ITS STRENGTH ARE TRUE, YOUR MANHATTAN IS IN THE GRAVEST DANGER, RICHARDS..."
WE'RE NOT READY FOR THIS, WE NEED MORE FIELD-TRAINING--
SUE AND JOHNNY FIRST, THEN NAMOR, THEN THIS LEVIATHAN--
STAY IN TOUCH, ALYSSA--
I'LL DO THE SAME--
I-- I GOTTA DO SOMETHING...
BENJAMIN JACOB GRIMM DON'T SIT OUT FIGHTS, 'SPECIALLY WHEN LIVES ARE AT STAKE--

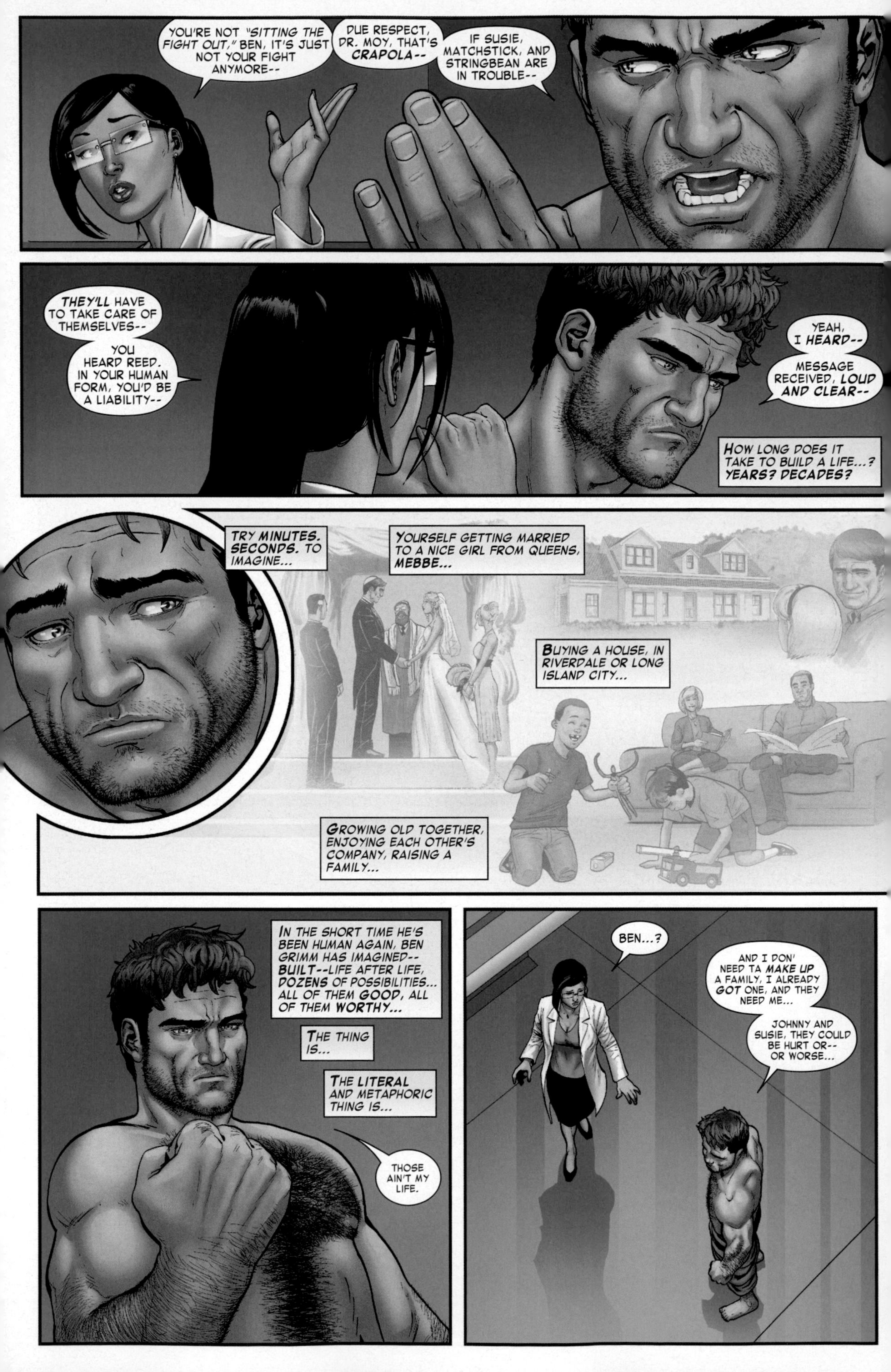

YOU'RE NOT "SITTING THE FIGHT OUT," BEN, IT'S JUST NOT YOUR FIGHT ANYMORE--
DUE RESPECT, DR. MOY, THAT'S CRAPOLA--
IF SUSIE, MATCHSTICK, AND STRINGBEAN ARE IN TROUBLE--
THEY'LL HAVE TO TAKE CARE OF THEMSELVES--
YOU HEARD REED. IN YOUR HUMAN FORM, YOU'D BE A LIABILITY--
YEAH, I HEARD--
MESSAGE RECEIVED, LOUD AND CLEAR--
HOW LONG DOES IT TAKE TO BUILD A LIFE...? YEARS? DECADES?
TRY MINUTES. SECONDS. TO IMAGINE...
YOURSELF GETTING MARRIED TO A NICE GIRL FROM QUEENS, MEBBE...
BUYING A HOUSE, IN RIVERDALE OR LONG ISLAND CITY...
GROWING OLD TOGETHER, ENJOYING EACH OTHER'S COMPANY, RAISING A FAMILY...
IN THE SHORT TIME HE'S BEEN HUMAN AGAIN, BEN GRIMM HAS IMAGINED-- BUILT--LIFE AFTER LIFE, DOZENS OF POSSIBILITIES... ALL OF THEM GOOD, ALL OF THEM WORTHY...
THE THING IS...
THE LITERAL AND METAPHORIC THING IS...
THOSE AIN'T MY LIFE.
BEN...?
AND I DON' NEED TA MAKE UP A FAMILY, I ALREADY GOT ONE, AND THEY NEED ME...
JOHNNY AND SUSIE, THEY COULD BE HURT OR-- OR WORSE...

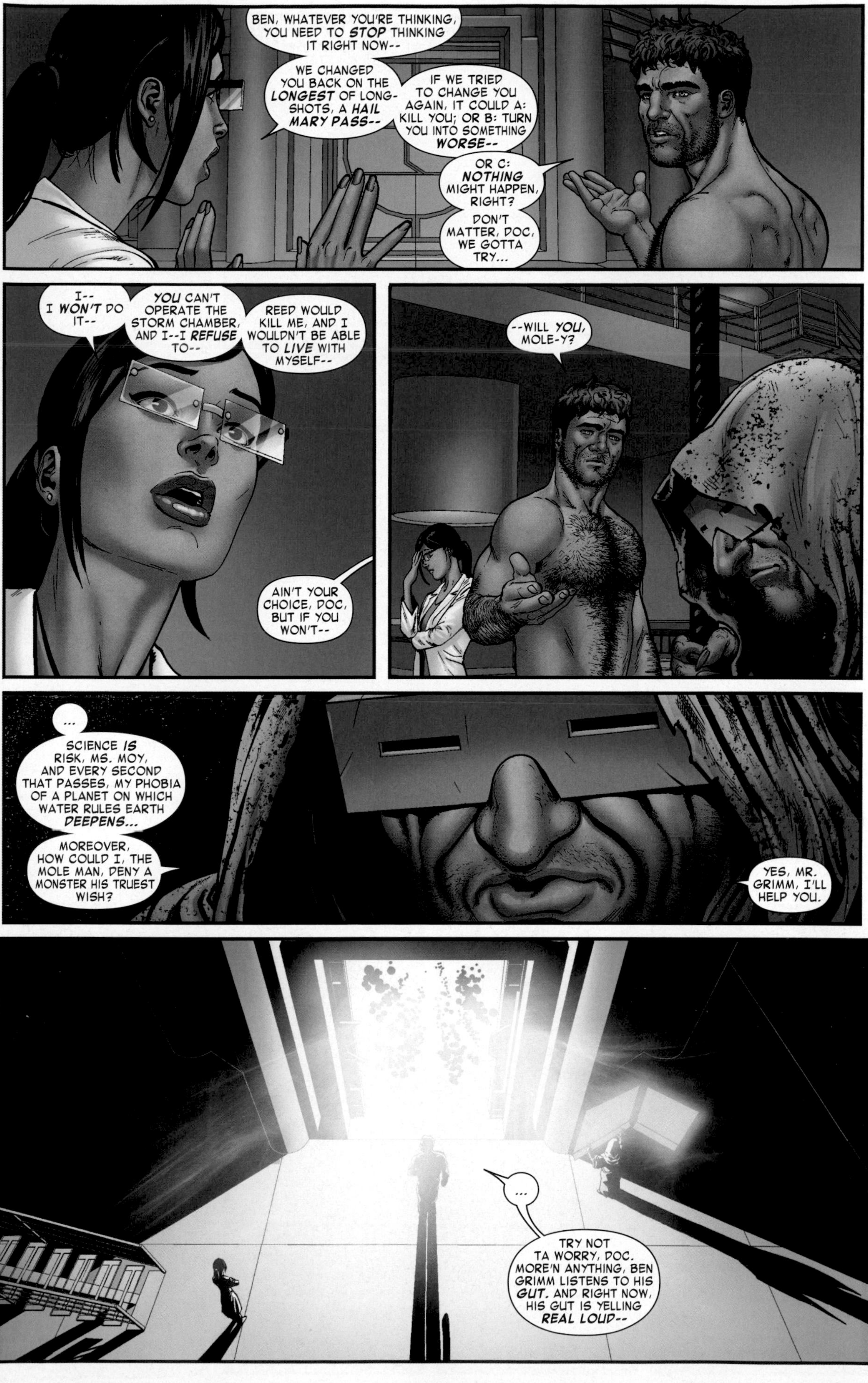
BEN, WHATEVER YOU'RE THINKING, YOU NEED TO STOP THINKING IT RIGHT NOW--
WE CHANGED YOU BACK ON THE LONGEST OF LONG-SHOTS, A HAIL MARY PASS--
IF WE TRIED TO CHANGE YOU AGAIN, IT COULD A: KILL YOU; OR B: TURN YOU INTO SOMETHING WORSE--
OR C: NOTHING MIGHT HAPPEN, RIGHT?
DON'T MATTER, DOC, WE GOTTA TRY...
I-- I WON'T DO IT--
YOU CAN'T OPERATE THE STORM CHAMBER, AND I--I REFUSE TO--
REED WOULD KILL ME, AND I WOULDN'T BE ABLE TO LIVE WITH MYSELF--
AIN'T YOUR CHOICE, DOC, BUT IF YOU WON'T--
--WILL YOU, MOLE-Y?
...
SCIENCE IS RISK, MS. MOY, AND EVERY SECOND THAT PASSES, MY PHOBIA OF A PLANET ON WHICH WATER RULES EARTH DEEPENS...
MOREOVER, HOW COULD I, THE MOLE MAN, DENY A MONSTER HIS TRUEST WISH?
YES, MR. GRIMM, I'LL HELP YOU.
...
TRY NOT TA WORRY, DOC. MORE'N ANYTHING, BEN GRIMM LISTENS TO HIS GUT. AND RIGHT NOW, HIS GUT IS YELLING REAL LOUD--

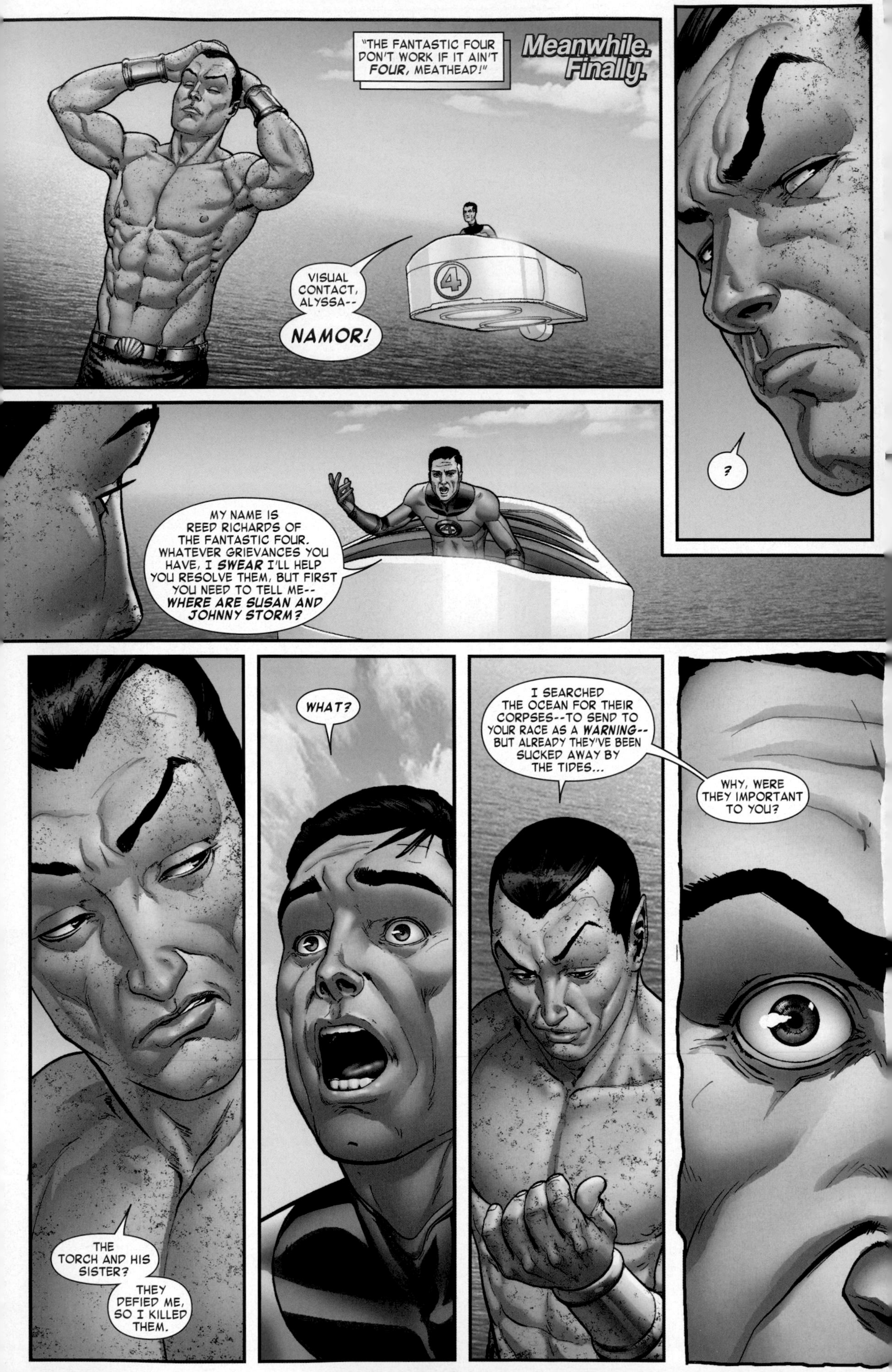
"THE FANTASTIC FOUR DON'T WORK IF IT AIN'T FOUR, MEATHEAD!"
Meanwhile. Finally.
VISUAL CONTACT, ALYSSA--
NAMOR!
?
MY NAME IS REED RICHARDS OF THE FANTASTIC FOUR. WHATEVER GRIEVANCES YOU HAVE, I SWEAR I'LL HELP YOU RESOLVE THEM, BUT FIRST YOU NEED TO TELL ME-- WHERE ARE SUSAN AND JOHNNY STORM?
THE TORCH AND HIS SISTER?
THEY DEFIED ME, SO I KILLED THEM.
WHAT?
I SEARCHED THE OCEAN FOR THEIR CORPSES--TO SEND TO YOUR RACE AS A WARNING-- BUT ALREADY THEY'VE BEEN SUCKED AWAY BY THE TIDES...
WHY, WERE THEY IMPORTANT TO YOU?

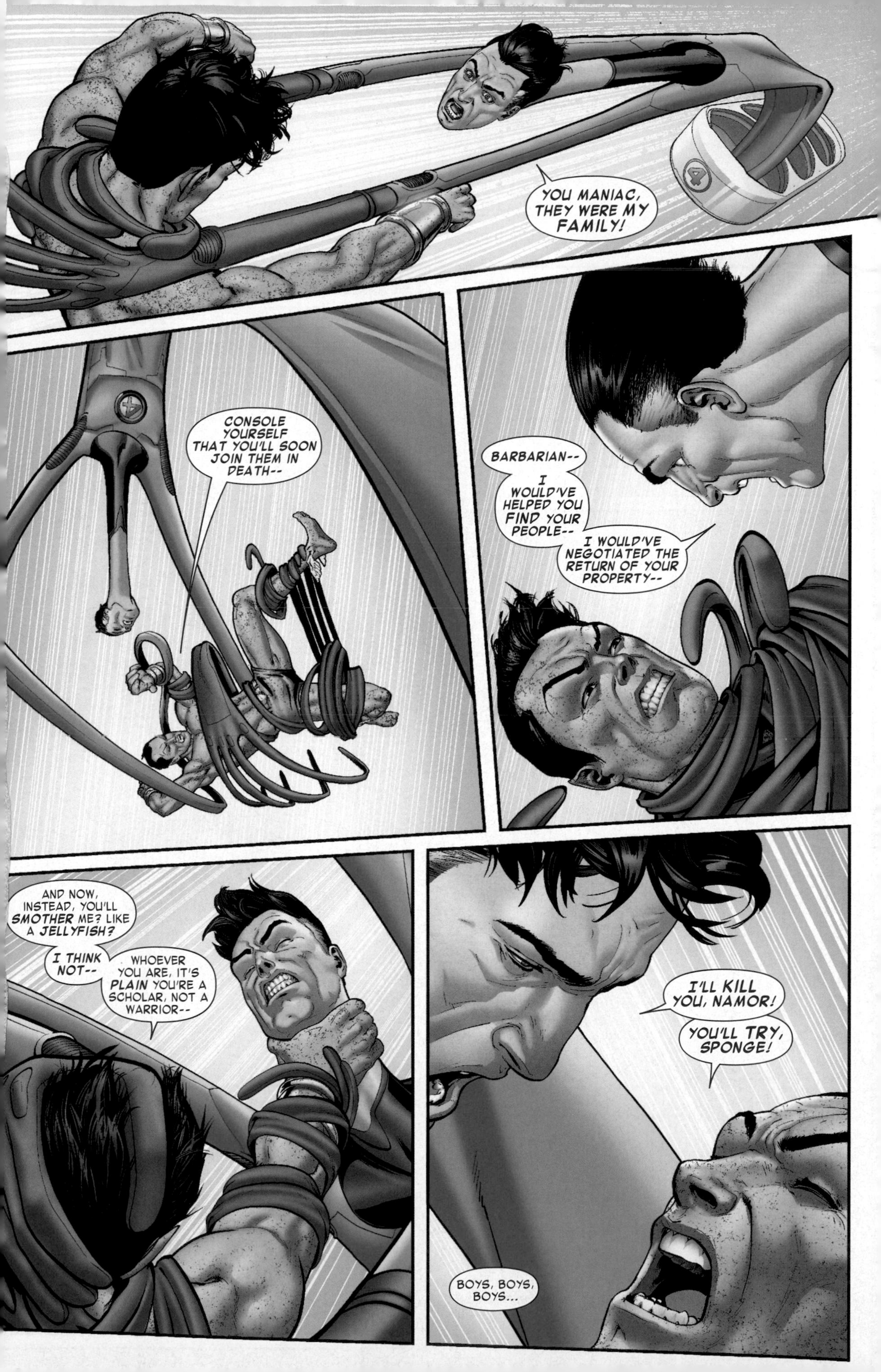
YOU MANIAC, THEY WERE MY FAMILY!
CONSOLE YOURSELF THAT YOU'LL SOON JOIN THEM IN DEATH--
BARBARIAN--
I WOULD'VE HELPED YOU FIND YOUR PEOPLE--
I WOULD'VE NEGOTIATED THE RETURN OF YOUR PROPERTY--
AND NOW, INSTEAD, YOU'LL SMOTHER ME? LIKE A JELLYFISH?
I THINK NOT--
WHOEVER YOU ARE, IT'S PLAIN YOU'RE A SCHOLAR, NOT A WARRIOR--
I'LL KILL YOU, NAMOR!
YOU'LL TRY, SPONGE!
BOYS, BOYS, BOYS...

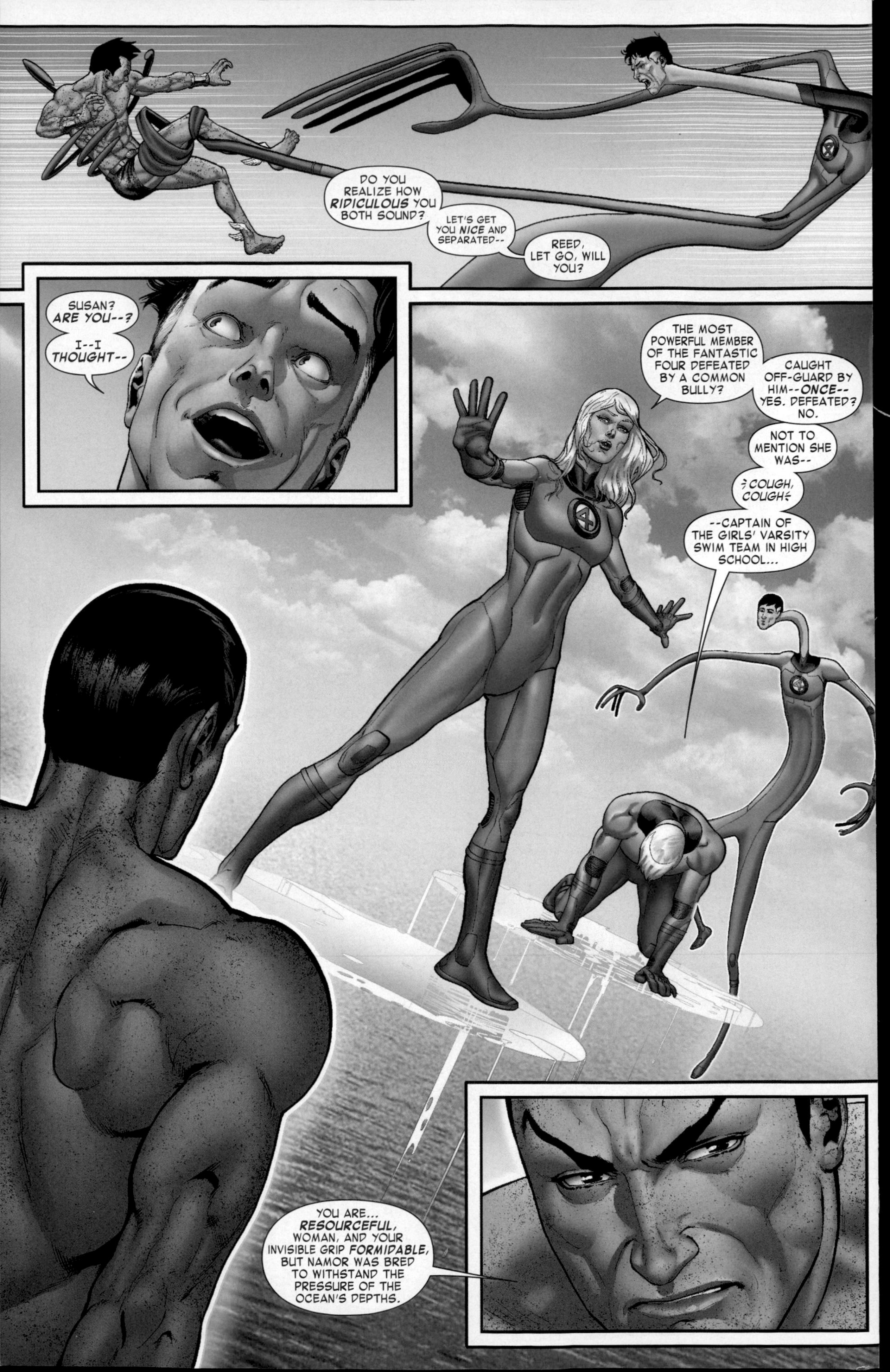

DO YOU REALIZE HOW RIDICULOUS YOU BOTH SOUND?
LET'S GET YOU NICE AND SEPARATED--
REED, LET GO, WILL YOU?
SUSAN? ARE YOU--?
I--I THOUGHT--
THE MOST POWERFUL MEMBER OF THE FANTASTIC FOUR DEFEATED BY A COMMON BULLY?
CAUGHT OFF-GUARD BY HIM--ONCE--YES. DEFEATED? NO.
NOT TO MENTION SHE WAS--
COUGH, COUGH
--CAPTAIN OF THE GIRLS' VARSITY SWIM TEAM IN HIGH SCHOOL...
YOU ARE... RESOURCEFUL, WOMAN, AND YOUR INVISIBLE GRIP FORMIDABLE, BUT NAMOR WAS BRED TO WITHSTAND THE PRESSURE OF THE OCEAN'S DEPTHS.

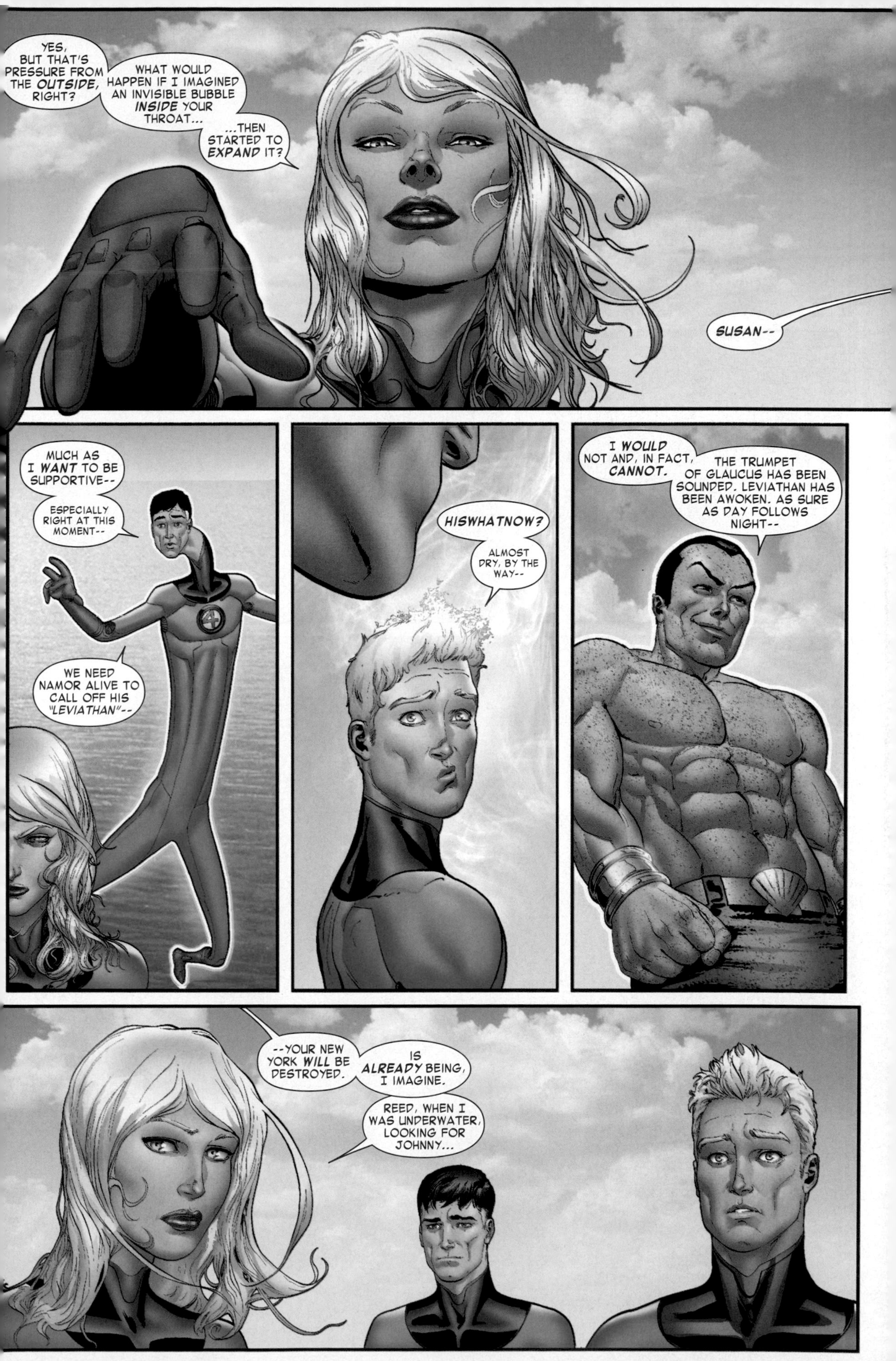

YES, BUT THAT'S PRESSURE FROM THE *OUTSIDE*, RIGHT?
WHAT WOULD HAPPEN IF I IMAGINED AN INVISIBLE BUBBLE *INSIDE* YOUR THROAT...
...THEN STARTED TO *EXPAND* IT?
SUSAN--
MUCH AS I *WANT* TO BE SUPPORTIVE--
ESPECIALLY RIGHT AT THIS MOMENT--
WE NEED NAMOR ALIVE TO CALL OFF HIS *"LEVIATHAN"*--
HISWHATNOW?
ALMOST DRY, BY THE WAY--
I *WOULD* NOT AND, IN FACT, *CANNOT.*
THE TRUMPET OF GLAUCUS HAS BEEN SOUNDED. LEVIATHAN HAS BEEN AWOKEN. AS SURE AS DAY FOLLOWS NIGHT--
--YOUR NEW YORK *WILL* BE DESTROYED.
IS *ALREADY* BEING, I IMAGINE.
REED, WHEN I WAS UNDERWATER, LOOKING FOR JOHNNY...

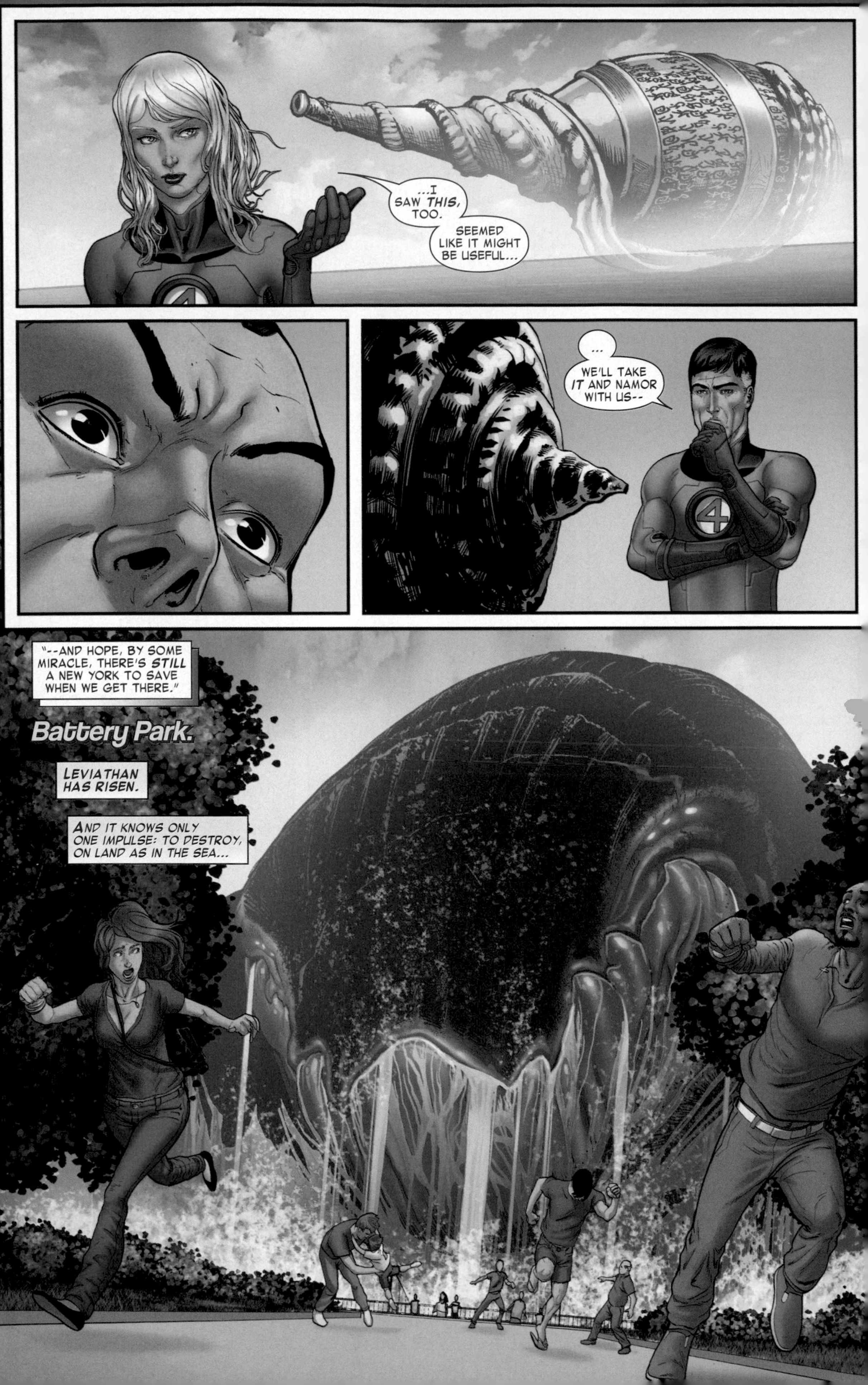

...I SAW THIS, TOO.
SEEMED LIKE IT MIGHT BE USEFUL...
...
WE'LL TAKE IT AND NAMOR WITH US--
"--AND HOPE, BY SOME MIRACLE, THERE'S STILL A NEW YORK TO SAVE WHEN WE GET THERE."
Battery Park.
LEVIATHAN HAS RISEN.
AND IT KNOWS ONLY ONE IMPULSE: TO DESTROY, ON LAND AS IN THE SEA...

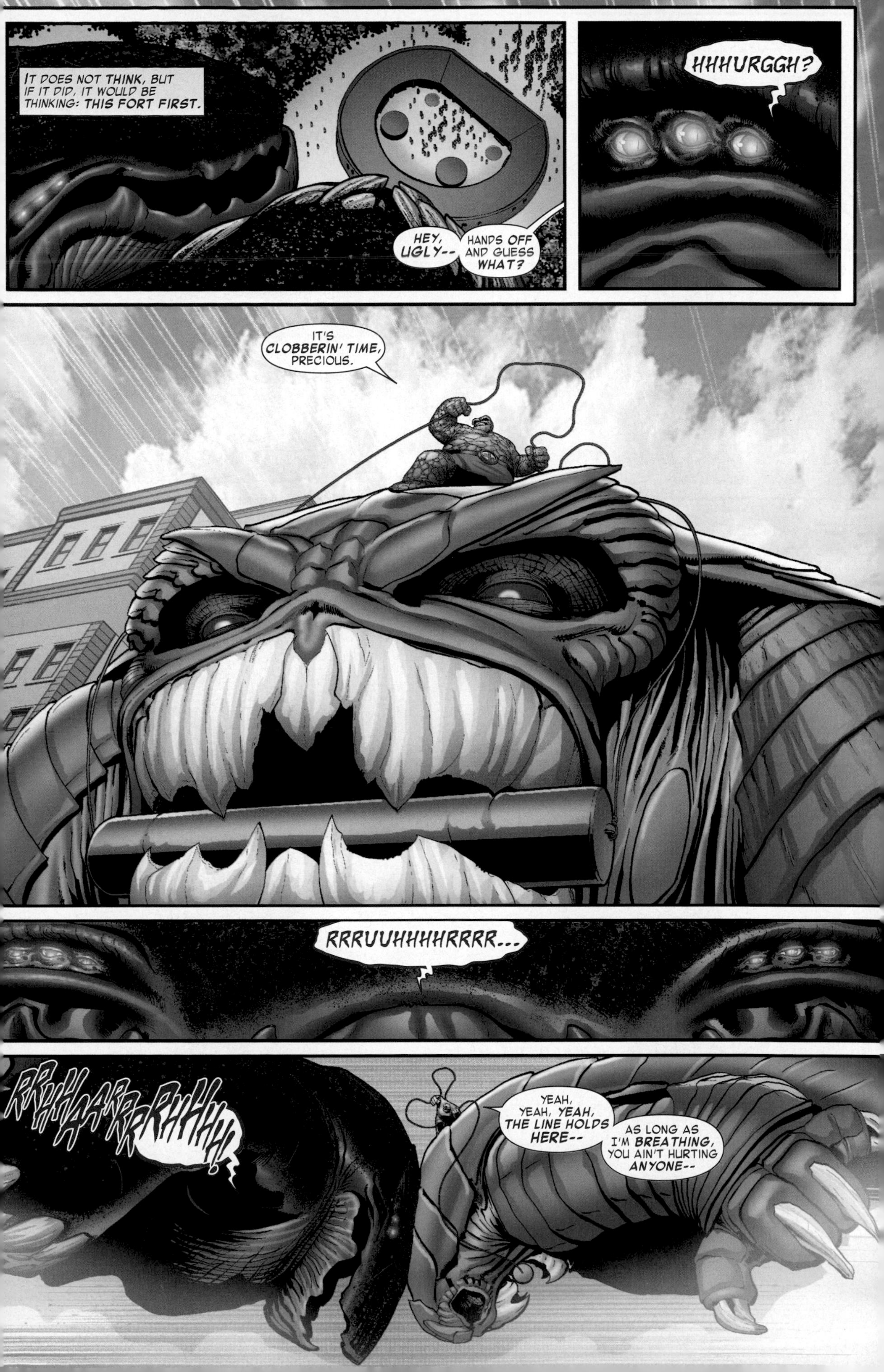
IT DOES NOT THINK, BUT IF IT DID, IT WOULD BE THINKING: THIS FORT FIRST.
HEY, UGLY--
HANDS OFF AND GUESS WHAT?
HHHURGGH?
IT'S CLOBBERIN' TIME, PRECIOUS.
RRRUUHHHHRRRR...
YEAH, YEAH, YEAH, THE LINE HOLDS HERE--
AS LONG AS I'M BREATHING, YOU AIN'T HURTING ANYONE--

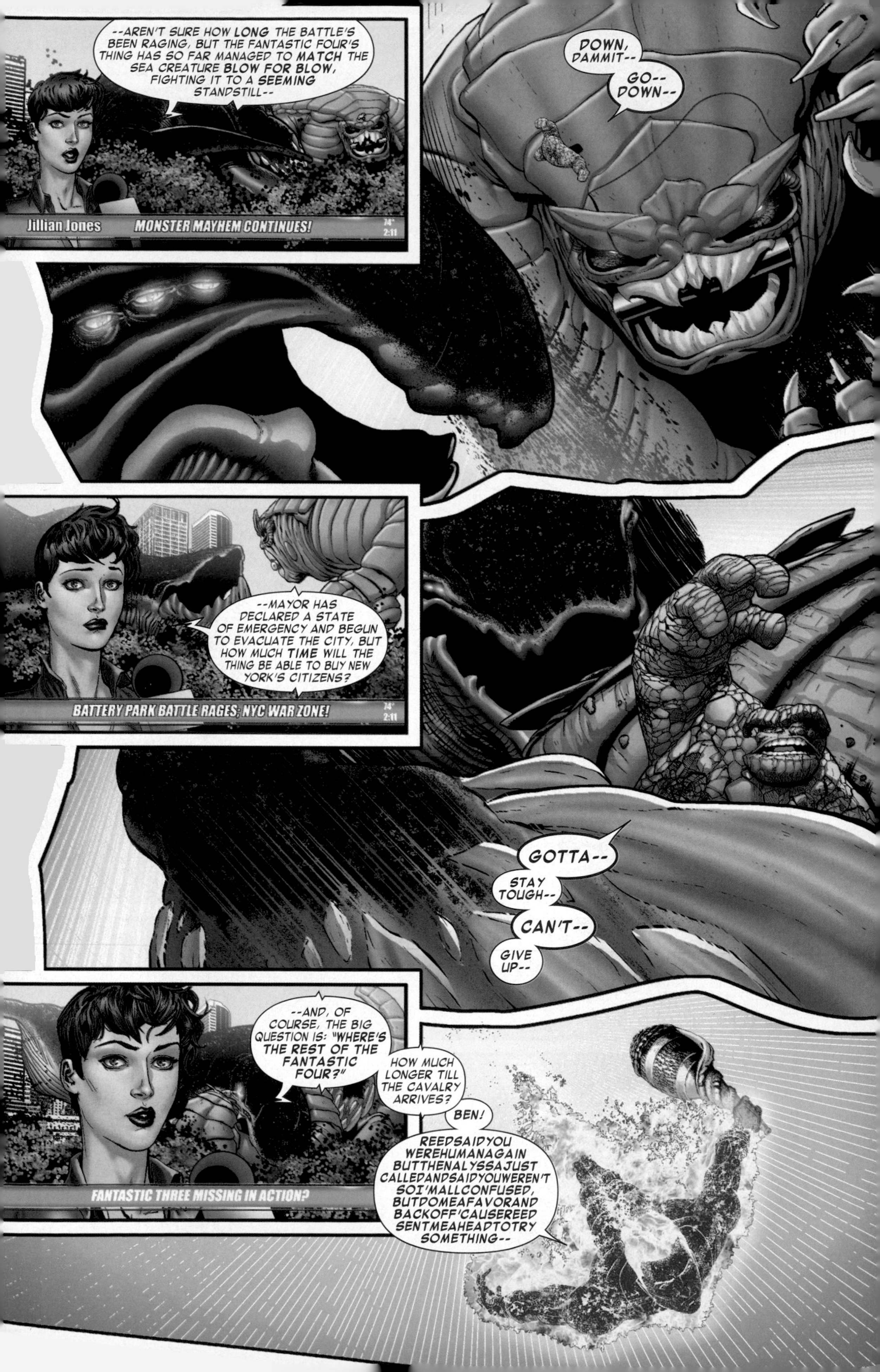

--AREN'T SURE HOW LONG THE BATTLE'S BEEN RAGING, BUT THE FANTASTIC FOUR'S THING HAS SO FAR MANAGED TO MATCH THE SEA CREATURE BLOW FOR BLOW, FIGHTING IT TO A SEEMING STANDSTILL--
Jillian Jones
MONSTER MAYHEM CONTINUES!
74°
2:11
DOWN, DAMMIT--
GO-- DOWN--
--MAYOR HAS DECLARED A STATE OF EMERGENCY AND BEGUN TO EVACUATE THE CITY, BUT HOW MUCH TIME WILL THE THING BE ABLE TO BUY NEW YORK'S CITIZENS?
BATTERY PARK BATTLE RAGES; NYC WAR ZONE!
74°
2:11
GOTTA--
STAY TOUGH--
CAN'T--
GIVE UP--
--AND, OF COURSE, THE BIG QUESTION IS: "WHERE'S THE REST OF THE FANTASTIC FOUR?"
FANTASTIC THREE MISSING IN ACTION?
HOW MUCH LONGER TILL THE CAVALRY ARRIVES?
BEN!
REEDSAIDYOU WEREHUMANAGAIN BUTTHENALYSSAJUST CALLEDANDSAIDYOUWEREN'T SOI'MALLCONFUSED, BUTDOMEAFAVORAND BACKOFF'CAUSEREED SENTMEAHEADTOTRY SOMETHING--

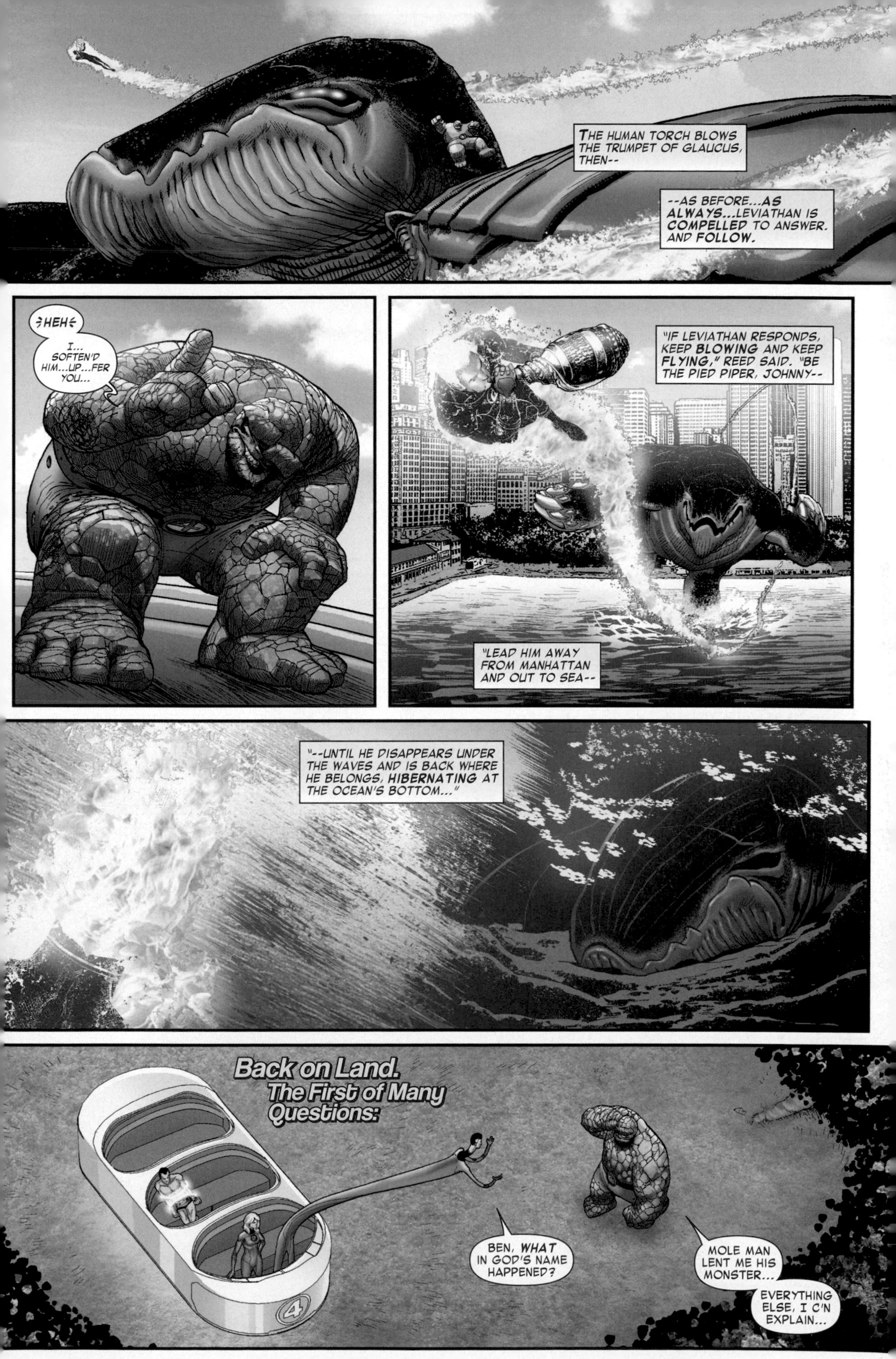
THE HUMAN TORCH BLOWS THE TRUMPET OF GLAUCUS, THEN--
--AS BEFORE...AS ALWAYS...LEVIATHAN IS COMPELLED TO ANSWER. AND FOLLOW.
HEH
I... SOFTEN'D HIM...UP...FER YOU...
"IF LEVIATHAN RESPONDS, KEEP BLOWING AND KEEP FLYING," REED SAID. "BE THE PIED PIPER, JOHNNY--
"LEAD HIM AWAY FROM MANHATTAN AND OUT TO SEA--
"--UNTIL HE DISAPPEARS UNDER THE WAVES AND IS BACK WHERE HE BELONGS, HIBERNATING AT THE OCEAN'S BOTTOM..."
Back on Land. The First of Many Questions:
BEN, WHAT IN GOD'S NAME HAPPENED?
MOLE MAN LENT ME HIS MONSTER...
EVERYTHING ELSE, I C'N EXPLAIN...

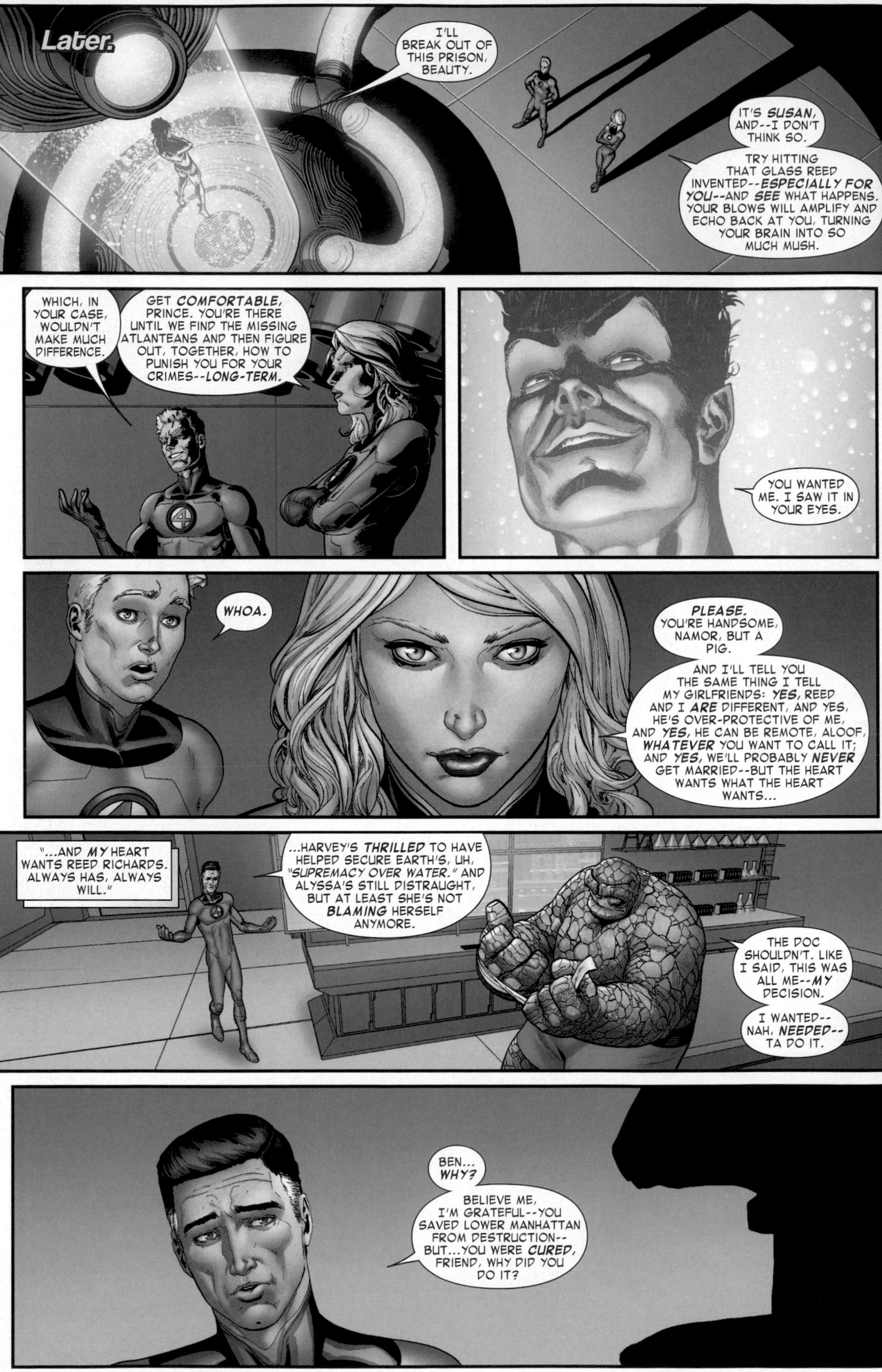
Later.
I'LL BREAK OUT OF THIS PRISON, BEAUTY.
IT'S SUSAN, AND--I DON'T THINK SO.
TRY HITTING THAT GLASS REED INVENTED--ESPECIALLY FOR YOU--AND SEE WHAT HAPPENS. YOUR BLOWS WILL AMPLIFY AND ECHO BACK AT YOU, TURNING YOUR BRAIN INTO SO MUCH MUSH.
WHICH, IN YOUR CASE, WOULDN'T MAKE MUCH DIFFERENCE.
GET COMFORTABLE, PRINCE. YOU'RE THERE UNTIL WE FIND THE MISSING ATLANTEANS AND THEN FIGURE OUT, TOGETHER, HOW TO PUNISH YOU FOR YOUR CRIMES--LONG-TERM.
YOU WANTED ME. I SAW IT IN YOUR EYES.
WHOA.
PLEASE. YOU'RE HANDSOME, NAMOR, BUT A PIG.
AND I'LL TELL YOU THE SAME THING I TELL MY GIRLFRIENDS: YES, REED AND I ARE DIFFERENT, AND YES, HE'S OVER-PROTECTIVE OF ME, AND YES, HE CAN BE REMOTE, ALOOF, WHATEVER YOU WANT TO CALL IT; AND YES, WE'LL PROBABLY NEVER GET MARRIED--BUT THE HEART WANTS WHAT THE HEART WANTS...
"...AND MY HEART WANTS REED RICHARDS. ALWAYS HAS, ALWAYS WILL."
...HARVEY'S THRILLED TO HAVE HELPED SECURE EARTH'S, UH, "SUPREMACY OVER WATER." AND ALYSSA'S STILL DISTRAUGHT, BUT AT LEAST SHE'S NOT BLAMING HERSELF ANYMORE.
THE DOC SHOULDN'T. LIKE I SAID, THIS WAS ALL ME--MY DECISION.
I WANTED--NAH, NEEDED--TA DO IT.
BEN... WHY?
BELIEVE ME, I'M GRATEFUL--YOU SAVED LOWER MANHATTAN FROM DESTRUCTION--BUT...YOU WERE CURED, FRIEND, WHY DID YOU DO IT?

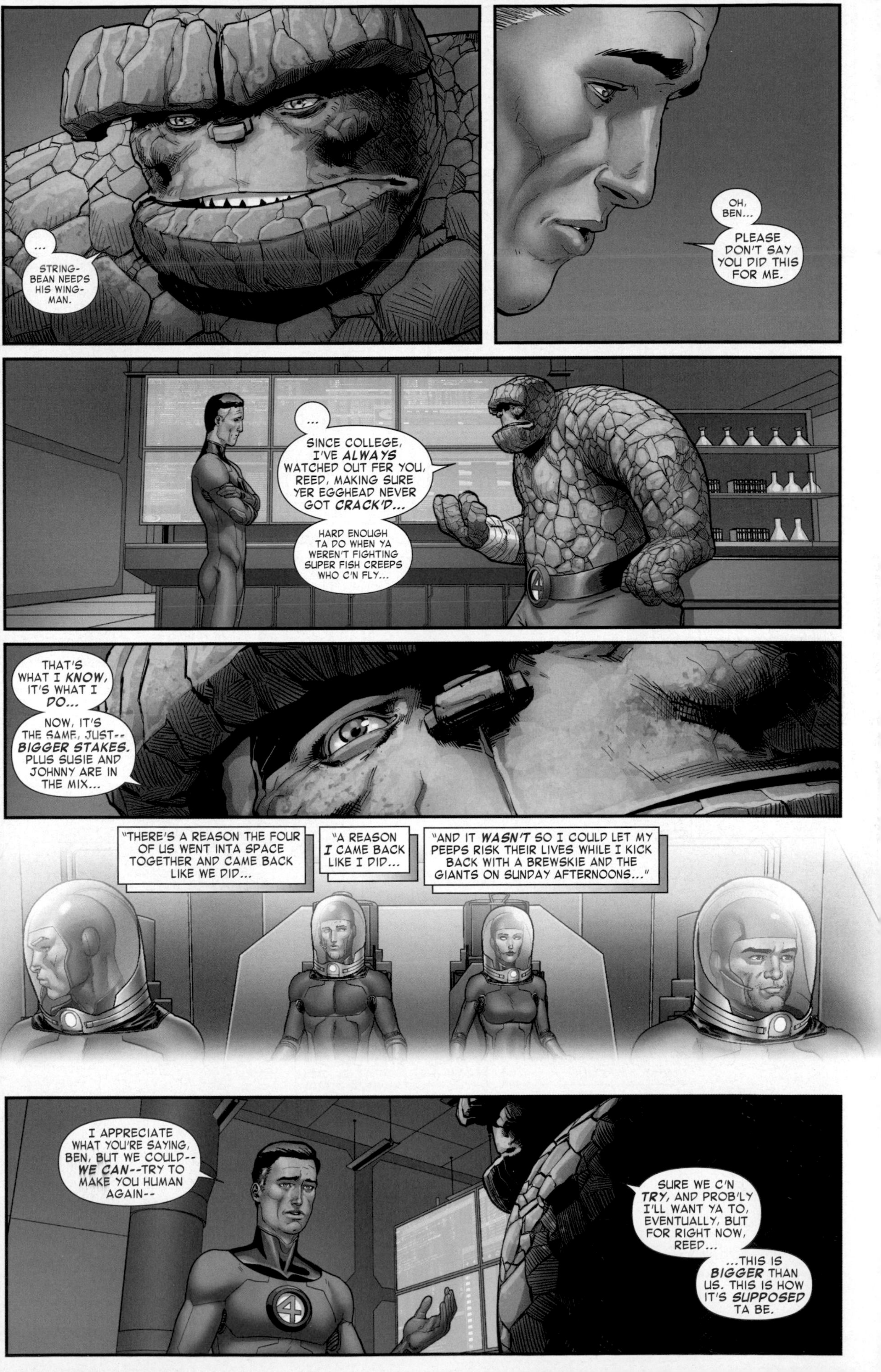
...
STRING-BEAN NEEDS HIS WING-MAN.
OH, BEN...
PLEASE DON'T SAY YOU DID THIS FOR ME.
...
SINCE COLLEGE, I'VE ALWAYS WATCHED OUT FER YOU, REED, MAKING SURE YER EGGHEAD NEVER GOT CRACK'D...
HARD ENOUGH TA DO WHEN YA WEREN'T FIGHTING SUPER FISH CREEPS WHO C'N FLY...
THAT'S WHAT I KNOW, IT'S WHAT I DO...
NOW, IT'S THE SAME, JUST--BIGGER STAKES. PLUS SUSIE AND JOHNNY ARE IN THE MIX...
"THERE'S A REASON THE FOUR OF US WENT INTA SPACE TOGETHER AND CAME BACK LIKE WE DID...
"A REASON I CAME BACK LIKE I DID...
"AND IT WASN'T SO I COULD LET MY PEEPS RISK THEIR LIVES WHILE I KICK BACK WITH A BREWSKIE AND THE GIANTS ON SUNDAY AFTERNOONS..."
I APPRECIATE WHAT YOU'RE SAYING, BEN, BUT WE COULD--WE CAN--TRY TO MAKE YOU HUMAN AGAIN--
SURE WE C'N TRY, AND PROB'LY I'LL WANT YA TO, EVENTUALLY, BUT FOR RIGHT NOW, REED...
...THIS IS BIGGER THAN US. THIS IS HOW IT'S SUPPOSED TA BE.

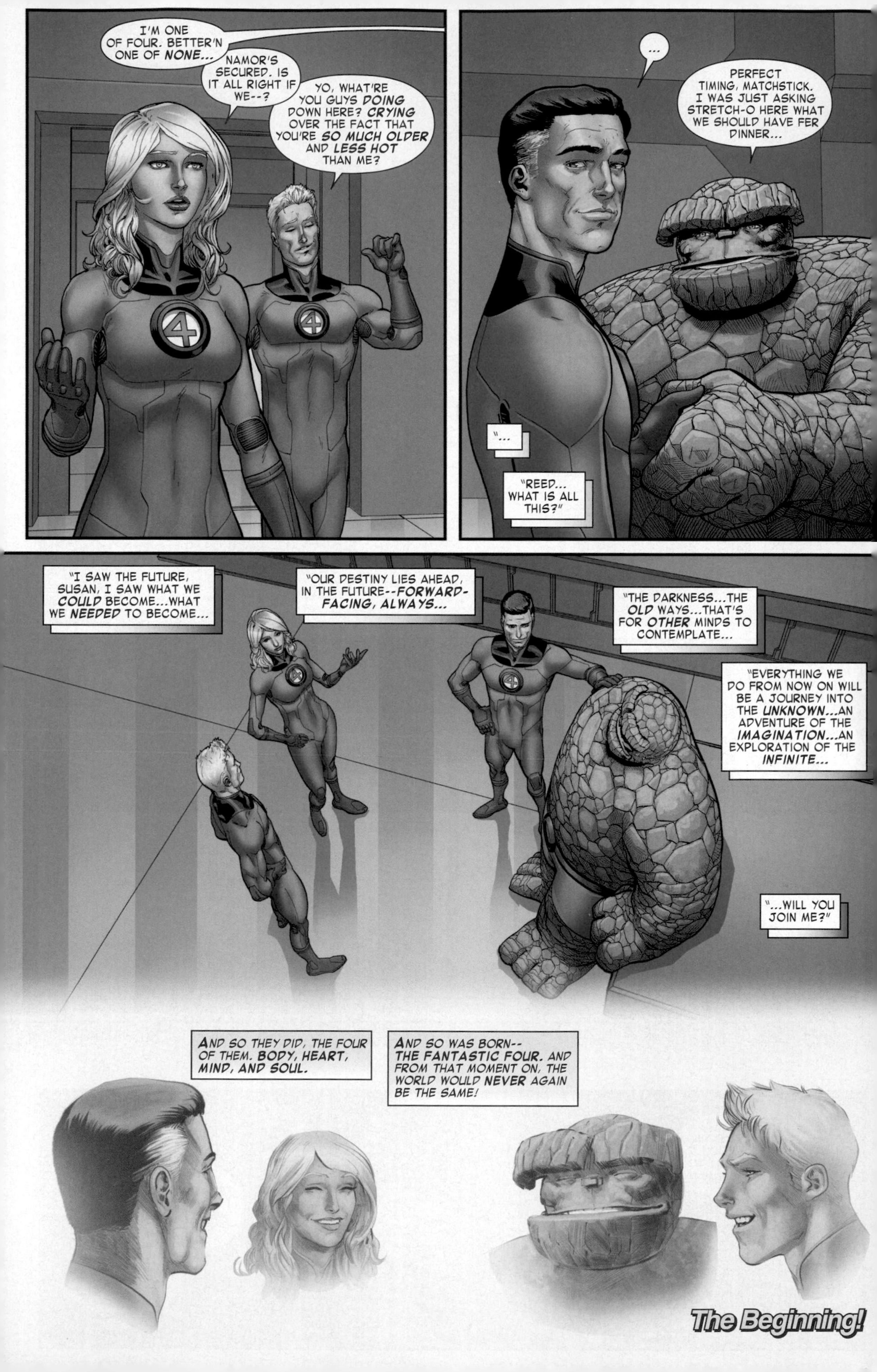

I'M ONE OF FOUR. BETTER'N ONE OF NONE...
NAMOR'S SECURED. IS IT ALL RIGHT IF WE--?
YO, WHAT'RE YOU GUYS DOING DOWN HERE? CRYING OVER THE FACT THAT YOU'RE SO MUCH OLDER AND LESS HOT THAN ME?
...
PERFECT TIMING, MATCHSTICK. I WAS JUST ASKING STRETCH-O HERE WHAT WE SHOULD HAVE FER DINNER...
"...
"REED... WHAT IS ALL THIS?"
"I SAW THE FUTURE, SUSAN, I SAW WHAT WE COULD BECOME...WHAT WE NEEDED TO BECOME...
"OUR DESTINY LIES AHEAD, IN THE FUTURE--FORWARD-FACING, ALWAYS...
"THE DARKNESS...THE OLD WAYS...THAT'S FOR OTHER MINDS TO CONTEMPLATE...
"EVERYTHING WE DO FROM NOW ON WILL BE A JOURNEY INTO THE UNKNOWN...AN ADVENTURE OF THE IMAGINATION...AN EXPLORATION OF THE INFINITE...
"...WILL YOU JOIN ME?"
AND SO THEY DID, THE FOUR OF THEM. BODY, HEART, MIND, AND SOUL.
AND SO WAS BORN-- THE FANTASTIC FOUR. AND FROM THAT MOMENT ON, THE WORLD WOULD NEVER AGAIN BE THE SAME!
The Beginning!

FANTASTIC FOUR #570 (2009) IT'S ADVENTURE, IT'S FAMILY, IT'S TOUGH QUESTIONS IN DARK TIMES... SEE WHAT HAPPENS WHEN REED RICHARDS TRIES TO SOLVE EVERYTHING IN THE FIRST ISSUE OF WRITER JONATHAN HICKMAN'S LANDMARK RUN!

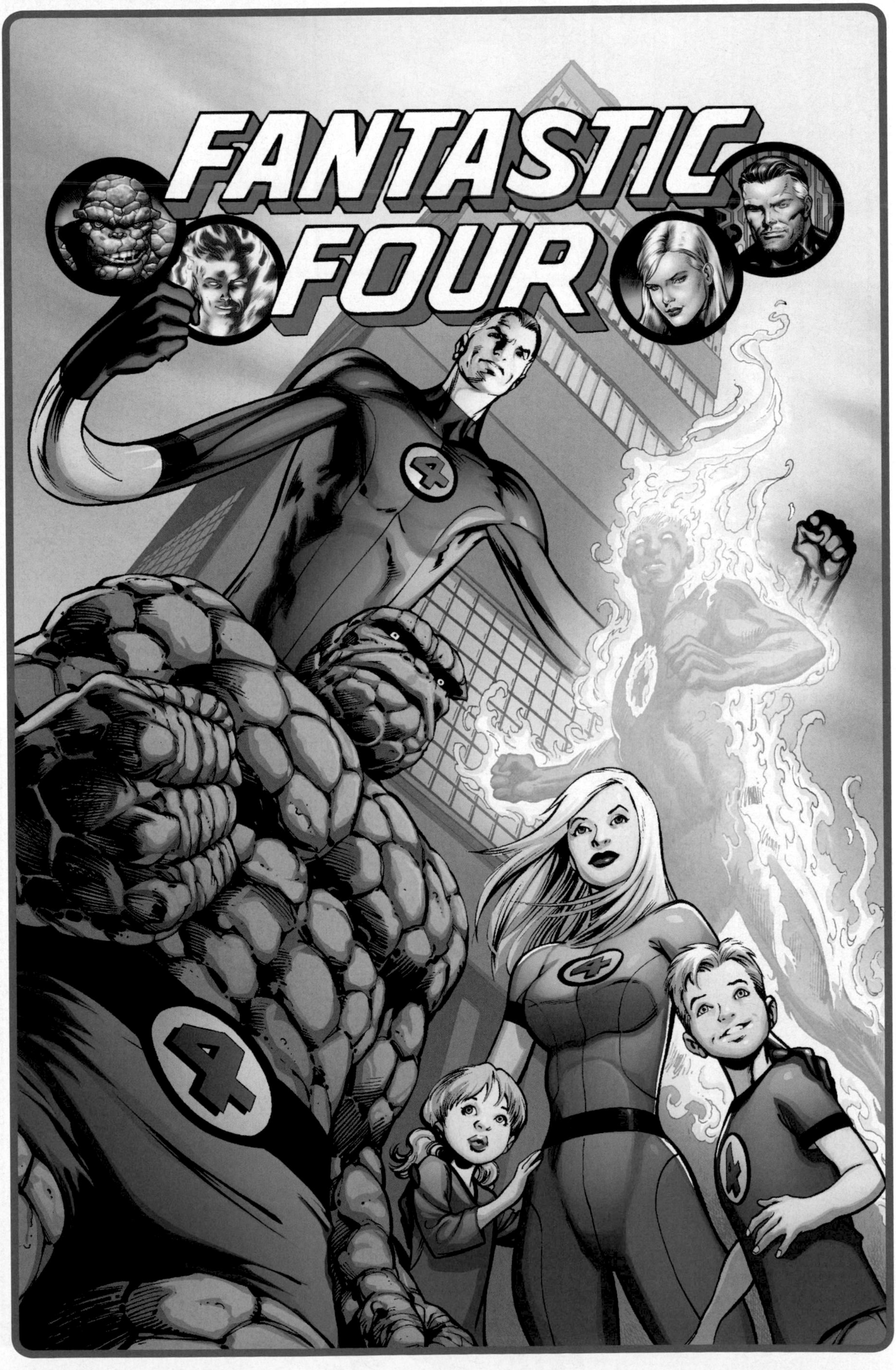
FANTASTIC
FOUR

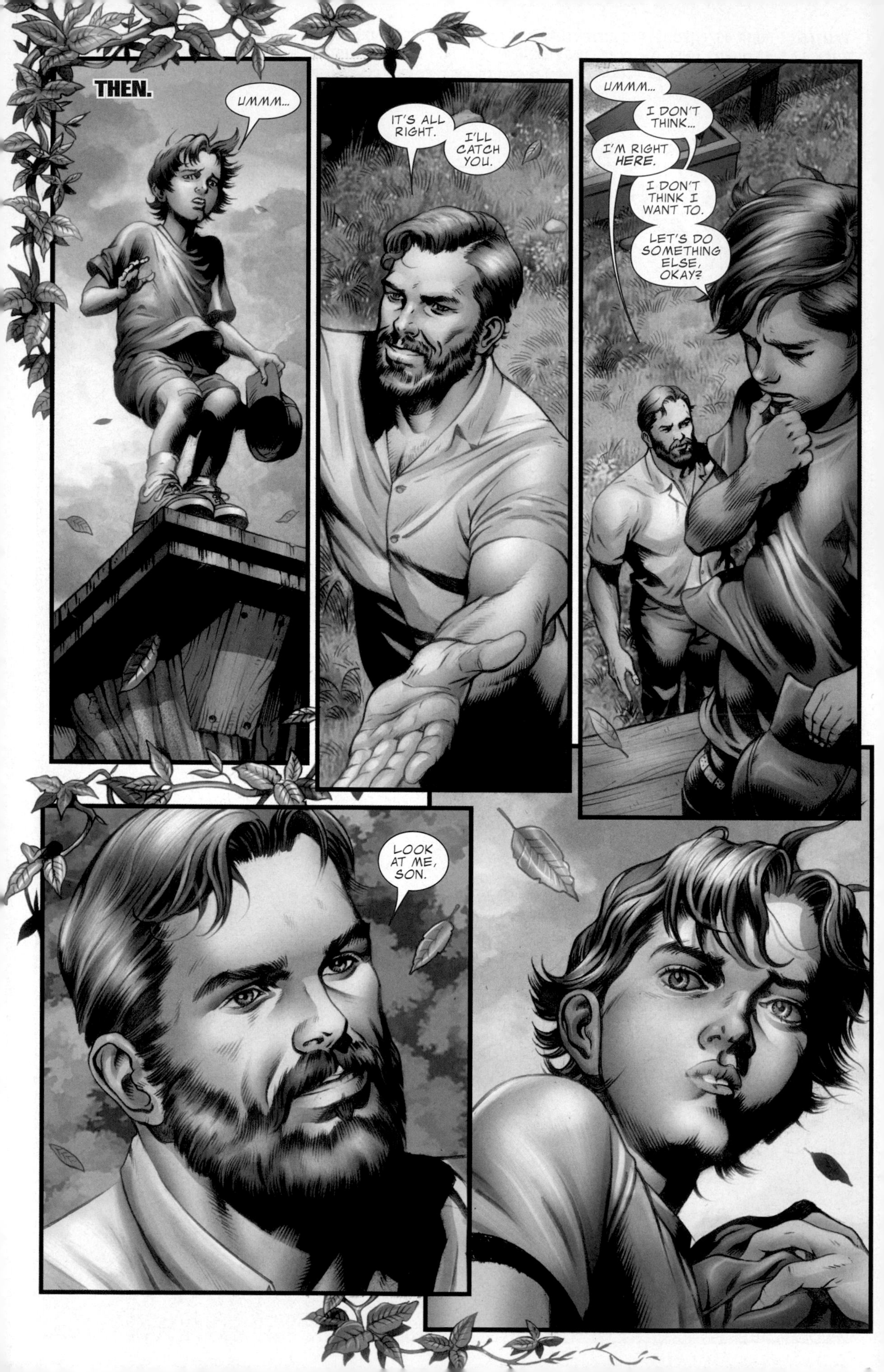
THEN.
UMMM...
IT'S ALL RIGHT.
I'LL CATCH YOU.
UMMM...
I DON'T THINK...
I'M RIGHT HERE.
I DON'T THINK I WANT TO.
LET'S DO SOMETHING ELSE, OKAY?
LOOK AT ME, SON.

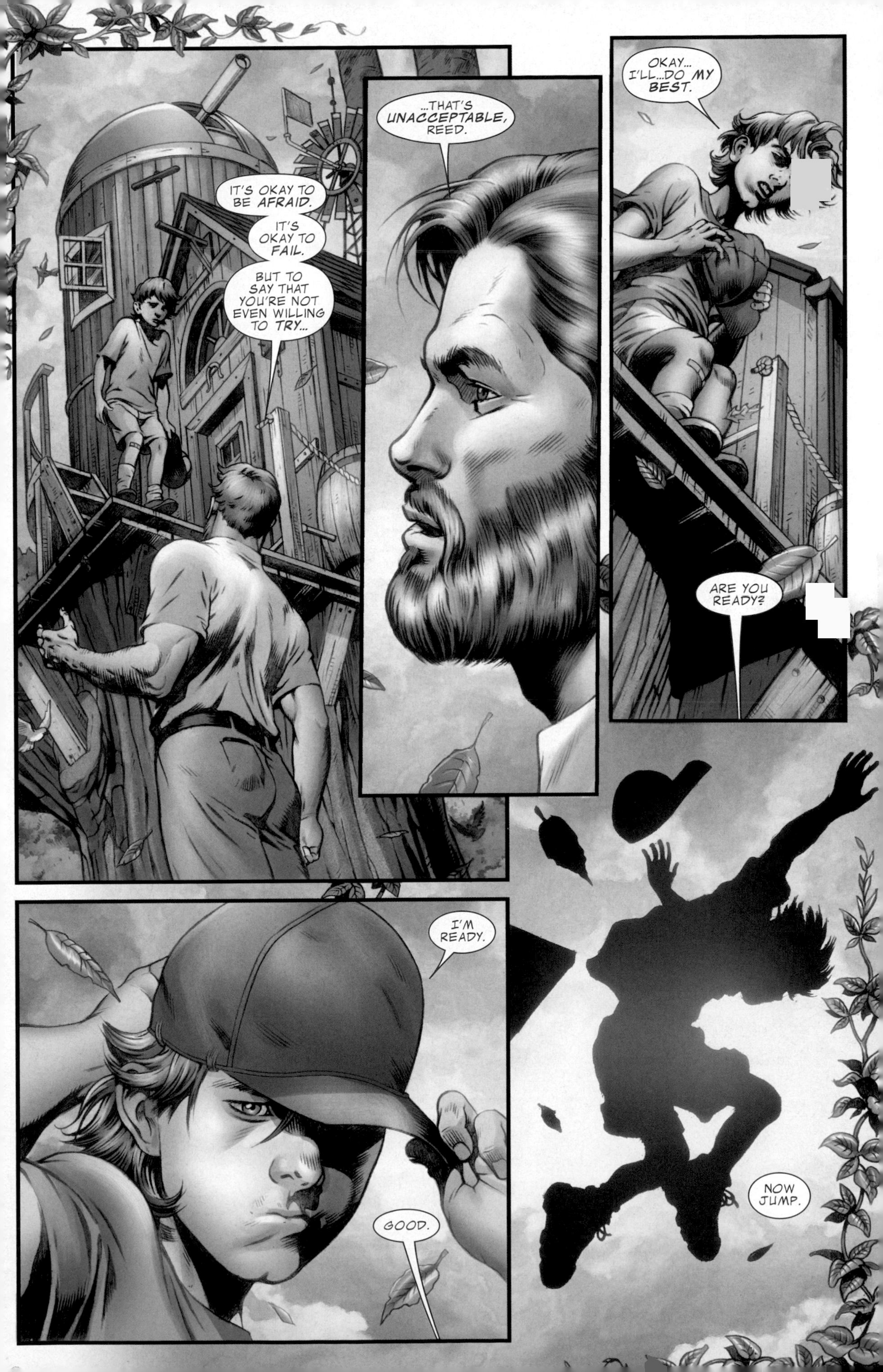
IT'S OKAY TO BE AFRAID.
IT'S OKAY TO FAIL.
BUT TO SAY THAT YOU'RE NOT EVEN WILLING TO TRY...
...THAT'S UNACCEPTABLE, REED.
OKAY... I'LL...DO MY BEST.
ARE YOU READY?
I'M READY.
GOOD.
NOW JUMP.

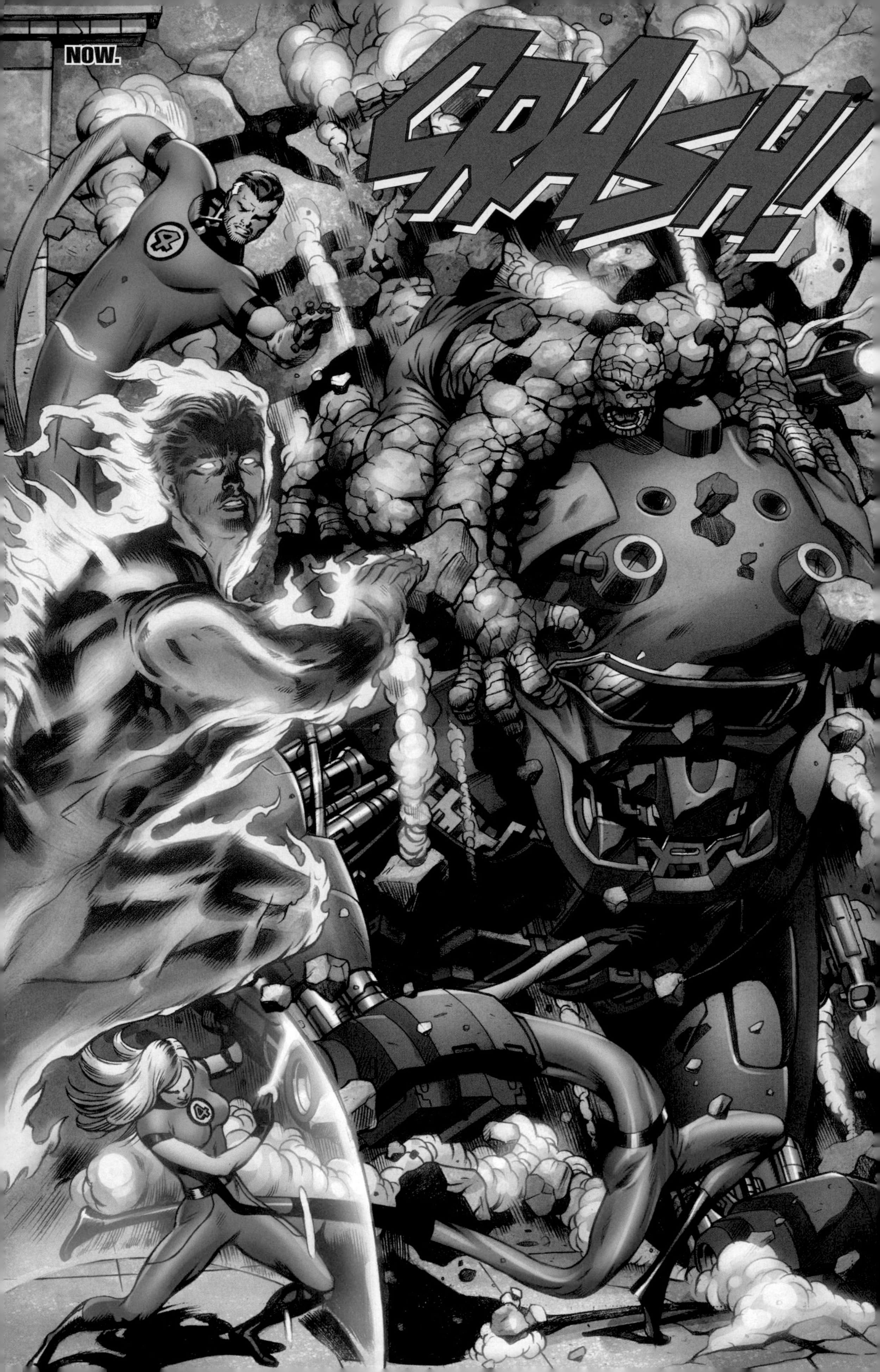
NOW.
CRASH!

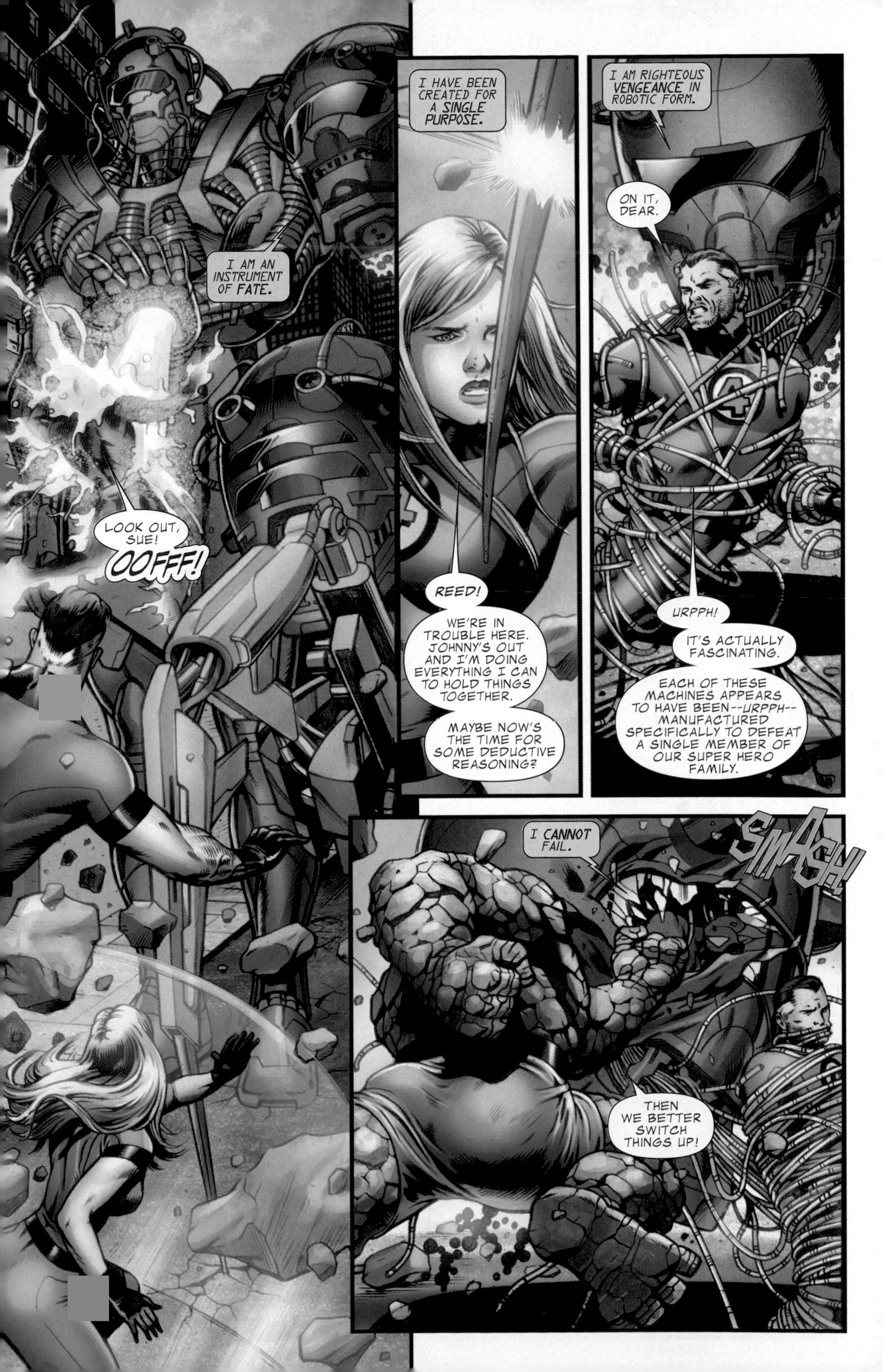
I AM AN INSTRUMENT OF FATE.
LOOK OUT, SUE!
OOFFF!
I HAVE BEEN CREATED FOR A SINGLE PURPOSE.
REED!
WE'RE IN TROUBLE HERE. JOHNNY'S OUT AND I'M DOING EVERYTHING I CAN TO HOLD THINGS TOGETHER.
MAYBE NOW'S THE TIME FOR SOME DEDUCTIVE REASONING?
I AM RIGHTEOUS VENGEANCE IN ROBOTIC FORM.
ON IT, DEAR.
URPPH!
IT'S ACTUALLY FASCINATING.
EACH OF THESE MACHINES APPEARS TO HAVE BEEN--URPPH--MANUFACTURED SPECIFICALLY TO DEFEAT A SINGLE MEMBER OF OUR SUPER HERO FAMILY.
I CANNOT FAIL.
SMASH!
THEN WE BETTER SWITCH THINGS UP!

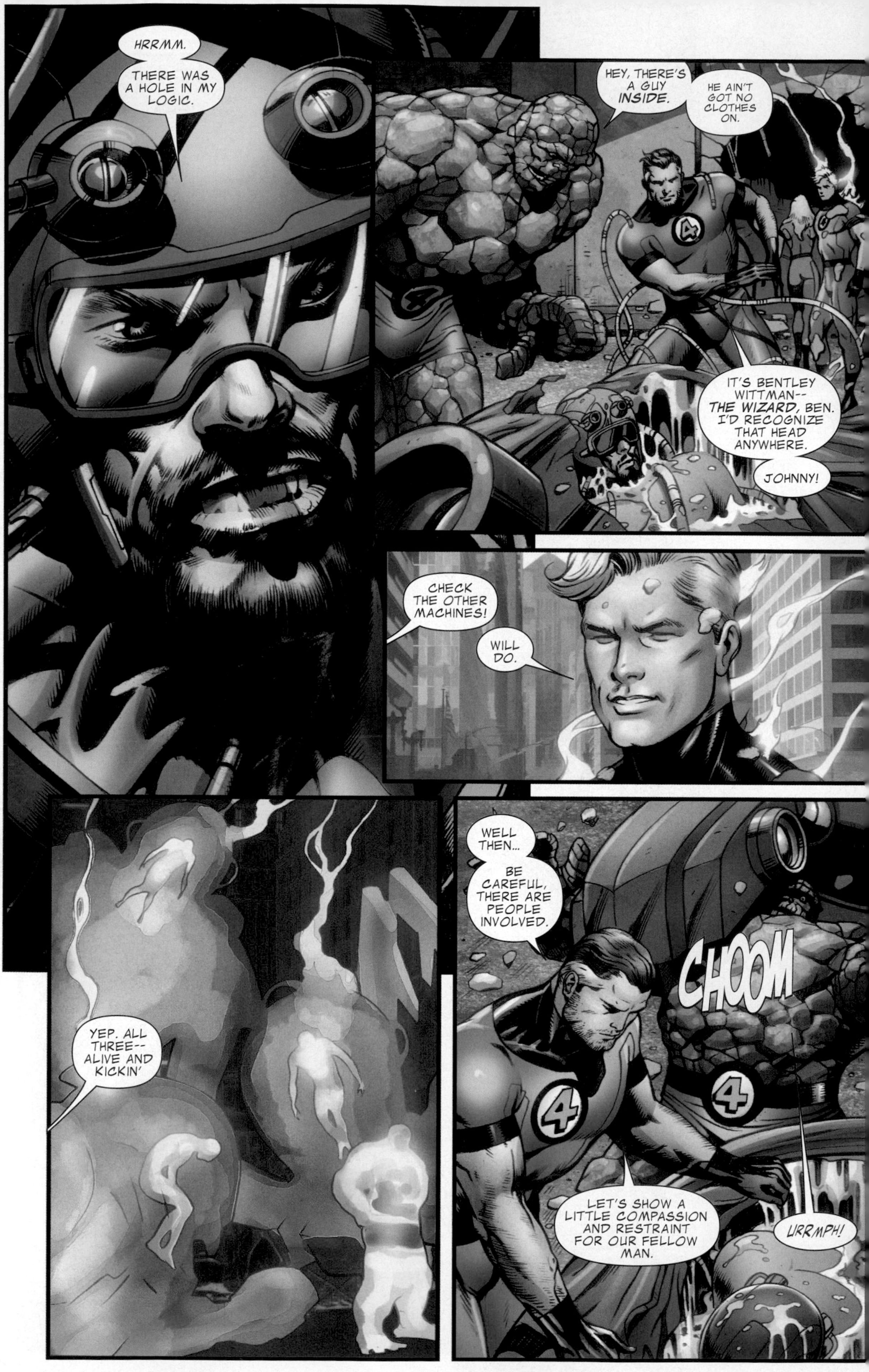
HRRMM.
THERE WAS A HOLE IN MY LOGIC.
HEY, THERE'S A GUY INSIDE.
HE AIN'T GOT NO CLOTHES ON.
IT'S BENTLEY WITTMAN-- THE WIZARD, BEN. I'D RECOGNIZE THAT HEAD ANYWHERE.
JOHNNY!
CHECK THE OTHER MACHINES!
WILL DO.
YEP. ALL THREE-- ALIVE AND KICKIN'
WELL THEN...
BE CAREFUL, THERE ARE PEOPLE INVOLVED.
CHOOM
LET'S SHOW A LITTLE COMPASSION AND RESTRAINT FOR OUR FELLOW MAN.
URRMPH!

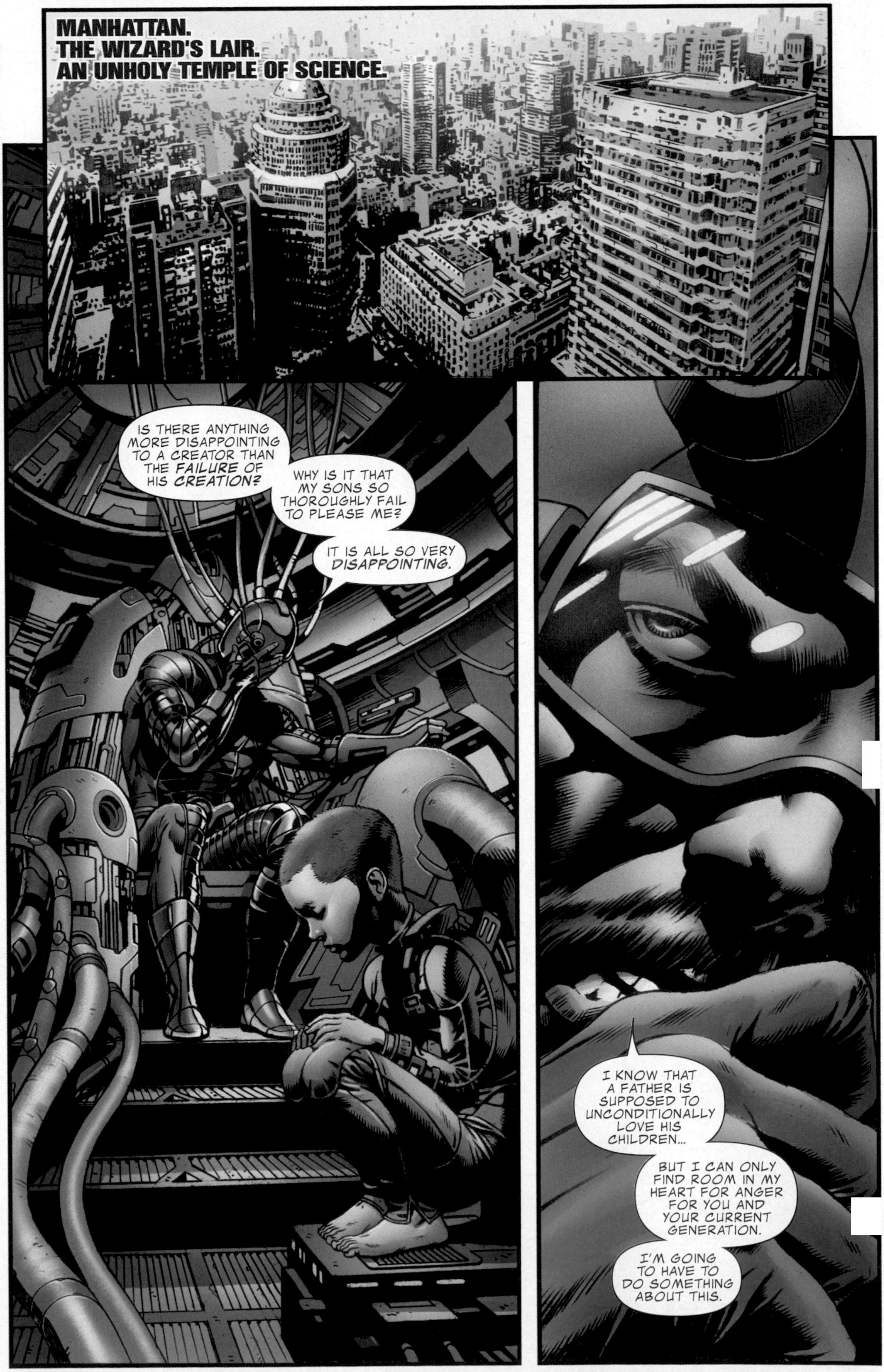
MANHATTAN.
THE WIZARD'S LAIR.
AN UNHOLY TEMPLE OF SCIENCE.
IS THERE ANYTHING MORE DISAPPOINTING TO A CREATOR THAN THE FAILURE OF HIS CREATION?
WHY IS IT THAT MY SONS SO THOROUGHLY FAIL TO PLEASE ME?
IT IS ALL SO VERY DISAPPOINTING.
I KNOW THAT A FATHER IS SUPPOSED TO UNCONDITIONALLY LOVE HIS CHILDREN...
BUT I CAN ONLY FIND ROOM IN MY HEART FOR ANGER FOR YOU AND YOUR CURRENT GENERATION.
I'M GOING TO HAVE TO DO SOMETHING ABOUT THIS.

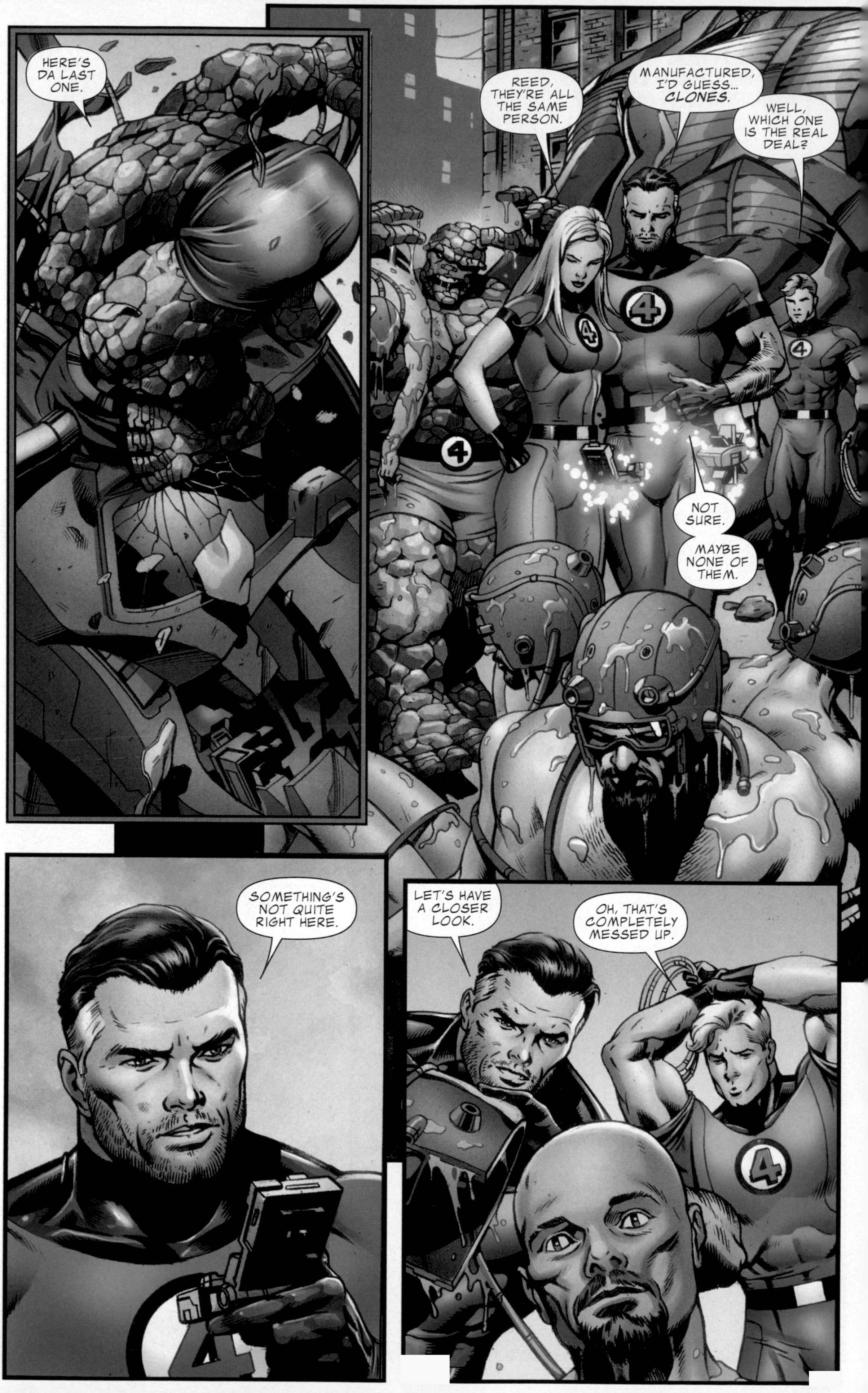
HERE'S DA LAST ONE.
REED, THEY'RE ALL THE SAME PERSON.
MANUFACTURED, I'D GUESS... CLONES.
WELL, WHICH ONE IS THE REAL DEAL?
NOT SURE.
MAYBE NONE OF THEM.
SOMETHING'S NOT QUITE RIGHT HERE.
LET'S HAVE A CLOSER LOOK.
OH, THAT'S COMPLETELY MESSED UP.

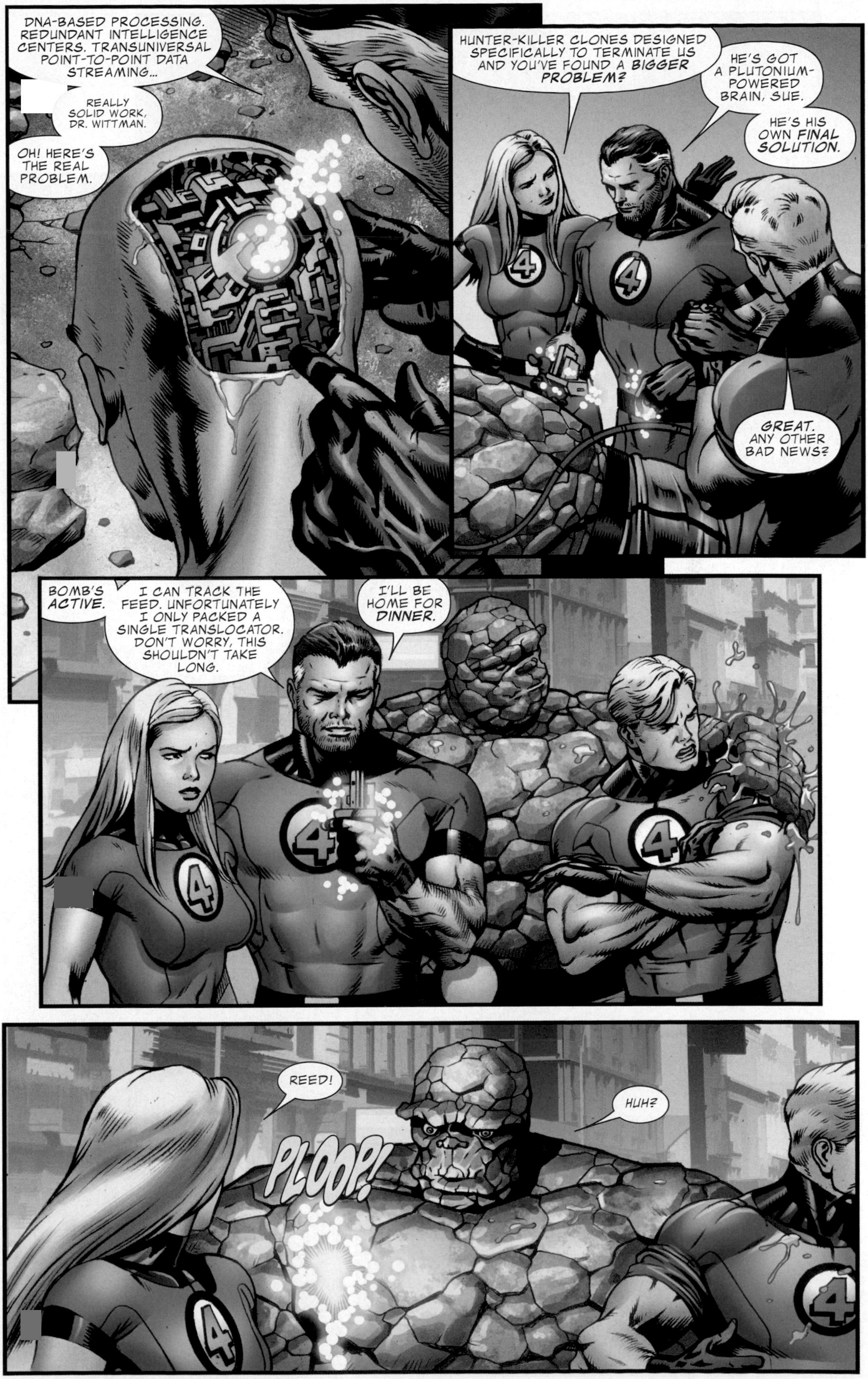

DNA-BASED PROCESSING. REDUNDANT INTELLIGENCE CENTERS. TRANSUNIVERSAL POINT-TO-POINT DATA STREAMING...
REALLY SOLID WORK, DR. WITTMAN.
OH! HERE'S THE REAL PROBLEM.
HUNTER-KILLER CLONES DESIGNED SPECIFICALLY TO TERMINATE US AND YOU'VE FOUND A BIGGER PROBLEM?
HE'S GOT A PLUTONIUM-POWERED BRAIN, SUE.
HE'S HIS OWN FINAL SOLUTION.
GREAT. ANY OTHER BAD NEWS?
BOMB'S ACTIVE.
I CAN TRACK THE FEED. UNFORTUNATELY I ONLY PACKED A SINGLE TRANSLOCATOR. DON'T WORRY, THIS SHOULDN'T TAKE LONG.
I'LL BE HOME FOR DINNER.
REED!
HUH?
PLOOP!

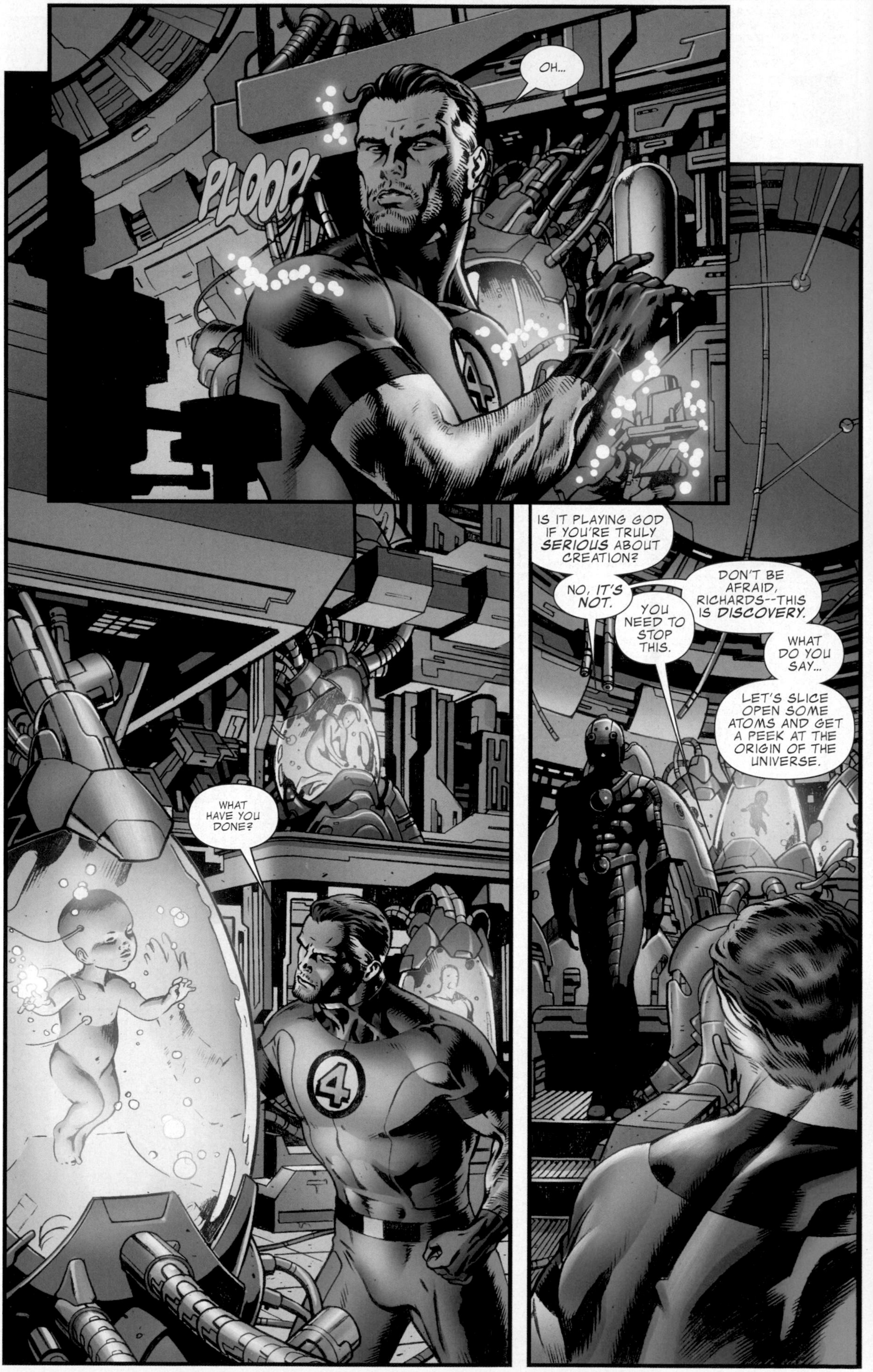
OH...
PLOOP!
WHAT HAVE YOU DONE?
IS IT PLAYING GOD IF YOU'RE TRULY SERIOUS ABOUT CREATION?
NO, IT'S NOT.
YOU NEED TO STOP THIS.
DON'T BE AFRAID, RICHARDS--THIS IS DISCOVERY.
WHAT DO YOU SAY...
LET'S SLICE OPEN SOME ATOMS AND GET A PEEK AT THE ORIGIN OF THE UNIVERSE.

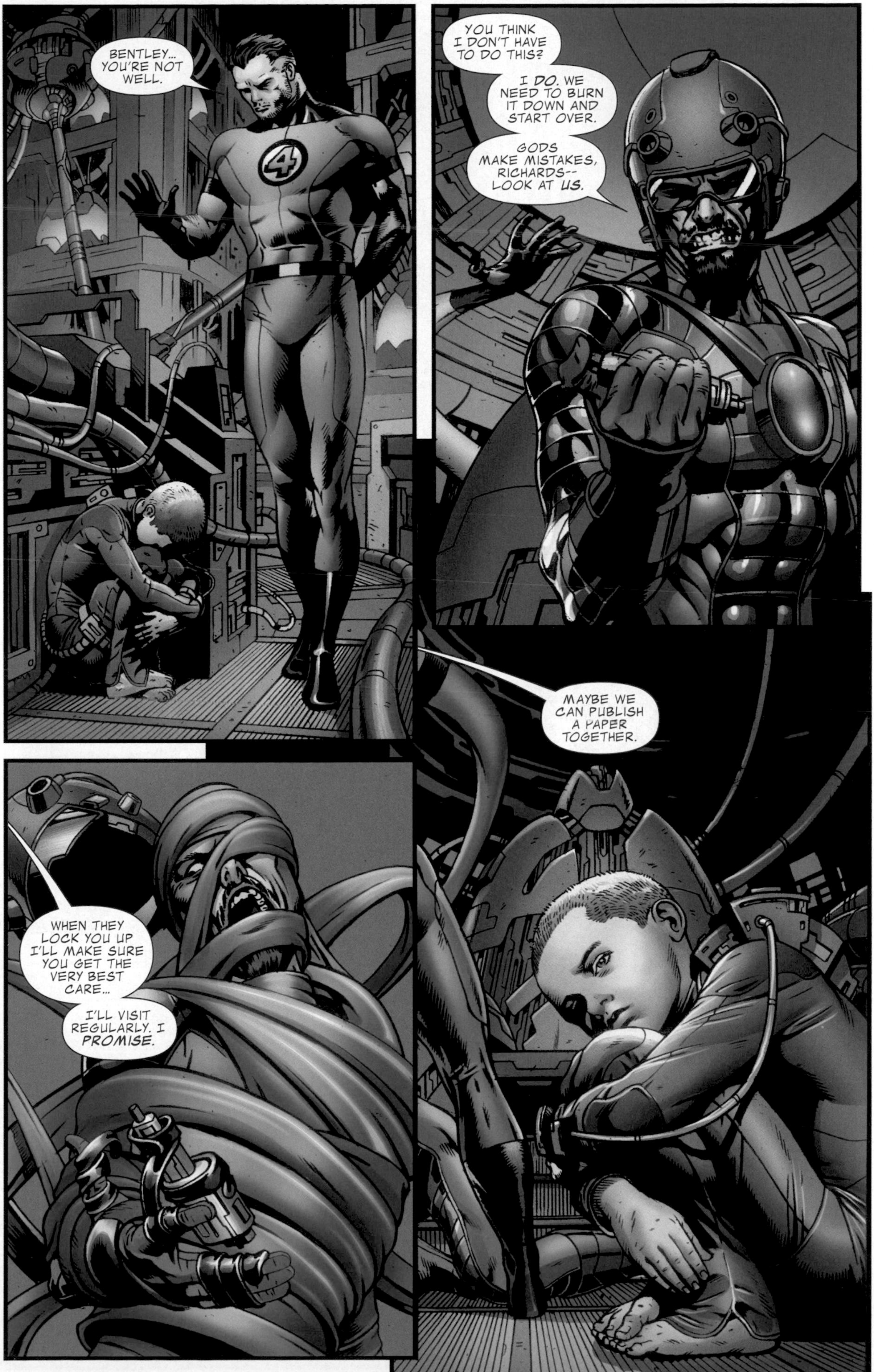
BENTLEY... YOU'RE NOT WELL.
YOU THINK I DON'T HAVE TO DO THIS?
I DO. WE NEED TO BURN IT DOWN AND START OVER.
GODS MAKE MISTAKES, RICHARDS-- LOOK AT US.
MAYBE WE CAN PUBLISH A PAPER TOGETHER.
WHEN THEY LOCK YOU UP I'LL MAKE SURE YOU GET THE VERY BEST CARE...
I'LL VISIT REGULARLY. I PROMISE.

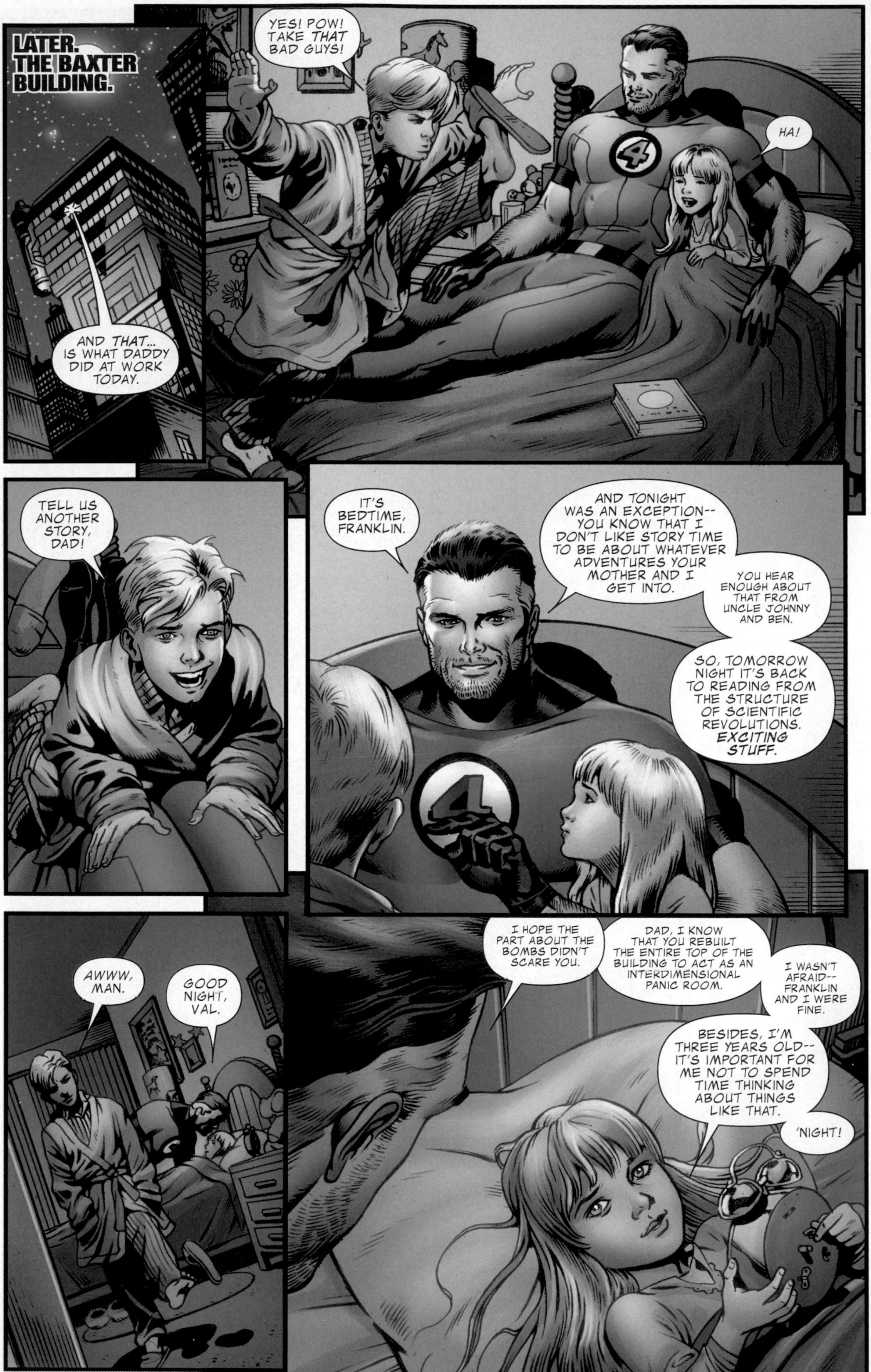
LATER. THE BAXTER BUILDING.
AND THAT... IS WHAT DADDY DID AT WORK TODAY.
YES! POW! TAKE THAT BAD GUYS!
HA!
TELL US ANOTHER STORY, DAD!
IT'S BEDTIME, FRANKLIN.
AND TONIGHT WAS AN EXCEPTION-- YOU KNOW THAT I DON'T LIKE STORY TIME TO BE ABOUT WHATEVER ADVENTURES YOUR MOTHER AND I GET INTO.
YOU HEAR ENOUGH ABOUT THAT FROM UNCLE JOHNNY AND BEN.
SO, TOMORROW NIGHT IT'S BACK TO READING FROM THE STRUCTURE OF SCIENTIFIC REVOLUTIONS. EXCITING STUFF.
AWWW, MAN.
GOOD NIGHT, VAL.
I HOPE THE PART ABOUT THE BOMBS DIDN'T SCARE YOU.
DAD, I KNOW THAT YOU REBUILT THE ENTIRE TOP OF THE BUILDING TO ACT AS AN INTERDIMENSIONAL PANIC ROOM.
I WASN'T AFRAID-- FRANKLIN AND I WERE FINE.
BESIDES, I'M THREE YEARS OLD-- IT'S IMPORTANT FOR ME NOT TO SPEND TIME THINKING ABOUT THINGS LIKE THAT.
'NIGHT!

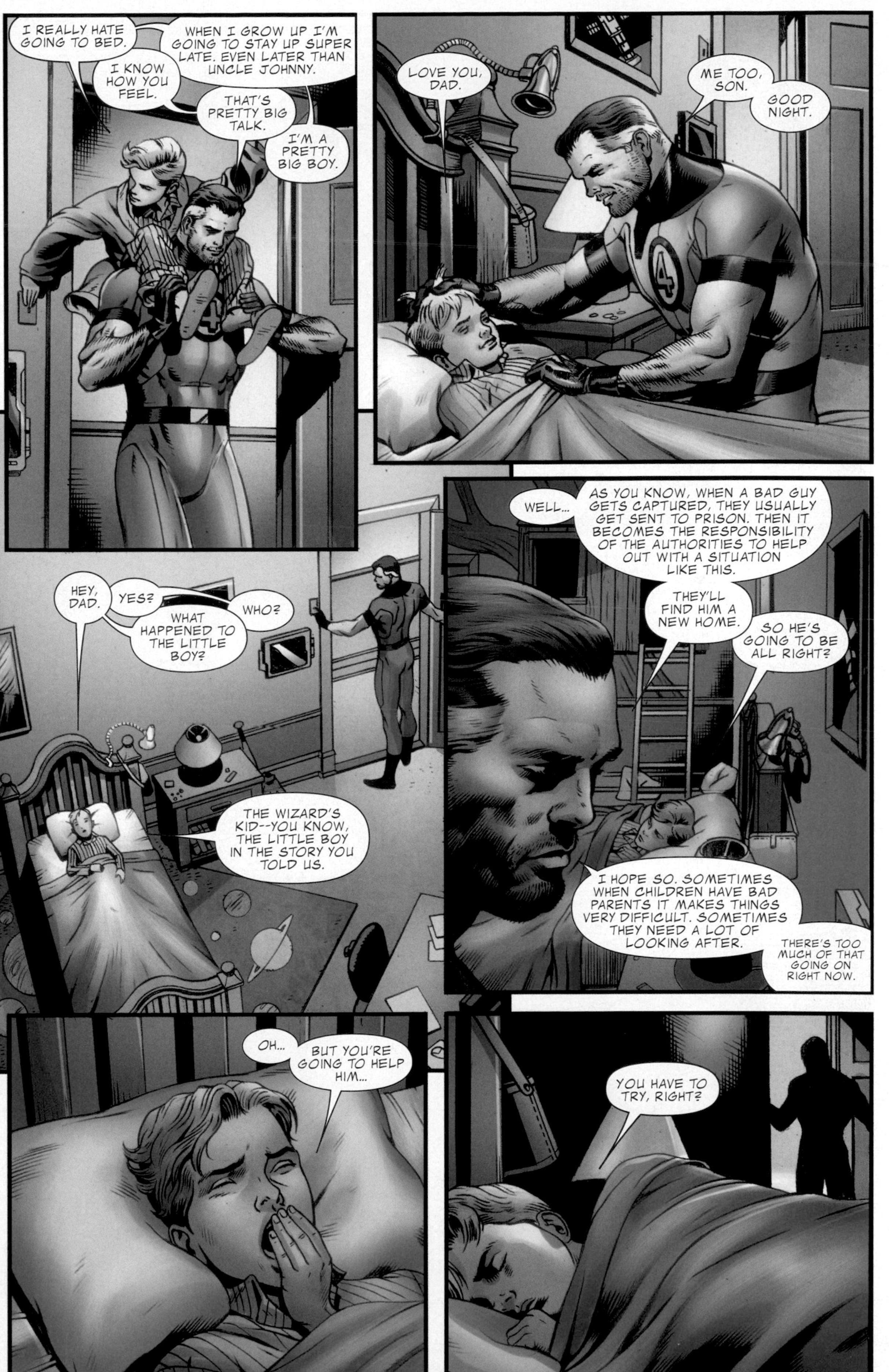
I REALLY HATE GOING TO BED.
WHEN I GROW UP I'M GOING TO STAY UP SUPER LATE. EVEN LATER THAN UNCLE JOHNNY.
I KNOW HOW YOU FEEL.
THAT'S PRETTY BIG TALK.
I'M A PRETTY BIG BOY.
LOVE YOU, DAD.
ME TOO, SON.
GOOD NIGHT.
HEY, DAD.
YES?
WHAT HAPPENED TO THE LITTLE BOY?
WHO?
THE WIZARD'S KID--YOU KNOW, THE LITTLE BOY IN THE STORY YOU TOLD US.
WELL...
AS YOU KNOW, WHEN A BAD GUY GETS CAPTURED, THEY USUALLY GET SENT TO PRISON. THEN IT BECOMES THE RESPONSIBILITY OF THE AUTHORITIES TO HELP OUT WITH A SITUATION LIKE THIS.
THEY'LL FIND HIM A NEW HOME.
SO HE'S GOING TO BE ALL RIGHT?
I HOPE SO. SOMETIMES WHEN CHILDREN HAVE BAD PARENTS IT MAKES THINGS VERY DIFFICULT. SOMETIMES THEY NEED A LOT OF LOOKING AFTER.
THERE'S TOO MUCH OF THAT GOING ON RIGHT NOW.
OH...
BUT YOU'RE GOING TO HELP HIM...
YOU HAVE TO TRY, RIGHT?

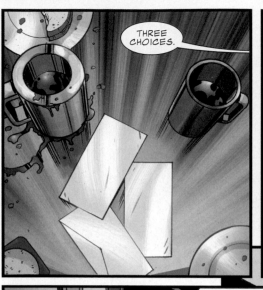

THREE CHOICES.

IN EACH ENVELOPE IS AN ALL-EXPENSES-PAID VACATION. EACH ONE TO A LUXURIOUS, REMOTE AND SECLUDED LOCATION.

IT'S TIME TO CHOOSE, CONTESTANT NUMBER ONE--WHAT'S IT GOING TO BE?

I DUNNO ABOUT THIS.

WHAT'S TO KNOW?

YOU'RE UGLY, YOU'RE LONELY AND YOU'VE JUST HAD YOUR HEART BROKEN. TIME TO GET OUTTA TOWN, MAN.

PICK.

OKAY. UHH, DAT ONE.

KIDS ARE IN BED.

THANKS.

VAL FIGURED OUT THE CHANGES I MADE TO THE BUILDING.

HOW DID...

YOU SHOULD PLAN ON GETTING USED TO IT, SUSAN.

SHE'S GOING TO BE MUCH SMARTER THAN I AM.

WINNER, WINNER. CHICKEN DINNER!

3 DAYS, 2 NIGHTS ON BEAUTIFUL NU-WORLD WITH SUPER HERO/ CELEBRITY JOHNNY STORM.

OH, AND WHAT'S THIS, PRIZE INCLUDES FRUIT BASKET AND A SELECTION OF SCENTED OILS AND OTHER FINE BATH PRODUCTS.

VERY NICE, BENNY. WELL DONE.

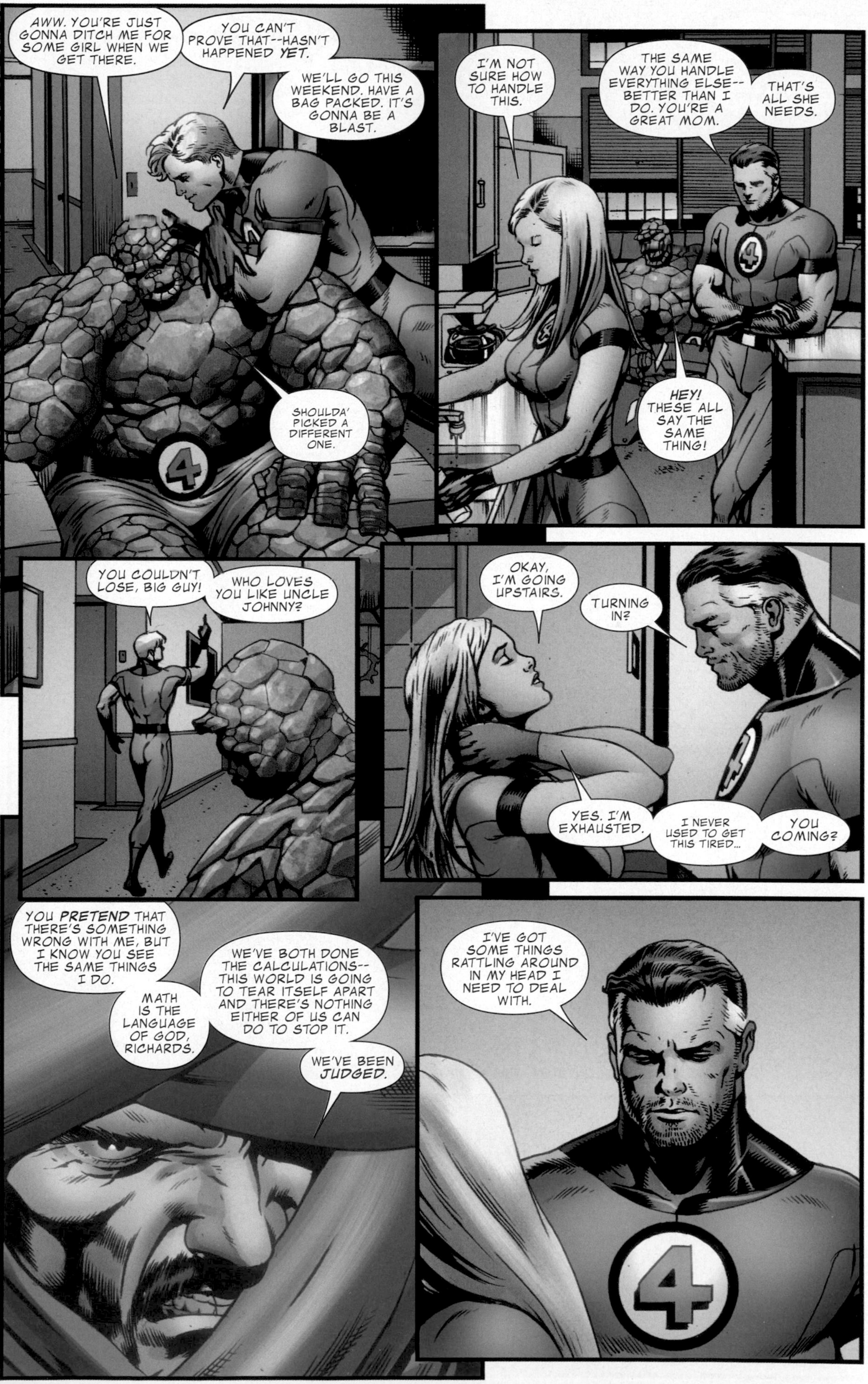

AWW. YOU'RE JUST GONNA DITCH ME FOR SOME GIRL WHEN WE GET THERE.
YOU CAN'T PROVE THAT--HASN'T HAPPENED *YET.*
WE'LL GO THIS WEEKEND. HAVE A BAG PACKED. IT'S GONNA BE A BLAST.
SHOULDA' PICKED A DIFFERENT ONE.
I'M NOT SURE HOW TO HANDLE THIS.
THE SAME WAY YOU HANDLE EVERYTHING ELSE--BETTER THAN I DO. YOU'RE A GREAT MOM.
THAT'S ALL SHE NEEDS.
HEY! THESE ALL SAY THE SAME THING!
YOU COULDN'T LOSE, BIG GUY!
WHO LOVES YOU LIKE UNCLE JOHNNY?
OKAY, I'M GOING UPSTAIRS.
TURNING IN?
YES. I'M EXHAUSTED.
I NEVER USED TO GET THIS TIRED...
YOU COMING?
YOU **PRETEND** THAT THERE'S SOMETHING WRONG WITH ME, BUT I KNOW YOU SEE THE SAME THINGS I DO.
MATH IS THE LANGUAGE OF GOD, RICHARDS.
WE'VE BOTH DONE THE CALCULATIONS--THIS WORLD IS GOING TO TEAR ITSELF APART AND THERE'S NOTHING EITHER OF US CAN DO TO STOP IT.
WE'VE BEEN *JUDGED.*
I'VE GOT SOME THINGS RATTLING AROUND IN MY HEAD I NEED TO DEAL WITH.

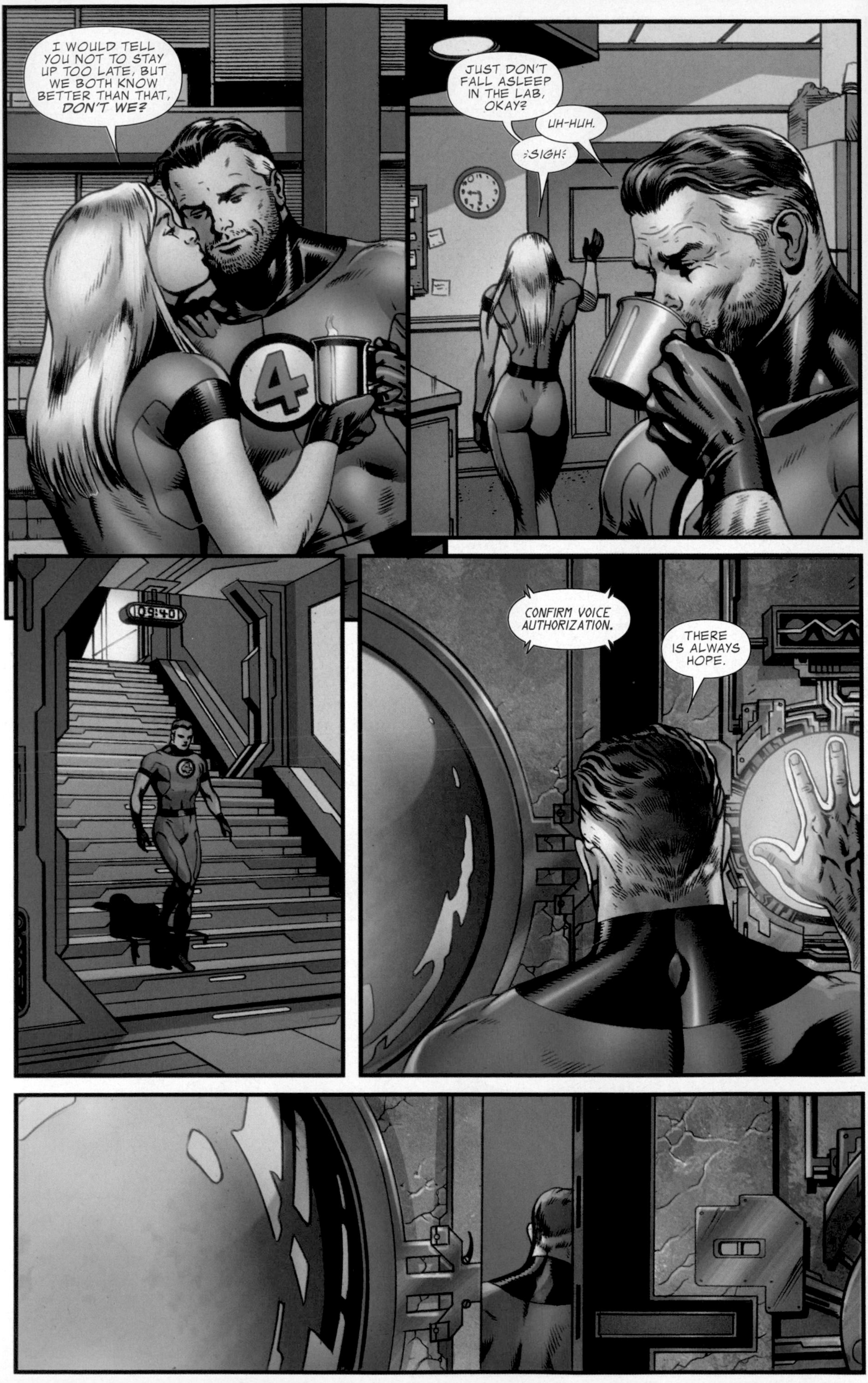
I WOULD TELL YOU NOT TO STAY UP TOO LATE, BUT WE BOTH KNOW BETTER THAN THAT, *DON'T WE?*
JUST DON'T FALL ASLEEP IN THE LAB, OKAY?
UH-HUH.
SIGH
09:40
CONFIRM VOICE AUTHORIZATION.
THERE IS ALWAYS HOPE.

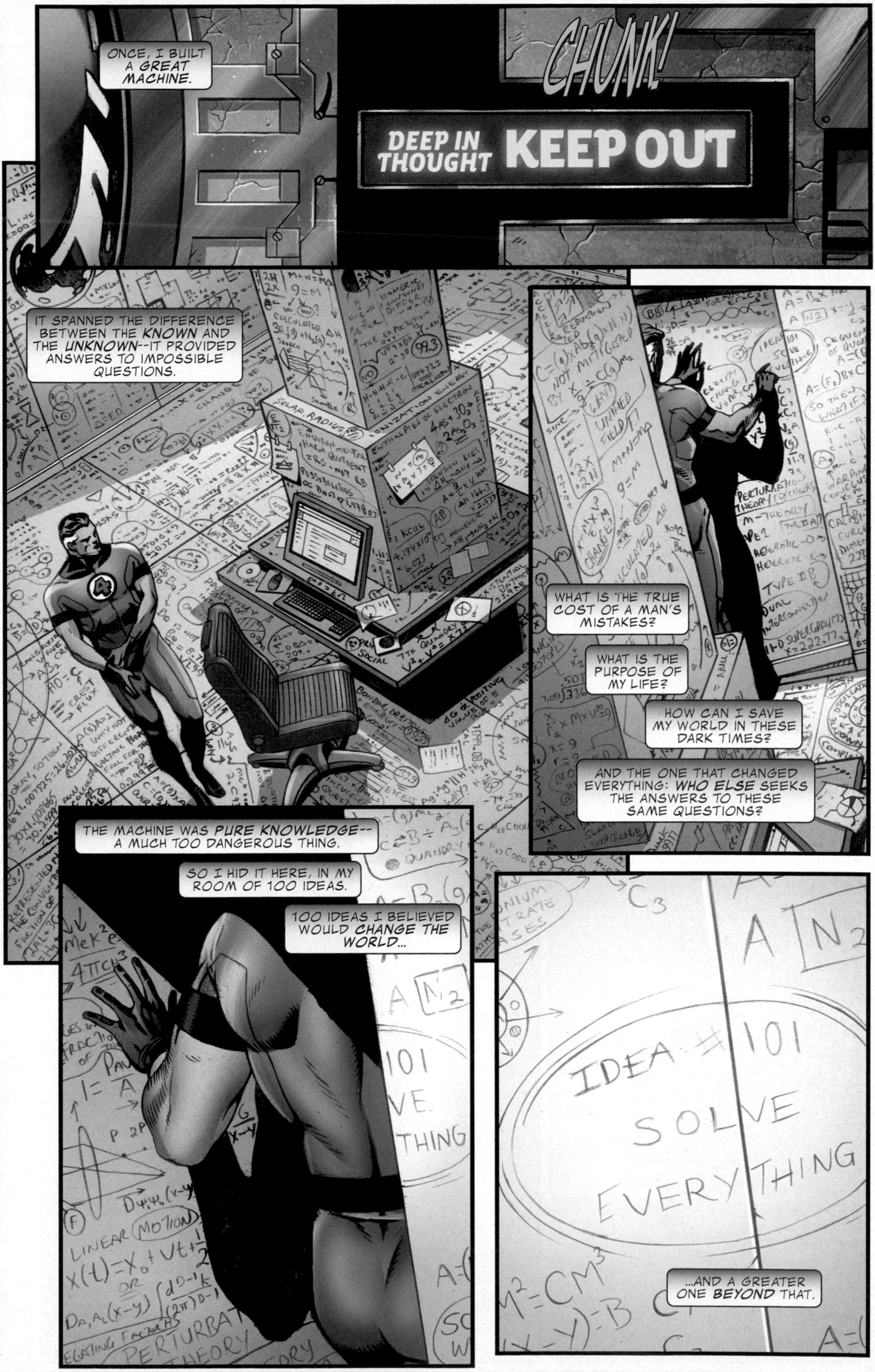

ONCE, I BUILT A GREAT MACHINE.
CHUNK!
DEEP IN THOUGHT
KEEP OUT
IT SPANNED THE DIFFERENCE BETWEEN THE KNOWN AND THE UNKNOWN--IT PROVIDED ANSWERS TO IMPOSSIBLE QUESTIONS.
WHAT IS THE TRUE COST OF A MAN'S MISTAKES?
WHAT IS THE PURPOSE OF MY LIFE?
HOW CAN I SAVE MY WORLD IN THESE DARK TIMES?
AND THE ONE THAT CHANGED EVERYTHING: WHO ELSE SEEKS THE ANSWERS TO THESE SAME QUESTIONS?
THE MACHINE WAS PURE KNOWLEDGE-- A MUCH TOO DANGEROUS THING.
SO I HID IT HERE, IN MY ROOM OF 100 IDEAS.
100 IDEAS I BELIEVED WOULD CHANGE THE WORLD...
IDEA #101
SOLVE
EVERYTHING
...AND A GREATER ONE BEYOND THAT.

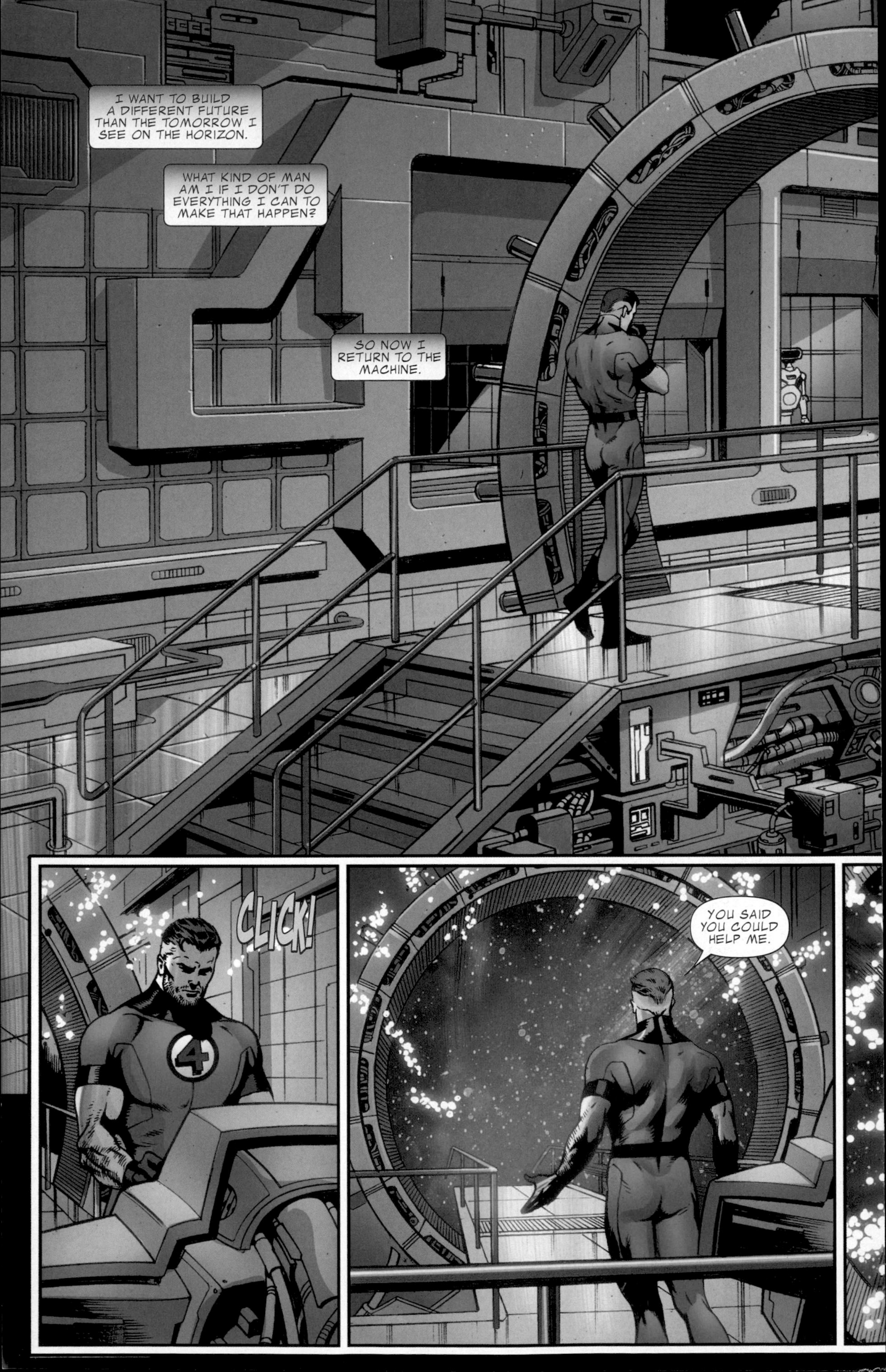
I WANT TO BUILD A DIFFERENT FUTURE THAN THE TOMORROW I SEE ON THE HORIZON.
WHAT KIND OF MAN AM I IF I DON'T DO EVERYTHING I CAN TO MAKE THAT HAPPEN?
SO NOW I RETURN TO THE MACHINE.
CLICK!
YOU SAID YOU COULD HELP ME.

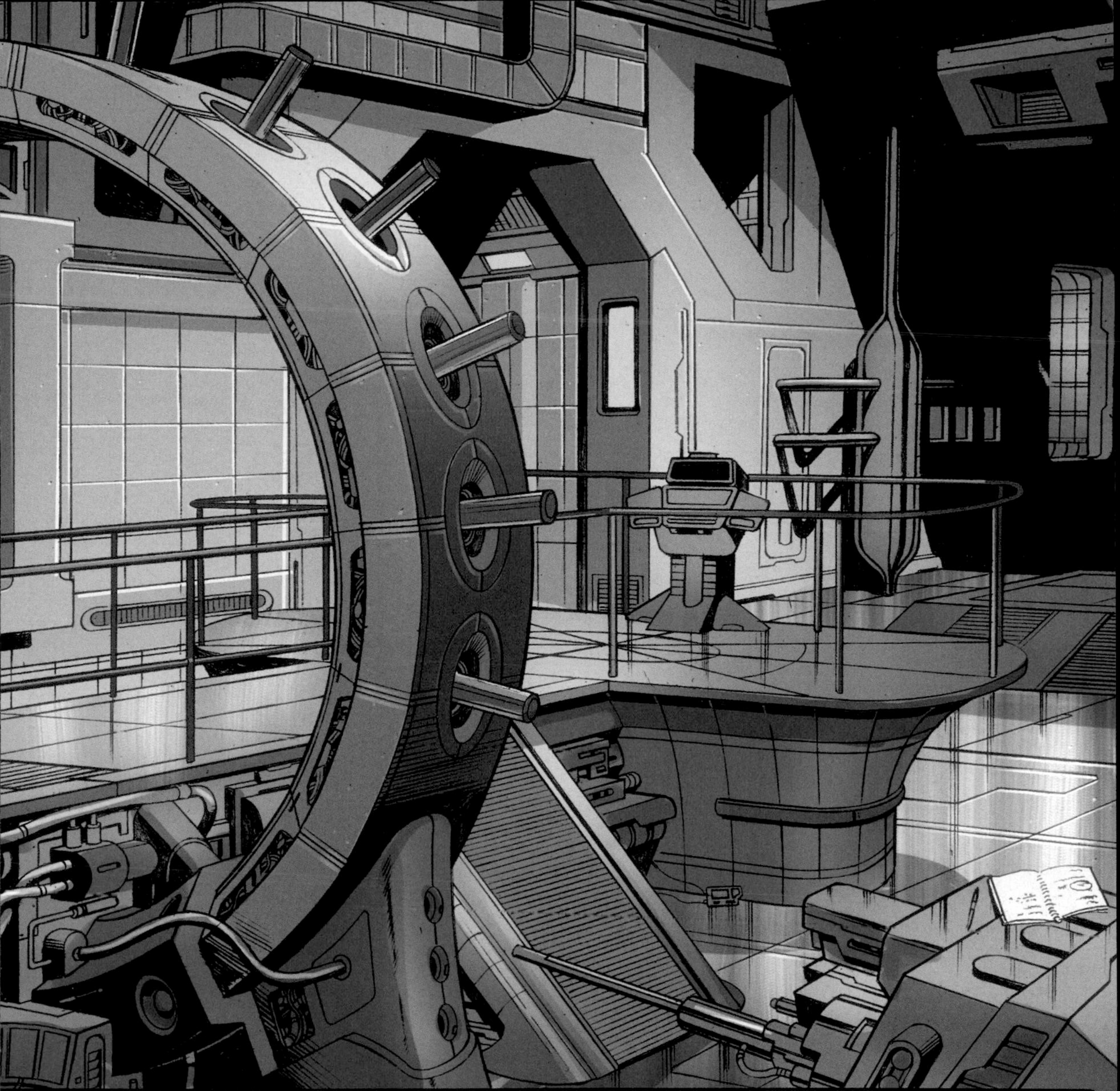

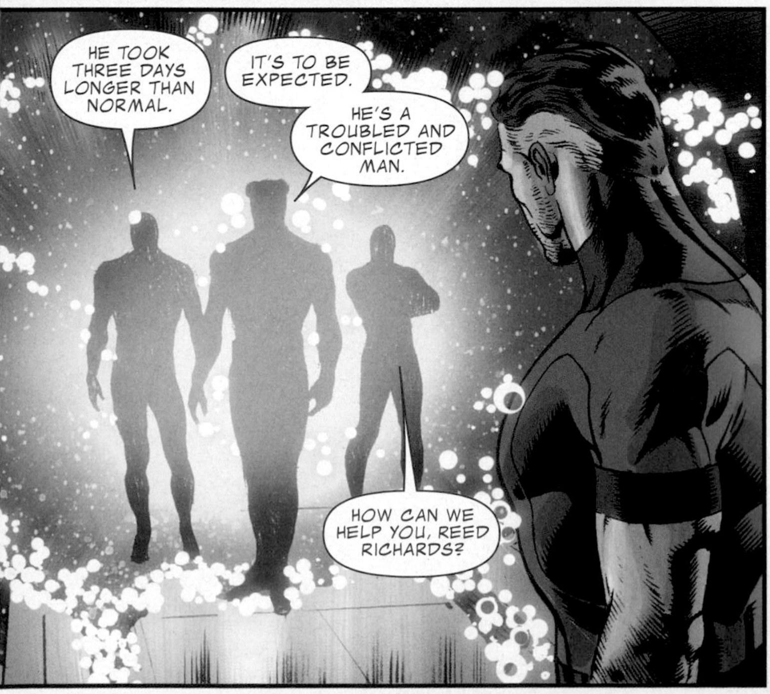
HE TOOK THREE DAYS LONGER THAN NORMAL.
IT'S TO BE EXPECTED.
HE'S A TROUBLED AND CONFLICTED MAN.
HOW CAN WE HELP YOU, REED RICHARDS?

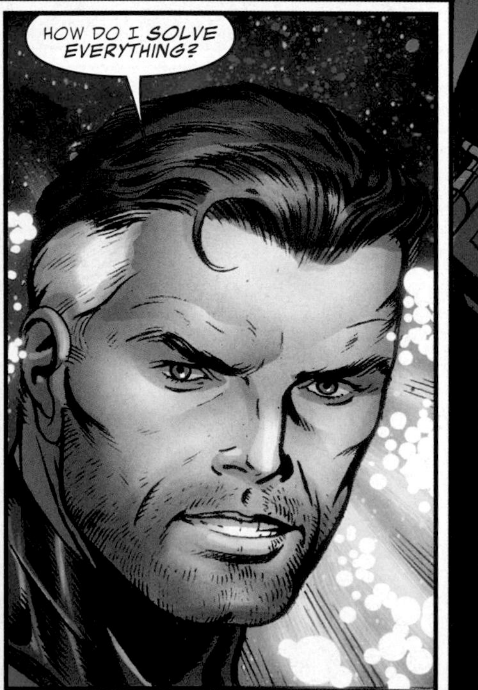
HOW DO I SOLVE EVERYTHING?

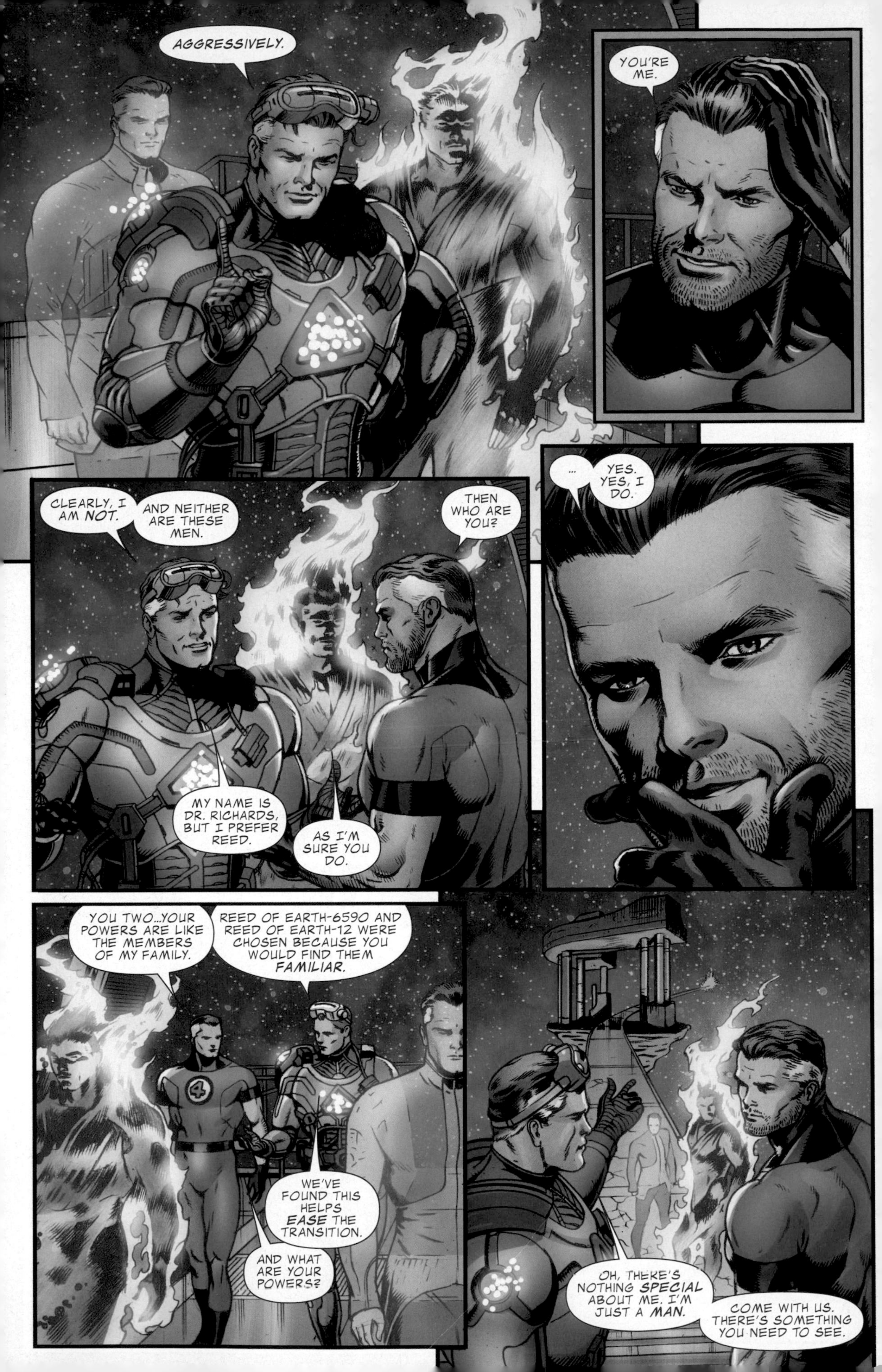
AGGRESSIVELY.
YOU'RE ME.
CLEARLY, I AM NOT.
AND NEITHER ARE THESE MEN.
THEN WHO ARE YOU?
MY NAME IS DR. RICHARDS, BUT I PREFER REED.
AS I'M SURE YOU DO.
... YES. YES, I DO.
YOU TWO...YOUR POWERS ARE LIKE THE MEMBERS OF MY FAMILY.
REED OF EARTH-6590 AND REED OF EARTH-12 WERE CHOSEN BECAUSE YOU WOULD FIND THEM FAMILIAR.
WE'VE FOUND THIS HELPS EASE THE TRANSITION.
AND WHAT ARE YOUR POWERS?
OH, THERE'S NOTHING SPECIAL ABOUT ME. I'M JUST A MAN.
COME WITH US. THERE'S SOMETHING YOU NEED TO SEE.

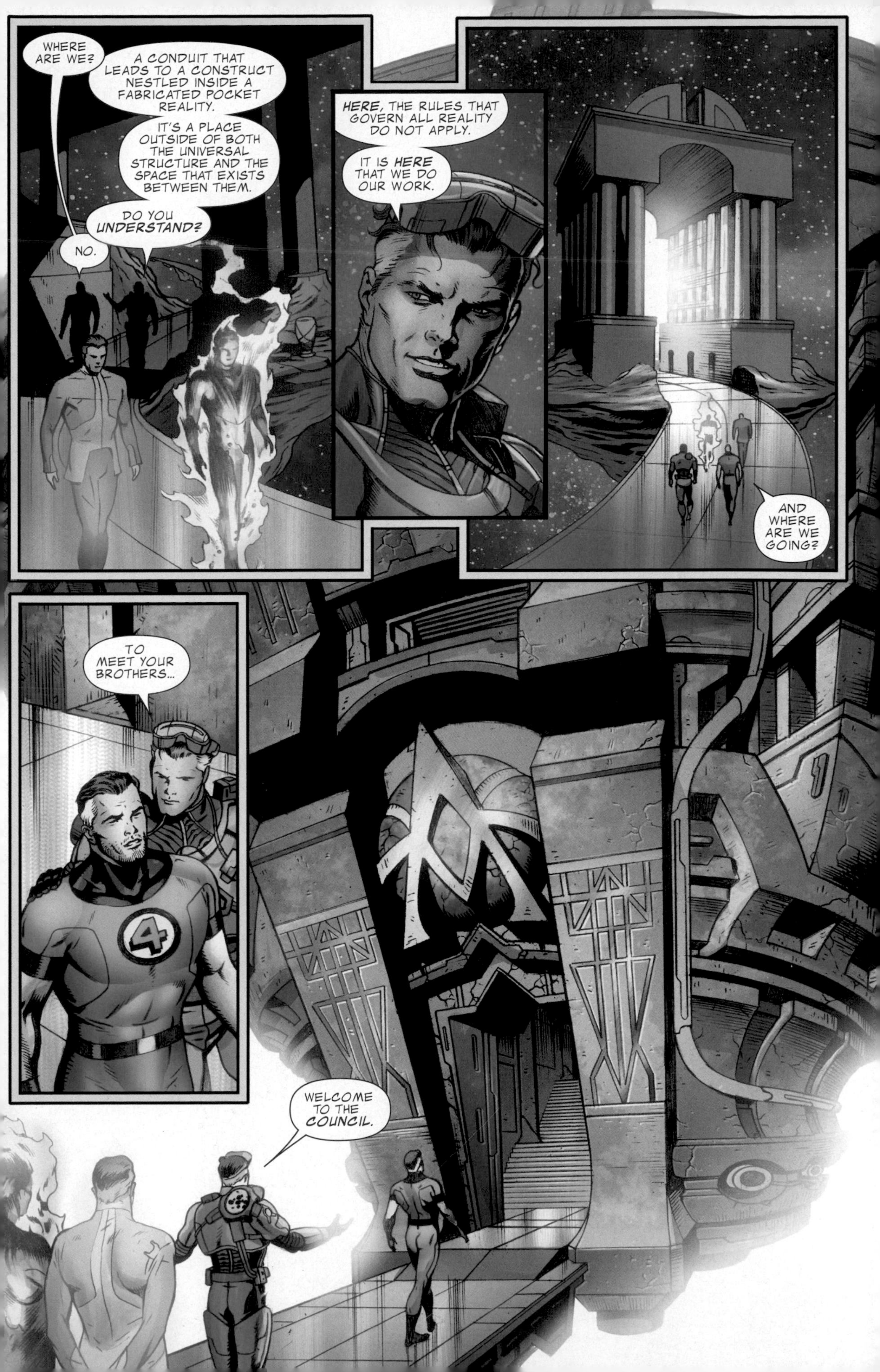

WHERE ARE WE?
A CONDUIT THAT LEADS TO A CONSTRUCT NESTLED INSIDE A FABRICATED POCKET REALITY.
IT'S A PLACE OUTSIDE OF BOTH THE UNIVERSAL STRUCTURE AND THE SPACE THAT EXISTS BETWEEN THEM.
DO YOU UNDERSTAND?
NO.
HERE, THE RULES THAT GOVERN ALL REALITY DO NOT APPLY.
IT IS HERE THAT WE DO OUR WORK.
AND WHERE ARE WE GOING?
TO MEET YOUR BROTHERS...
WELCOME TO THE COUNCIL.

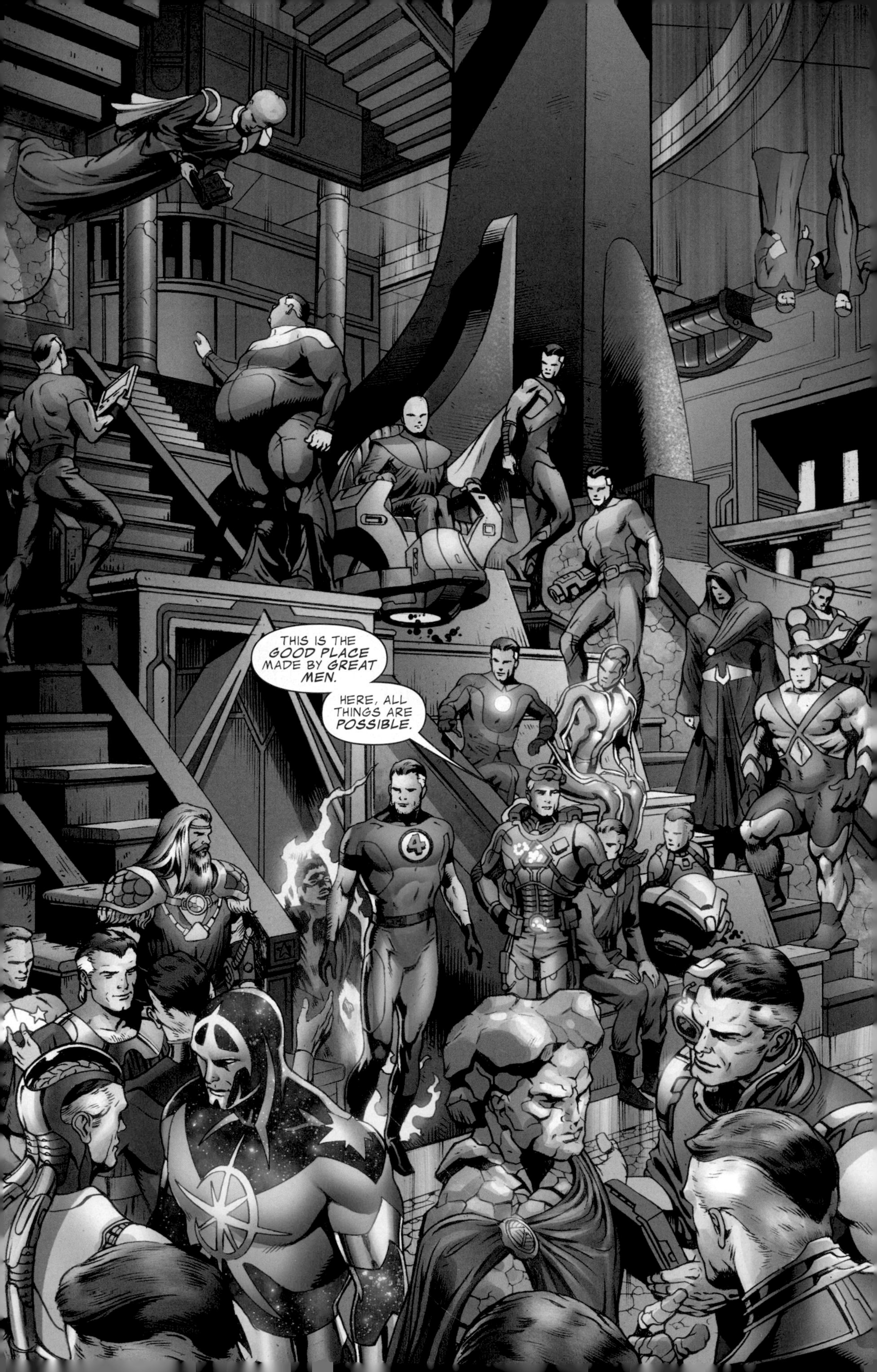
THIS IS THE GOOD PLACE MADE BY GREAT MEN.
HERE, ALL THINGS ARE POSSIBLE.

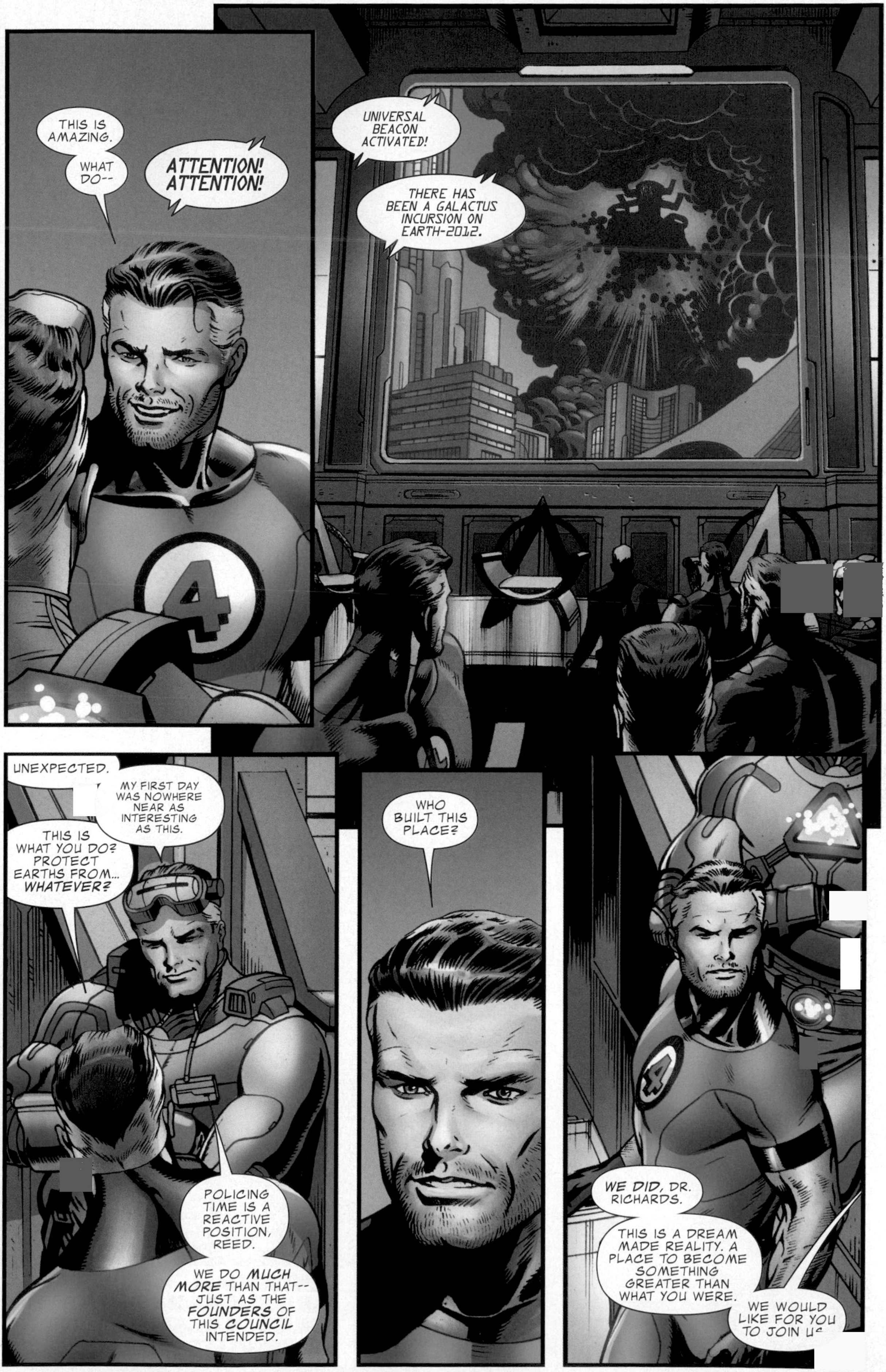
THIS IS AMAZING.
WHAT DO--
ATTENTION! ATTENTION!
UNIVERSAL BEACON ACTIVATED!
THERE HAS BEEN A GALACTUS INCURSION ON EARTH-2012.
UNEXPECTED.
MY FIRST DAY WAS NOWHERE NEAR AS INTERESTING AS THIS.
THIS IS WHAT YOU DO? PROTECT EARTHS FROM... WHATEVER?
POLICING TIME IS A REACTIVE POSITION, REED.
WE DO MUCH MORE THAN THAT-- JUST AS THE FOUNDERS OF THIS COUNCIL INTENDED.
WHO BUILT THIS PLACE?
WE DID, DR. RICHARDS.
THIS IS A DREAM MADE REALITY. A PLACE TO BECOME SOMETHING GREATER THAN WHAT YOU WERE.
WE WOULD LIKE FOR YOU TO JOIN US

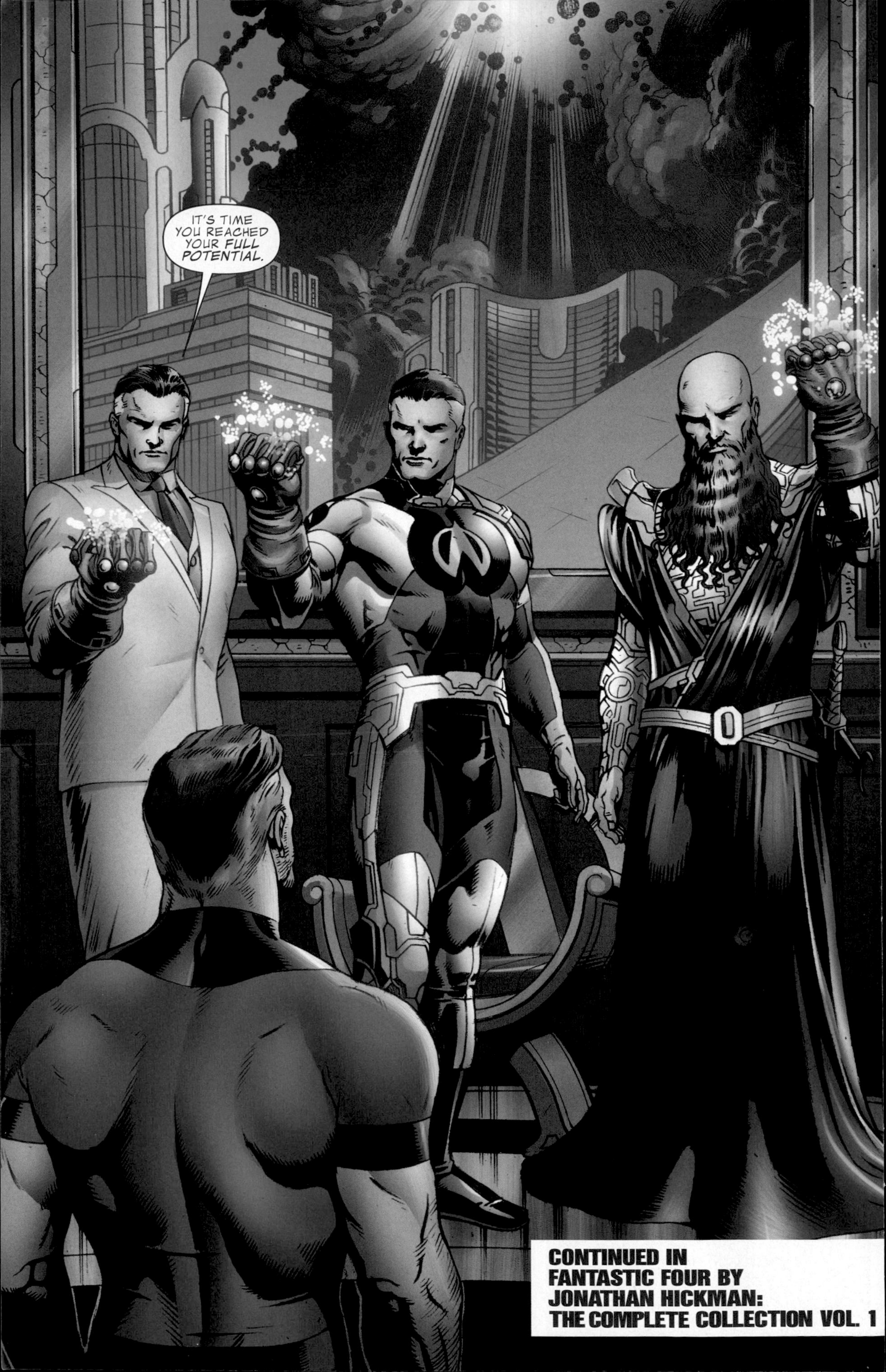
IT'S TIME YOU REACHED YOUR FULL POTENTIAL.
CONTINUED IN FANTASTIC FOUR BY JONATHAN HICKMAN: THE COMPLETE COLLECTION VOL. 1

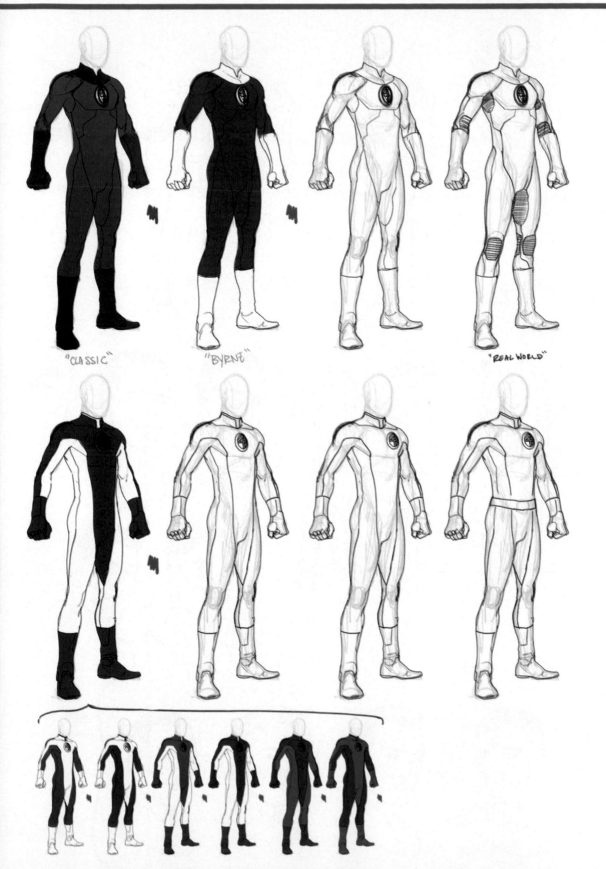

"CLASSIC" "BYRNE" "REAL WORLD"

COSTUME DESIGNS

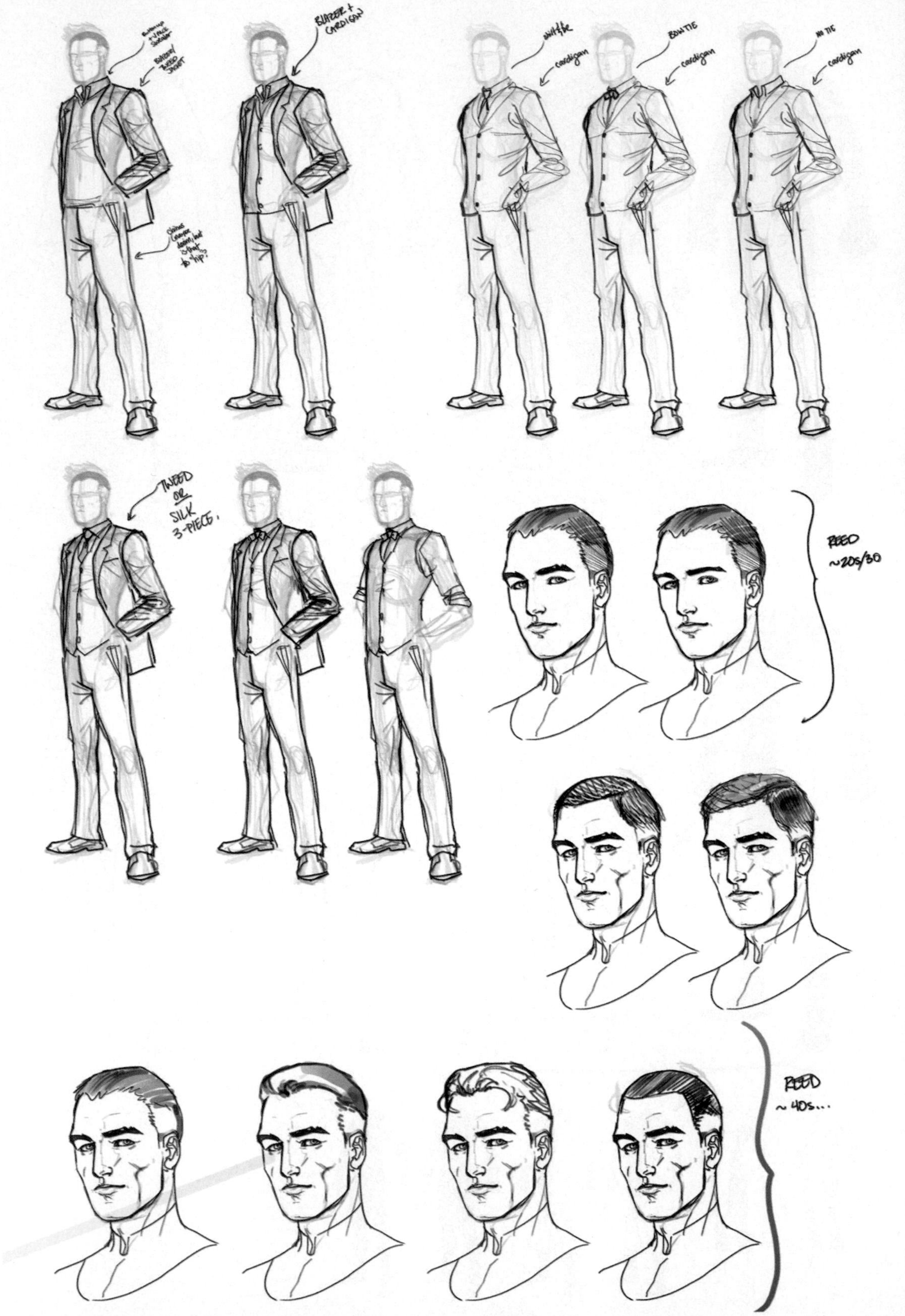
BLAZER + CARDIGAN
cardigan
BOWTIE
cardigan
NO TIE
cardigan
TWEED OR SILK 3-PIECE.
REED ~20s/30
REED ~40s...

REED RICHARDS

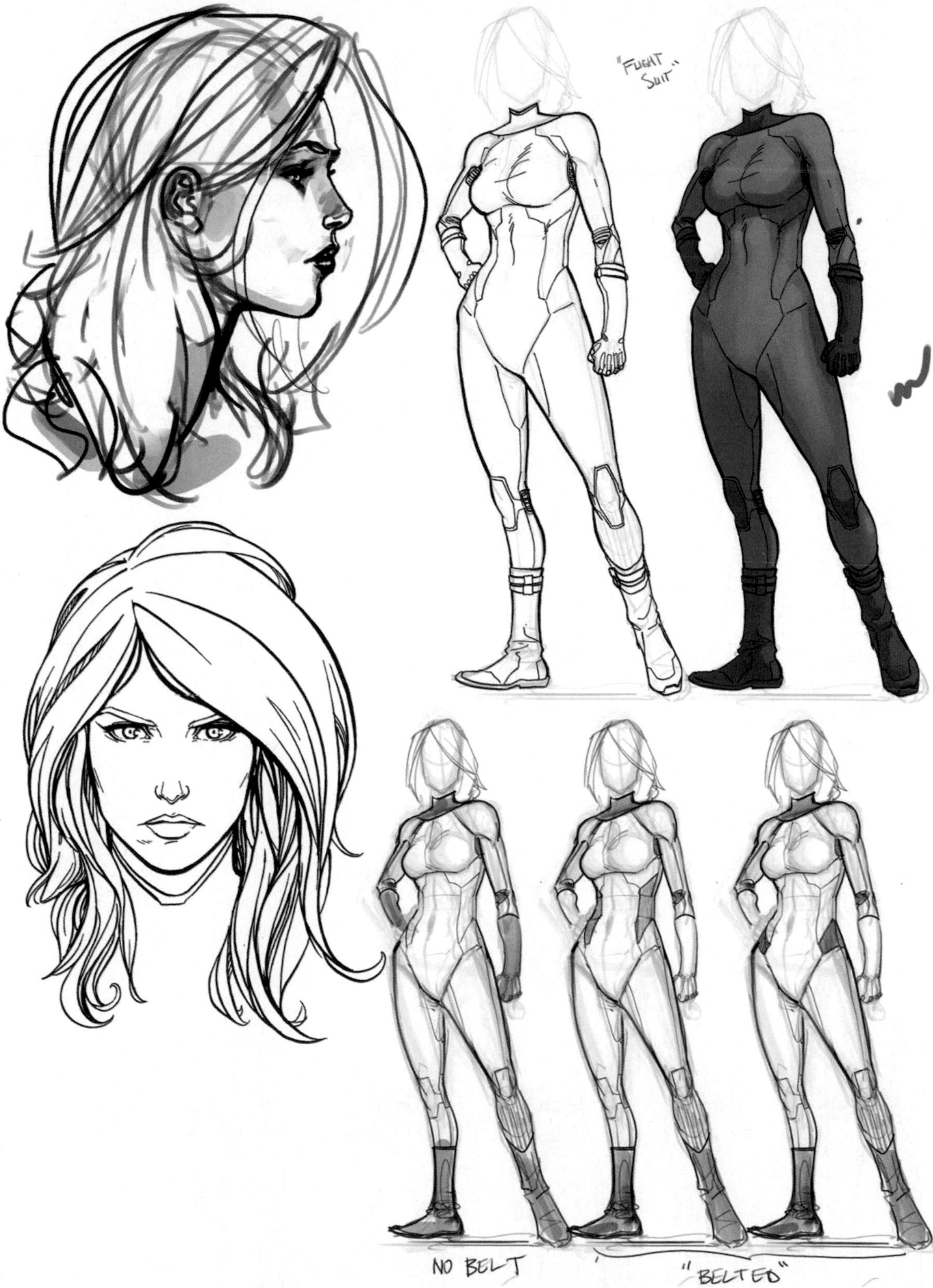
"FLIGHT SUIT"
NO BELT
"BELTED"

SUE STORM

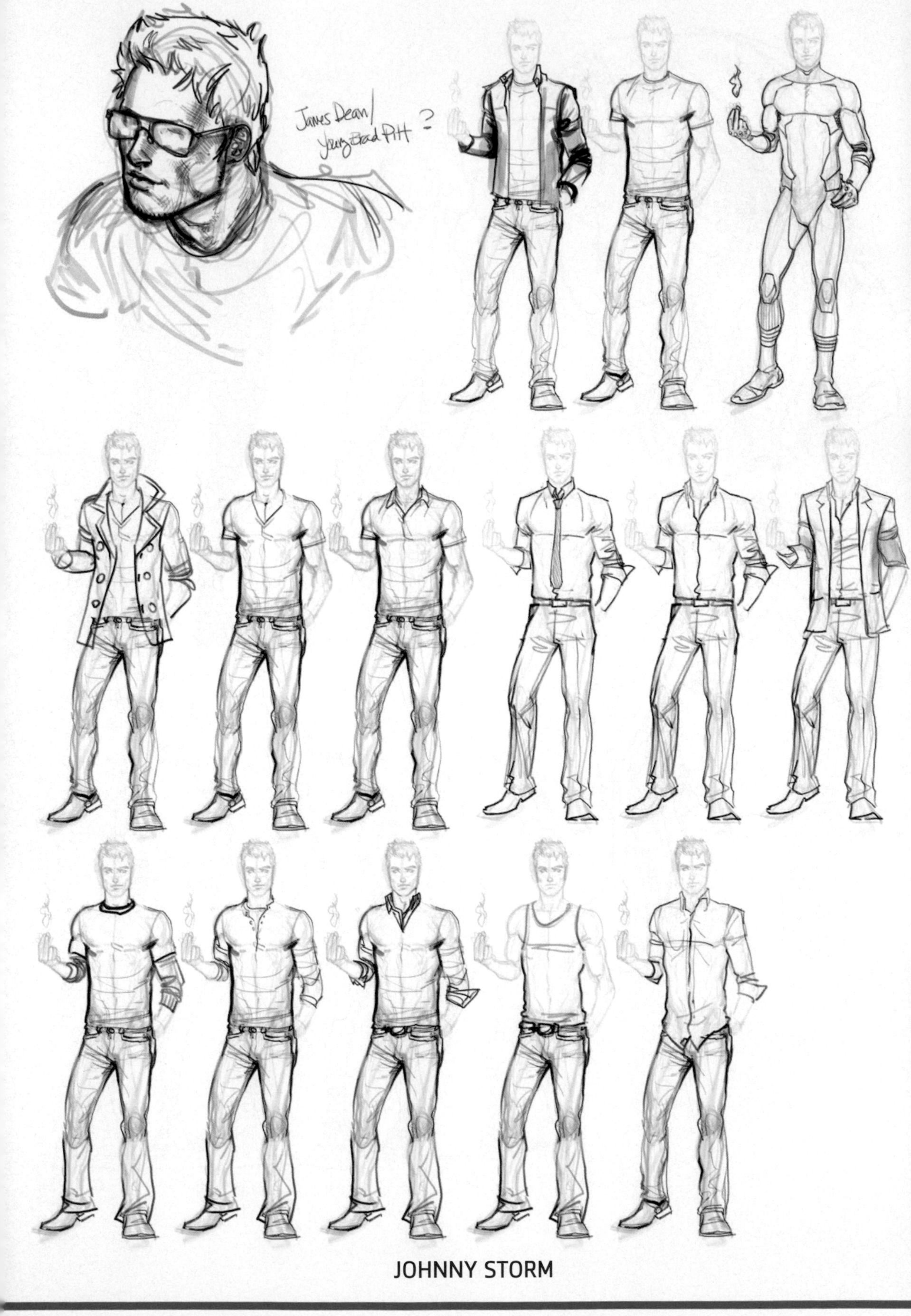
James Dean/
Young Brad Pitt ?

JOHNNY STORM

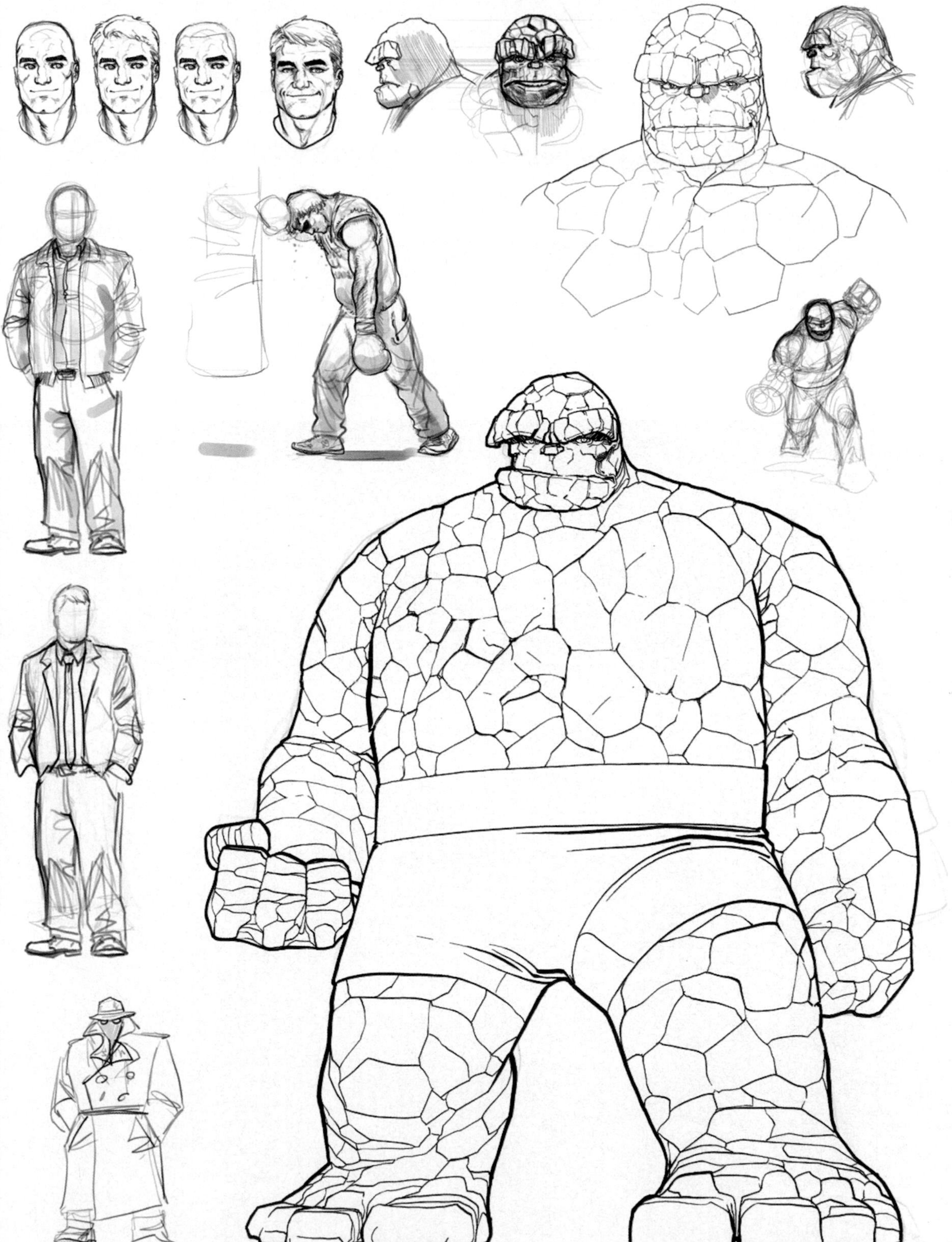

BENJAMIN GRIMM

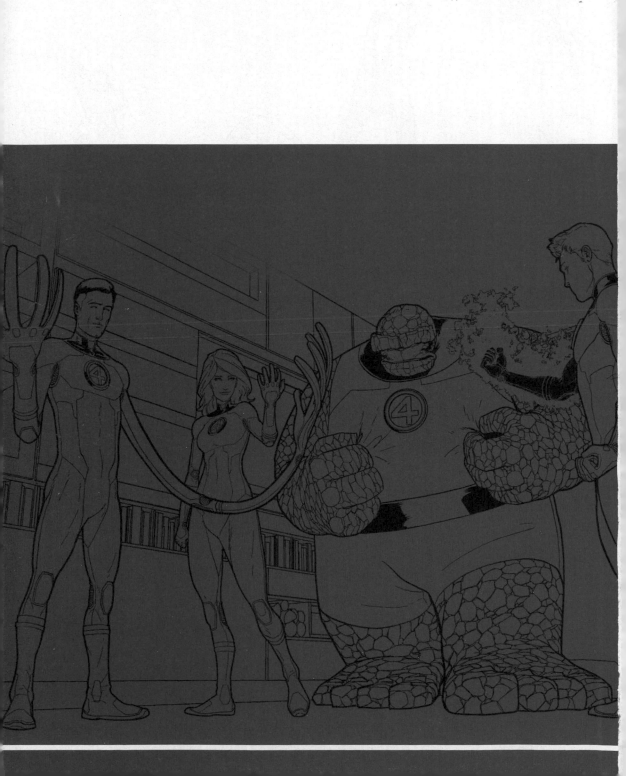